"A FINE BOOK . . .

"Ms. Robertson tells us about a change in storytellers, but also about a challenge to the received wisdom about what stories to tell."

The New York Times Book Review

"Robertson is uniquely qualified to report on what was for *The Times* a historic internal movement. . . . A heartrending story . . . thorough and balanced."

San Francisco Chronicle

"A history of women's rights and wrongs at *The Times* during the past century. The balcony is the cramped space in the National Press Club in Washington where, until 1971, women were forced to stand while covering political events because they were not allowed to become members. Ms. Robertson's account traces the journey of women from the balcony, at the newspaper where she spent most of her career."

The New York Times

"A lively look at the women who sued *The Times* for sex discrimination . . . It's the people in the book who make it easy for anyone to relate to the experience of working for the journalistic institution known as *The New York Times*. Each of the book's vivid characters virtually leaps off the page. . . . A landmark in the history of the advancement of women in the newspaper business."

Chicago Tribune

"AN ENGAGING, ENRAGING AND INSPIRING BOOK

on the time-honored misogyny and patronizing attitudes that permeate the newspaper of record . . . Robertson has unmasked a variety of evils and evil-doers. In so doing, she has written an explosive, colorful and pointed exposé that cuts to the bone of media mythology."

In These Times

"Women's struggle for equal work and equal pay at the newspaper of record is the subject of Pulitzer-winning Robertson's lively new book—a century-long tale of courage, despair, and outright mulishness told with wit, candor, and great affection. . . . A virtual celebration of feminism . . . Superlative journalism—sharp, detailed, and unsparing."

Kirkus Reviews (starred review)

"A landmark . . . This is a marvelous book—even-handed, compelling and gracefully written. Robertson fearlessly skewers the powers that be (and were) at *The Times,* . . . and she sketches the careers of a number of fascinating *Times*women, starting with foreign correspondent Anne O'Hare McCormick in the '20s and '30s, and leading up to columnist Anna Quindlen today."

The Buffalo News

"This book is an inspiration for [women] and a warning to those who seek to keep them out. Robertson shows women can not only work hard enough to earn their place among those above the glass ceiling, they are strong enough to throw the stones needed to break it."

The Tampa Tribune-Times

THE GIRLS
IN THE
BALCONY

WOMEN, MEN, AND
THE NEW YORK TIMES

Nan Robertson

FAWCETT COLUMBINE · NEW YORK

A Fawcett Columbine Book
Published by Ballantine Books

This edition published by arrangement with Random House, Inc.

Library of Congress Catalog Card Number: 92-97326

ISBN: 0-449-90793-7

Cover design by Susan Grube

Manufactured in the United States of America
First Ballantine Books Edition: May 1993

10 9 8 7 6 5 4 3 2 1

To brave women

Author's Note

Never has a book been more fun to research. My subjects were friends and colleagues at the newspaper where I spent most of my working life, the place I came to when I was twenty-eight years old and left after my hair had gone white. Every person on every level, women and men alike, was accessible to me and spoke, mostly, with candor. They had respect for fact and for history. They were trained observers and storytellers. They searched for the significant detail, the revealing quote. They dredged up old notebooks, old diaries and appointment books, tapes and transcripts of meetings held years before. I plunged into their memories, and into my own. The publisher, Punch Sulzberger, helped me measure the table in the Board Room. The records the *Times* opened to me were matchless: its private archives, the clippings morgue, the oral history project, the reference library with its sixty thousand volumes, the microfilms dating back one hundred and forty years to the paper's first days. More specific expressions of gratitude to the people who have served *The New York Times* and this book are in the Acknowledgments section.

Contents

THE GIRLS
IN THE
BALCONY

CHAPTER 1

THE EMPEROR'S HALL

The Board Room at the pinnacle of the New York Times Building is calculated to awe. It is a huge room, with a baronial fireplace sheathed in green marble at the far end, set against carved mahogany paneling that reaches from floor to ceiling. Over the mantel hangs an oil portrait of Adolph Simon Ochs, the newspaper's beetle-browed founding father and patriarch of the family that rules it still. The dark wood trim, the thick mahogany doors, the brass sconces, the soft neutral carpeting, the inscribed photographs of world-famous men massed along the walls—everything about it breathes dignity, power, tradition. It is quiet there; a hush that enfolds the entire fourteenth floor, a world away from the restless reporters and messy desks and ringing phones in the city room eleven floors below, from the inky-faced men who sweat and curse every night amid the thunder and clangor of the presses deep beneath the sidewalks of West Forty-third Street. It is so still up there on the publisher's floor that one can hear the *tock, tock, tock, tock* of the stately grandfather clock that the grateful leading citizens of Chattanooga gave to Adolph Ochs in 1892, after he had built them the gold-domed headquarters of the Chattanooga *Times*. That newspaper, too, still belongs to Ochs's heirs.

A table dominates the Board Room. It overwhelms the Board Room. It is twenty-five feet long, two feet six inches longer than the table in the Cabinet Room of the White House. It stretches from one end to the other of this august chamber, a slab of magnificent inlaid mahogany, uplifted on clusters of curving feet, whose gleaming surface perfectly mirrors the brass chandeliers above and the faces of those who sit along its edges. It swells in the middle, wide enough for an adult to lie across it, and tapers toward the ends. The thing is excessive, and it is mesmerizing.

The vast majority of those who have worked for *The New York Times* and spent their lives in the building, and even most of the celebrated public figures who have lunched in the private dining rooms with the publisher, have never visited the fourteenth floor. Even fewer have been in the Board Room. Until Ochs's death in 1935, it was his office, with a smaller table for meetings and a long, long walk to his desk at the far end. The room so daunted and perhaps even offended the aristocratic Arthur Hays Sulzberger, Ochs's son-in-law and successor as publisher—unlike the self-made Ochs, a man born to old money and status—that he chose a tiny office for himself next to the Board Room. Arthur Hays Sulzberger's only son moved into the same little office when he became publisher in 1963.

···········

On a steamy Wednesday morning in July 1972, with the temperature outside climbing into the nineties and the humidity rising to the saturation point, that only son, Arthur Ochs Sulzberger, sat at the head of the table in the Board Room. Five men in dark suits were ranged along one side of the table, their backs to the window wall where light streamed through filmy curtains. Sulzberger, whom everybody except his second wife called Punch—she thought the nickname undignified—was the only man there who seemed entirely at home.

A handsome, sunny, open-featured fellow, as friendly as a cocker spaniel, with his mother's big dark eyes and generous mouth, he had toddled as a little boy around his grandfather Ochs's desk in this very room. He rarely seemed to take himself seriously, and for a long time, many of those who worked for him agreed that, indeed, Punch was not to be taken seriously. When his sister Judy telephoned to congratulate him right after his promotion to publisher, following the shockingly unexpected death of Punch's predecessor and brother-in-law Orvil Dryfoos at the age of fifty, Punch told her: "I have just made my first top-level decision. I have decided not to throw up." By contrast, the men who sat on his right hand that July day in 1972 in the Board Room, all powerful executives and editors of *The New York Times,* seemed stiff, formal and slightly ill at ease.

Into this sanctum stepped a dozen women in groups of two and three, representing the newly formed Women's Caucus. Ruth Block, a picture researcher from the Sunday department, who had started as a secretary and had spent half her life at the *Times,* came through the door and thought, "My God! Just look at this place!" The elegance of the room made her feel subdued; the table was the most beautiful she had ever seen. To her friend Ursula Mahoney, the table "seemed to go on forever; it seemed to go on as long as the eye could see." She thought, "This room is overpowering—is it because they're taking us seriously? Or are they trying to intimidate us?" Joan Cook, a reporter with a broad, smiling Celtic face and a motherly manner, found her eyes riveted on the gleaming table. "Here we are," she said to herself, "in the emperor's hall at last!" She had never been in the Board Room before. None of the women had been in the room before.

In came Grace Lichtenstein, tiny and full of beans, her blond hair in a shining waterfall down her back, eyes opened wide behind her huge round glasses; at thirty, she was one of the youngest of the group. Edith Evans Asbury, even tinier, white-haired, with a hair-trigger temper, a newspaper reporter since 1929, greeted Punch breezily and thought: "I've known this guy since he was a kid."

Grace Glueck, the wittiest woman in the newsroom, arrived. Dressed as usual in something chic and sharp-edged (a friend always imagined Grace as a sophisticated Nora Charles figure in the *Thin Man* movie series, wearing a tilted forties hat with a sleek green feather), she dropped a quip on Punch and seated herself with the other women on the side of the table across from the dark-suited men. The window light fell full on the women's faces, disorienting them slightly.

Betsy Wade came in. Punch immediately signaled for her to take the seat next to him on his left. It was known already that she was the leader, that she would present the women's complaints to the men who ran the *Times*. Dark, serious, with an air of grave courtesy, she usually commanded respect—not just because she was chief copy editor on the foreign desk, the first woman ever to hold so high a position in the newsroom of *The New York Times,* and was so good at the job, but also because of her manner, the way her deep gaze locked into yours, her precise way of thinking and speaking, her obvious intelligence. The night before, she had hardly noticed it was her forty-third birthday, too busy and too tired to celebrate properly with her husband and sons. She had come home late, after a meeting of the Women's Caucus had made her leadership official. Betsy, the most clearheaded and articulate member, the one who had the facts, would speak for them all at the unprecedented Board Room confrontation—for the women who had dropped the bomb on the management of *The New*

York Times two months before, on the next to last day of May 1972.

The bomb was a five-page letter signed by fifty women on the daily and Sunday news staffs, setting out in dramatic detail the sorry lot of female workers at a newspaper whose public image—whose image of itself—was that of a liberal and benevolent institution. Separate copies of the letter had been delivered the day after the Memorial Day weekend to Sulzberger, his three older sisters, Marian, Ruth, and Judith, and his mother, Iphigene, all directors of the New York Times Company. It began by saying that women across the country were beginning to assert their rights and seek redress of their grievances. It said that *The New York Times* was and always had been negligent about putting women in vital, decision-making jobs.

The letter pointed out that there was not one woman executive on the masthead. There was not one woman among the vice presidents, nor any in a position to aspire to a vice presidency. Two of the three women in top editorial positions, the editor and deputy editor of the family/style department, were in jobs traditionally held by women, with a staff overwhelmingly made up of women. Only the third, Betsy Wade, head of the foreign news desk, was in a position traditionally held by men. There were forty women reporters to three hundred and eighty-five men reporters, and eleven of those women were in family/style. Of twenty-two national correspondents, not one was a woman. Of thirty-three foreign correspondents, only three were women. There was only one woman bureau chief, just appointed to Paris. In the Washington bureau, with thirty-five reporters, only three were women; the number had not gone up in nine years, although the staff had nearly doubled in that time. There were no women photographers. Of thirty-one critics in culture news, only four were women. Reviewers of drama, music, movies, television, and books were all male. The sports department had one woman and twenty-three men. There were no women on the editorial board, which had eleven members. There were no women columnists. Of the seventy-five copy editors on the daily paper, four were women. Almost all the lower-paying, lower-ranking jobs were confined to women.

But the part that made Sulzberger really sit up and take notice was a paragraph saying that a breakdown of salaries showed "compellingly" that across the entire range of jobs at *The New York Times,* women with comparable education, ability, and years of service were paid less than men for doing the same work. The *Times,* the letter made clear, was subject, like other businesses, to the Civil Rights Act of 1964 and should adopt an affirmative action plan for reaching equality between men and women. The paper should make full use of the talents of women already on the staff and should look for more women to hire, to promote, and to bring into jobs from which they were completely excluded.

The message was clear. *The New York Times* was unjust. For the first time in the history of the most important newspaper in America, a paper that set the highest standards for fairness and moral tone, its women had banded together to say "You are unfair. You are hypocritical." They asked the publisher to meet with them.

Punch Sulzberger reread the letter and was astonished. It had never crossed his mind that people thought his newspaper was anti-women. Having three sisters and a strong-minded mother, he thought that he knew what women wanted, that he had been completely sensitized to their concerns. He was, in fact, hurt. He called for a meeting, on Wednesday, July 19, 1972. By the time that day rolled around, Sulzberger and his managers had studied the letter, had done some homework of their own, and thought they were ready.

On the management side of the table, their backs to the windows, sat a group of genial and polished men—Seymour Topping, a former foreign editor and now assistant managing editor for news, an outspoken admirer of Betsy Wade's work;

Peter Millones, a rather priggish younger assistant managing editor who held the most hated job in the newsroom, the one with hiring, promotion, and punishment powers over the news staff; John Mortimer and Howard Bishow, the *Times'*s chief labor negotiators, both accommodating men, chary of combat; and Daniel Schwarz, the perpetually smiling Sunday editor, who had been the Sunday staff's crying towel for decades when he was deputy to the tyrannical Lester Markel.

Some of the women there that day had no idea who some of the men sitting opposite them were. They all knew Punch, however, and thought of him as Punch, not Mr. Sulzberger, born though he was to be lord of the *Times.* There was nothing pompous about Punch. When asked to do a log of his activities for a book called *A Day in the Life of The New York Times,* he sent a memo to its author, Ruth Adler, the editor of the paper's house organ. It contained this notation: "9:36 to 9:37 A.M. Threw out a dead tulip."

The women all knew who was *not* there—the managing editor whose meteoric rise at the *Times* had dazzled and burned those in his way and left tension and turbulence, excitement and awe and fear at every turn. They also knew by then that he was angry with them. The publisher seemed to anticipate the women's unasked question. "Abe Rosenthal wanted me to give you his regrets," Punch told them. "He can't make it today, he's out of town." Sy Topping was there as Abe's representative.

Punch began the meeting by mentioning the May letter from the Women's Caucus. The women had asked for an affirmative action program. Well, said Punch, they would have one, and the *Times* management wanted their help in developing it. But there were problems. The *Times* was in an economic squeeze—not broke, mind you, but the staff was being cut. And everything the *Times* did for women they must do also for blacks and Puerto Ricans. Now, the *Times* had looked over the salaries of women who signed the letter in May, and in fact had reviewed the salaries of both men and women in the news and Sunday departments, and *had* found some inequities, but they seemed to be fairly evenly balanced between men and women, Punch said.

The publisher was in the midst of this opening statement when Eileen Shanahan and I burst into the Board Room. Punch, whose back was to the door, swiveled around to see who was interrupting so noisily. His eyes widened. His chin dropped. We apologized, out of breath from running—we had taken the morning's first Eastern shuttle flight from Washington, but the plane and our taxi had been delayed by heavy traffic. There were no more seats on the women's side of the table. The publisher motioned us to two empty chairs just to his right, facing Betsy, Grace Glueck, and Joan Cook.

Sulzberger's face is vividly expressive when his guard is down—emotions chase their way across it like clouds across a March sky. He was showing surprise, consternation, puzzlement. I could almost hear him thinking: "Nan? Eileen? All the way from Washington? What are *they* mad about?" Punch and I were the same age, forty-six, and we had been friends since the mid-1950s, when I was a young fashion reporter and Punch was trying to find things to do around the newspaper. His father, Arthur Hays Sulzberger, was then in his vigorous prime. Few believed in the fifties that Punch was capable of being publisher; his thoughtful and competent brother-in-law Orvil Dryfoos was the heir apparent. Punch to me then was not the dauphin but simply a delightful luncheon companion in a little coterie of my newsroom pals. Now he was publisher and I was a feature and news writer in the Washington bureau, covering the White House family.

Eileen was a superstar who had arrived at the *Times* in Washington in 1962, just a few months before I did. Reporters with steel egos quailed when she was on a story in a field monopolized by men—economics, big money, taxes, business. She had endless energy, enthusiasm, and an intellect of singular clarity. She explained extremely complicated things in simple language and told why the reader should pay attention.

When her Irish was up, which was often, her green eyes practically shot sparks and her voice soared into Valkyrie-like arias of anger. That morning she was unusually jittery—she hated flying, she was pathologically afraid of it, but she had a big story brewing in the capital. There was no other way to make the New York meeting and get back to Washington in time.

A wide smile cracked right across Joan Cook's face. "How wonderful!" she thought. "The Washington bureau is here!" The bureau was heavily male and elitist, and it tried to distance itself from New York in every way. To have two members from that snootiest of outposts gratified Joan.

The meeting unrolled in an atmosphere of civility. Betsy made a calm, dignified initial presentation. It was as if she and Punch were alone together, exchanging thoughts aloud down there at the end of the table. They were the protagonists, the others as still as the heavy chairs they sat in. Millones or Mortimer supplied short answers to the publisher's occasional specific questions. Eileen answered one query about the law. Grace Glueck and Joan spoke briefly. Punch rambled amiably on: There was no shortage of qualified women. They would get a fair shake. Lists would be drawn up, job openings scrutinized, negotiating committees formed. Betsy began boring in: There were gross inequities in the hiring, promotion, and wages of women all over the *Times* building. Women were overlooked and ignored. Even the committee Punch had just appointed to find qualified women to fill higher executive jobs consisted only of men: "Why are there no women on this committee?"

"Oh, sure there could be," said Punch. "There's absolutely no problem in that. I just took the three top people—the editor of the editorial page, the Sunday editor, and the managing editor—and with them the vice president of personnel. It just happens by chance they're all men."

"You haven't got a woman you could field on your side, have you?" Betsy asked. Of course, the publisher said, he could have gotten three or four women in executive jobs to serve, but it didn't seem to make sense. Besides, the women were rather lower down on the ladder, and the committees should include top-ranking people.

Betsy insisted. There had to be some input from women on the management side. "There *must* be. . . . Mrs. Heiskell [Marian Heiskell, the oldest of Punch's three sisters, a member of the Times board of directors] would not be interested in sitting on your side?"

"Sure she would, if I can ever find her," Punch replied. "I can't find any of my sisters or my mother; they're all away—which is nice."

Betsy asked Punch to invite Mrs. Heiskell. No problem, the publisher replied. He added, with a sigh, "I'll have to leave messages all over town."

"Yes, boss," Betsy said, just loud enough for me and a couple of others to hear. It was an impertinence, lightly delivered, just pointed enough to underline the difference in rank that separated Betsy and Punch.

She shuffled through a little sheaf of notes. She was looking at salary figures. She had spent long hours at the New York office of the Newspaper Guild crunching numbers, using a huge, clunky calculator with a crank on the side like a slot machine, while Guild officials looked on. Joan Cook and Grace Glueck were with her, as well as other Caucus members. They needed the figures for negotiations, the women said. All names would be expunged. Harry Fisdell, the local Guild vice president, read the salaries off an immense sheet. They ranked all the salaries in descending order. Betsy thought then, This is going to be damning.

"I think our intention was not to discuss individual salaries," broke in Peter Millones, the assistant managing editor for news personnel, his face stiff with disapproval.

"I'm talking about *patterns*," Betsy said. "I'm not talking about individual salaries." The Caucus had chosen to look at the salaries of a group of general assignment *Times* reporters, men and women. The average weekly salary of eighty-eight men was $454. The average weekly salary of twenty-six women was $395. Six of the eighty-eight men were working at the minimum salary scale for reporters. Six of the twenty-six women were working at the minimum salary scale. "The federal Civil Rights Act, Peter, refers to patterns of salary discrimination, and what we're talking about here is patterns," Betsy said. "On a percentage basis we have a strikingly larger number of women working on the minimum than we have men."

Betsy went relentlessly on. The gap between the average salaries of the examined group of men reporters and women reporters was $59 a week; the New York Times–Guild Pension Fund, of which Betsy was a trustee, showed salary discrimination throughout all departments in the building.

"It's all there," Betsy said. "All of us are afraid in our pocketbooks. It hurts you over your lifetime earnings, it hurts you in your pension, it hurts every way. And of course, the individual woman can do little to remedy this. She goes to her boss or to her manager and she says, 'Look, I'm turning the same turret lathe as the guy sitting here and I'm making less.' And he says, 'Well, you just don't turn the turret lathe quite so well.' "

One woman could not fight such a response, Betsy said, but the federal government would be interested in a pattern of discrimination. "These pension figures—which I know you're not familiar with, and I'm sorry you're not—are buildingwide figures graded by age and experience. And you know, the women show up in the minus column, column after column after column. . . . I think we women have discovered in talking to each other that our problems—which we thought were individual—turned out to be . . . universal. We all thought we had gone through an isolated experience, and it turns out that we've all gone through the same experience."

The publisher looked stunned. A difference of $59 a week between the average salaries of men and women in this group meant that each woman received $3,000 a year less than her male counterpart. If similar discrepancies existed in other departments, merit raises for the roughly 550 women employees at *The New York Times* could cost the company almost $2 million a year.

Down the table, the peppery Edith Evans Asbury was beginning to burn all over again. She had first heard about the salary gap at a Women's Caucus meeting days before, and she had figured out from the Guild list that at least nineteen men in the city room were making more than she, Edith, a proven, seasoned reporter who had already had twenty-three years of experience when she joined the *Times* in 1952. The next morning she had stood up from her seat in the city room and gazed with outrage at the sea of men all around her. She had thought, "There are not nineteen men in this room better than I am. There are not nineteen men as good as I am." In fact, she saw only two she conceded were as good as or better than she—Homer Bigart and Peter Kihss, both legendary reporters.

Grace Glueck spoke. "At the risk of breaking open a hornet's nest," she began, each word crisply, perfectly enunciated, "it seems to me that this whole discussion . . . is really not getting at the heart of the problem." The problem was, she said, what the men who were in positions of command on the *Times* expected and demanded of the women who worked under them.

"A woman cannot be in a position of deserving a merit raise unless she is given the kinds of assignments that can show her as being worthy of a merit raise. And I don't think the men in power on this newspaper think of women as capable of doing the jobs that they assign men to do."

Further, there were no women in the pipeline for power—which, at least in the newsroom, led through the editors' desks, said Betsy. "There is a battalion of assistant city editors and there is no woman assistant city editor. I mean, it seems to me it's as bald as that."

Punch was looking more and more aghast. Now Dan

Schwarz, the eternally reassuring Uncle Dan, as some on his staff called him, began to argue. There was a solid representation of women in his Sunday department, many with editors' jobs. He had a list right with him of twenty-five or thirty women that he was moving right along.

"Secretaries!" blurted out Ruth Block, across the table.

"No, no!" protested Schwarz, his smile fading.

Barbara Wyden, an editor in the Sunday department, leaned forward. The last time Schwarz had hired a woman editor, she said, was when *she* came on the staff—and that had been ten years ago.

Schwarz's eyes popped. He drew back, the dumbfounded look on his face so stark that almost the entire table burst into laughter. Punch was among those laughing. The Sunday editor started to protest again; Punch cut him short and turned to Betsy, asking her what the next step should be. They agreed on more meetings within days, more specifics, small committees.

As the group rose from the table, Grace Glueck thought, "I'm very proud of us. I think we've managed it very well." She thought that at times Punch had seemed like a little boy who had been caught doing something he shouldn't have. She experienced what she later described as "a little victory twinge." She was gratified that at last the publisher had been confronted with some hard truths about the women toiling on the Sulzberger plantation. It was high time for the self-righteous *Times* to put its own house in order.

Despite her outward aspect of calm, Betsy Wade had been very nervous during the meeting. She stepped into the elevator going down from the fourteenth floor feeling a mixture of fright, heartburn, and gross fatigue.

Grace Lichtenstein's emotions were in tumult. Like Eileen Shanahan, she had been covering the burgeoning women's liberation movement for two years. Like Eileen, she had had to ask her uninterested male editors for permission to cover women's politics, and when she got permission, she often had to cover them in her spare time, when her regular reporting was done. As one of the earliest members of the Women's Caucus, she had become aware of inequities on her own newspaper. Still, she was idealistic about the *Times*. It was a great institution. You almost had to work there to know how great it really was. She had thought, "The men who run this place are not really male chauvinists. They may be blind or ignorant, but they're not stupid—they're not men who consciously want to put women down." She had thought it would be immediately evident to the *Times* management that the women had a strong case, that changes should be made. It was not a matter of idle griping among a bunch of discontented females. But Dan Schwarz's sudden truculence and Punch's maddening vagueness had shaken her. The meeting itself, the formality of the setting, had given her a sense of trepidation.

"I felt like I was on the edge of a diving board about to make my first dive," she said later. "I felt it was clear, when we got up from that table, that there would be no going back."

MISTRESS McCORMICK

For as many years as anyone can remember, there has been a long L-shaped corridor lined with huge black-and-white photographs on the eleventh floor of *The New York Times*. It meant glory to me when I was young. I used to wander there, curious and awed, gazing into the faces of men I did not know, reading next to each picture, over and over, the stories they had written that had won the ultimate medal of the newspaper trade. Near the southern end of the corridor is the cafeteria where the employees eat. Few walk north along the hall unless they are lunching at the other end, in the private dining rooms of the *Times,* reserved for the people who run the paper and their most important guests. I would make my pilgrimages between mealtimes, when the corridor was deserted—because, you see, I was a little ashamed of my obsession.

When I came to the *Times* in 1955, at the age of twenty-eight, there were twenty-one Pulitzer Prize portraits in the corridor, ranged in chronological order. The first man to win one for the paper was Alva Johnston, in 1923. The eighth face in the procession was the only woman.

Anne O'Hare McCormick had won the Pulitzer in 1937, when I was eleven years old, a tomboy playing at Tarzan in the trees (I never wanted to play his adoring mate, Jane) and wrestling the boys to the ground in my Chicago neighborhood. That very year, I and my best girlfriend had sworn to each other at her mother's storefront café that we would be newspaper reporters when we grew up. Now, in 1955, I had been a newswoman for seven years. To me, young upstart, Anne McCormick looked like someone's dear old granny, square-faced and plain, with a crimped, flat hairdo over serene eyes that said: "I know many things." I looked at her, Olympian yet comforting, and at all the men of the *Times* enshrined before her and after her. And I thought: "I will never be up there."

Anne McCormick was an icon, distant and untouchable. I could never be as good as she. But there was more to it, other reasons why only one woman was in that corridor among all the men. I knew that it was not the fault of the people who gave out the Pulitzers. In the mid-1950s when I was a cub at the *Times,* and for a long time thereafter, women were almost never sent to cover the kinds of stories that won the Pulitzer Prize—the kinds of stories that men in journalism, talented and untalented, energetic and lazy, were sent to cover as a matter of course. That was the way of the world then. It was distinctly the way of the *Times.* More than twenty years would pass before women would burst in any numbers from the ghettos inside the *Times* building in which they spent their working lives.

Those in the Women's Caucus who tried to change *The New York Times* loved the paper. They wanted it to live up to its ideals. The men who ran the world's most admired newspaper denied to the very end that anything was wrong.

There was a long history behind the unequal treatment of women on the *Times*. Even Anne McCormick, the most famous, the most universally admired, and one of the most gifted women ever to work for the paper, was not hired as long as Adolph S. Ochs, its greatest publisher, was alive. For forty years, from 1896 until his death in 1935, the man who brought the *Times* to its present eminence did not want women in the ranks of those who gathered and wrote the news. "We have almost a prohibition against the employment of women on our editorial staff," Ochs told another publisher during World War I, when many newspapers were bringing women in to fill the jobs left by men going off to the armed forces.

Anne O'Hare McCormick began doing riveting work for the *Times* in 1921 as a "regular contributor" and stringer, mostly from Europe. Ochs never put her on salary. She was paid by the piece. In the twenties and thirties she interviewed Stalin, Hitler, and Mussolini when resident foreign correspondents could not get near those dictators. President Franklin Delano Roosevelt, a far more accessible yet sometimes inscrutable leader, rejoiced in her company and repaid her with long, candid, private conversations.

She described the aging Italian king Victor Emmanuel III, kicking his royal footstool away from him and then looking like "an unhappy small boy, dangling his legs" from a throne too big for him. She summoned up the majesty of the papacy and the tantrums of Italy's young Fascisti and the helpless despair of American men without work in the early days of the Great Depression, lying in the shadows of luxury hotels in New York and Los Angeles, rubbing a once-grassy park in the middle of Detroit bald as a board with their recumbent bodies. Everywhere she went, she made readers feel they were there, eavesdropping, peeping in on history

She had poetry in her, and the gift of prophecy. After hearing Mussolini's debutant speech in the Chamber of Deputies, a year before his Black Shirts seized Rome in 1922, she told another correspondent: "Italy has heard its master's voice." The veteran reporter and his colleagues had dismissed the man as a lout. They laughed at her.

Her talent shone forth in her very first stories for the *Times.* "She put a glow on everything she wrote," said James B. Reston, one of the most idolized reporters of his time, and of the *Times.* Adolph Ochs found her charming, and a writer of unusual power and grace. But he would not welcome Anne O'Hare McCormick on his staff.

His son-in-law and successor as publisher, Arthur Hays Sulzberger, could hardly wait to do the deed. Sulzberger had been secretly promising Mrs. McCormick a permanent arrangement since 1934, while Ochs was isolated in his second nervous breakdown and Sulzberger was acting in his place. Finally, on June 1, 1936, a year after Ochs's death, the new publisher put her on his payroll. She was fifty-six years old. He immediately named her the first woman member of the editorial board and soon gave Anne McCormick her own column on foreign affairs. Sulzberger called it "my first important official decision." Her peak earnings as a space-rate writer had been $200 for a *Times* magazine article and $62.50 for a daily newspaper piece measuring a column long. Her starting salary was $7,000 a year.

Her Pulitzer came less than a year later. It was not for one superlative piece. It was for distinguished foreign correspondence: her dispatches and features from Europe. Implicitly, the prize was for hundreds of articles written during the fifteen years she had knocked at the door of *The New York Times.* Only one other woman had won a Pulitzer in journalism before her: Minna Lewinson, who shared the prize in 1918 with Henry Beetle Hough for their history of the services the American press rendered to the public in 1917, the year the United States entered World War I. Anne McCormick was the first woman to win the Pulitzer for the *Times.* Thirty-three years would go by before a second *Times* woman was so honored.

How Mrs. McCormick got onto a major newspaper at all was something of a miracle. There was mystery, too, in the lady.

She did not like to talk about herself and would not be interviewed about her personal life; for years she refused to be listed in *Who's Who;* she would not tell how she managed, repeatedly and almost invariably, to get in to see the planet's most important people. She also believed, like almost every journalist of her generation, that the subject of a newspaper article was the subject, not the reporter. She did not want to be treated like a celebrity; it would interfere with what she called "the kind of impersonal and uncolored reporting . . . on which . . . a free press and therefore a free society depend." This was a laudable and sensible attitude, but Mrs. McCormick became world famous anyway.

She was so secretive about some fundamental facts—such as her exact age and formal education—that even *The New York Times* and the Pulitzer Prize committees had it wrong. When the nation's newspaper of record ran her front-page obituary the day after her death on May 29, 1954, her age was given as seventy-two. She was seventy-four. The *Times* listed her as a graduate of the College of St. Mary's of the Springs in Columbus, Ohio. She never went to college. Her convent high school was St. Mary's of the Springs Academy, from which she was graduated at the age of eighteen. (In 1924, the academy became a four-year college, and at its first commencement, in 1928, presented Anne McCormick with the first of her seventeen honorary degrees. It meant more to her, she told the sisters, than a degree from Oxford.)

Her Pulitzer fact-sheet in 1937 had mentioned more vaguely that she had been educated "at private schools in this country and Europe." Her education in Europe had come solely from the people she interviewed, the events she witnessed, and the books and newspapers she chose to read.

Anna Elizabeth O'Hare was born on May 16, 1880, in the town of Wakefield, Yorkshire, England, and was baptized there as a Roman Catholic. Shortly after her birth, her parents, Thomas and Teresa Beatrice Berry O'Hare, moved to the United States and settled in Columbus, Ohio. Anna, or Annie, as she was known when she was growing up, was the eldest of three daughters. When she was about fourteen, Thomas O'Hare, who had been a regional manager for the Home Life Insurance Company, "encountered business problems," as it was put delicately then. He abandoned the family and vanished forever from the scene.

The mother, a poet, went to work in a dry-goods store, determined that her daughters would get a soundly Catholic education. Anna had entered the Academy of St. Mary's of the Springs, run by Dominican sisters in a Columbus suburb, the year before her father's desertion. She was thirteen years old in 1893, a dainty five feet two inches tall, with red hair and what they called in those days a retroussé (turned up) nose. It was obvious to the sisters early on that Anna O'Hare was very, very bright and very, very studious.

Throughout her years at the academy, she led her classes. The 1897 yearbook shows her at the top with grades of 100 or near it in every subject from metaphysics and literature to composition, geometry, and chemistry.

The pupils were housed and taught in a tall, somber Victorian brick pile set on a hill. To prevent "all objectionable correspondence," every letter written or received by the young ladies was read by the mother superior. The boarders could entertain visitors only on Thursdays, under a sister's watchful eye. During the school year, the only vacation allowed was at Christmas.

To "encourage the dutiful in virtue and knowledge, and to stimulate the remiss," each pupil's report card for the month was read before the entire student body and faculty. Following public mortification or relief, honors were bestowed for correct deportment and diligent application.

In 1898, Anna O'Hare was graduated from St. Mary's Academy. She was, of course, the valedictorian. That same year, Anna's mother published a volume of her own poems, *Songs at Twilight,* and went around Columbus peddling it door-to-door.

Soon thereafter Mrs. O'Hare moved her family from Columbus to Cleveland and began writing a column and editing the women's section of the weekly *Catholic Universe Bulletin.* Her oldest daughter soon joined her on the staff, eventually becoming the *Bulletin*'s associate editor. Her career there lasted more than a decade.

On September 14, 1910, Anne O'Hare, thirty years old, married the man who would free her from constant worries about money and introduce her to the world.

Francis J. McCormick was eight years her senior, tall, lean and hawk-nosed, a courtly Irish Catholic, socially acceptable and rich. His father had made a fortune manufacturing, importing, and selling plumbing supplies in Dayton, Ohio. His mother was a cousin of James Cardinal Gibbons of Baltimore. After graduation from the University of Dayton, Frank McCormick entered his father's business.

The newlyweds settled in Dayton. They were never to have children, but the bride began to live a life that would give her fulfillment of another kind, beyond her wildest fantasies.

Frank McCormick spent months out of every year visiting Europe on business, sailing on the stateliest dowagers of the transatlantic fleets and putting up at the grandest hotels: the Savoy or Claridge's in London, the Bristol in Vienna, the Ritz or the Crillon in Paris. Everywhere he went he took his wife, drilled at St. Mary's in French and in Latin, which helped her in Italy. While her husband occupied himself with selling and buying, she went out into the cities—listening, looking, absorbing as she traversed Europe during the tumultuous years that preceded and followed the Great War that was to end all wars. She contributed occasional free-lance articles on her impressions to the *Catholic World* and *Reader Magazine.*

In 1917, the year the United States entered the war, Anne McCormick wrote an essay called "Journalism as a Profession for the Convent Graduate" for the St. Mary's yearbook. She was not sanguine:

In thinking of journalism for the convent graduate, it must be remembered that it is only in recent years that it has been a field at all hospitable to women workers. Even now, when the law and medicine have yielded with some reluctance to the feminine invasion, and the business world has resigned itself with more or less grace to the increasing competition of women, only the hardiest and most adventurous spirits have been able to force their way beyond that invisible but firmly established barrier which hedges in the masculine monopoly of the Fourth Estate.

Women writers languish over the Society column of the daily newspaper. They give advice to the lovelorn. They edit household departments. Clubs, cooking and clothes are recognized as subjects particularly fitted to their intelligence. They are graciously permitted to make the most out of the special article and the feature story. But only a determined few ever attain regular membership on the reportorial staff. And fewer still usurp the authority of an editorial desk, or achieve the dignity and influence of an editorial writer.

She could have written that essay fifty or sixty years later. It would still have been true of many newspapers, certainly of *The New York Times.*

In 1921, Anne McCormick herself took that leap she had warned all but the bravest not to attempt. She wrote a letter to Carr Van Anda, the managing editor of *The New York Times,* whom she had never met. Could she send him occasional stories from Europe on a space-rate basis? Van Anda wrote her back: "Try it."

Van Anda, in the finest *Times* tradition, thought women belonged at home. When he turned down one woman job applicant, she asked him in despair just how he thought single females could survive without jobs. He answered: "If I had my way about it, all unmarried men would be taxed to support indigent women."

Perhaps Van Anda was more receptive to Mrs. McCormick because Adolph Ochs was out of the picture at the time; he was in the throes of his first long nervous collapse and it was not known when he could resume work. Besides, this unknown woman with her unimpressive credentials would not be seen around the *Times* office or put on the payroll. She was obviously being supported by her husband. And Anne McCormick was marvelous at ingratiating herself with others, in person and on paper; her later letters to Arthur Hays Sulzberger and various *Times* editors exude both authority and warmth.

The *Times* has never had another managing editor to equal Van Anda for sheer force of intellect. He was a newspaper genius. A scholar of science and mathematics, an aloof figure with pale eyes behind rimless glasses and a stare of displeasure that the Pulitzer Prize–winning Alva Johnston described as a "death ray," he won no popularity contests with his staff. But their respect for his instincts and learning amounted to awe. It was Van Anda who urged on the *Times* to its superb coverage of polar exploration and the exploits of aviation, Van Anda who disputed the unsinkability of the *Titanic*. When the ship's radio went dead following an SOS call for help after the liner hit an iceberg in 1912, he was the only editor to surmise that she had plunged to the bottom. He prodded and pushed his reporters to a world scoop on the disaster, which took more than 1,500 lives in a single night. He read hieroglyphics and discovered a forgery one night while poring with a magnifying glass over photographs of a four-thousand-year-old inscription on King Tut's tomb.

He introduced American readers to Albert Einstein and his theory of relativity at a time when, according to a Princeton expert, the theory was understood only by "Dr. Einstein and by the Deity." Once, in a report about the great physicist's lectures, he discovered an error in one of Einstein's equations. The professor who had translated the lecture from the German stood by his notes, but went reluctantly back to Einstein. The scientist said: "Yes, Mr. Van Anda is right. I made a mistake in transcribing the equation on the blackboard."

This was the man Anne McCormick had asked for assignments. Van Anda soon gave her one that would have terrified the most seasoned reporter. On March 14, 1921, he sent this cable to her at the Hotel Regina in Rome: "WILL YOU GET ORLANDO'S OWN STORY SIGNED BY HIM OR IN QUOTATIONS COVERING HIGHLIGHTS OF CONFERENCES OF BIG FOUR AT PEACE CONFERENCE. . . . NONE OF BIG FOUR HAS YET TOLD WHO CONTROLLED AND WHAT HAPPENED SECRET SESSIONS. YOUR TASK TO GET FIRST."

Vittorio Orlando, a former premier of Italy, was one of the Big Four heads of government who had fashioned the destiny of the world at Versailles in 1919 along with President Woodrow Wilson of the United States, Britain's Lloyd George, and France's Georges Clemenceau. Anne McCormick had as an introduction only a letter from Van Anda, asking for the usual courtesies for a "special representative" of *The New York Times.* Four days later she cabled her reply: "SAW O. [Orlando] SEE AGAIN TOMORROW. WOULD TIMES CONSIDER MAKING HIM PROPOSITION FOR STATEMENT A SERIES REMINISCENCES. . . . THINK IT MIGHT APPEAL."

This self-possessed response came from a woman nearing her forty-first birthday, a woman totally untrained in daily newspaper work. It was a spectacular coup and McCormick's first scoop for the *Times.*

Anne McCormick would do it again and again, but she would never tell how she did it. That was part of her mystery. Her appeal was certainly not sexual—she had become dumpy in middle age and her red hair had darkened; she dressed well but conservatively, although she splurged on her hats, which were sometimes so elaborate that they look almost goofy to the modern eye. She listened eagerly and did not seek to dazzle by her talk. She was deeply religious, deeply Roman Catholic. "She sees me every time she comes to Rome," the pope said. It was not an ostentatious piety, but a kind of shining light at the center of her being—a rarity in an irreverent, blasphemous, frantic profession. Luther Huston, who read her copy as general manager of the *Times*'s Washington bureau, told of an occasion when Anne joined her gang of colleagues at a Chicago steak house after a national political convention. They had a few drinks at the bar, Anne sipping at her single old-fashioned, and then Huston stayed behind to pay the bill. When he joined the party, there was a seat saved for him at the head of the table. "I'll be father," he joked. "But I will not say grace." There was laughter, followed by silence. Anne McCormick said, "I'll say grace."

"All of us bowed our heads," Huston said, "and there in that saloon amid the whiskey fumes and the red-checked tablecloths, Anne McCormick said the most moving grace I ever heard. It was like a benediction. It wasn't forced. It didn't dampen or frost up the party. With her saying it, it was a perfectly normal and natural thing to do."

She was a quiet reporter in the midst of towering egos, often slipping in and out of European capitals on her news-gathering errands without letting the resident *Times* bureau chief know where she was staying, or even that she had been there. This way of operating—on a newspaper whose foreign correspondents are permanently attached by electronic umbilical cords to the home office—gave rise to some furious cables speeding back and forth across the Atlantic. The foreign desk demanded: "WHERE'S MISTRESS MCCORMICK NOW?" and got only: "MISTRESS MCCORMICK LONDONWARD WEEK AGO UNTRACE SINCE."

Even those who witnessed her in action were unable to explain how she got the interviews she did. Clifton Daniel couldn't explain it—Clifton Daniel of the soulful dark eyes and the Savile Row suits, the smoothest of reporters and editors, "the sheik of Fleet Street," who broke the heart of one titled Englishwoman after another and then married an American princess, Margaret Truman—even he could not pin Anne McCormick down.

"I was the *Times* bureau chief in Bonn after World War II and the McCormicks came to town very early one day," he recalled. "I went to the railroad station to greet them and offered the usual courtesies: Would you like a car? Can I arrange any appointments? She very politely said, 'No, thank you very much, I don't want to disturb you, I can take care of myself.' The next thing I knew, she had an appointment with everybody in town, from Konrad Adenauer [the augustly ancient chancellor of West Germany] on down. I'm sure Adenauer called her up and invited her to lunch. She never had to grovel for an appointment. It was rather prestigious to be interviewed by Mrs. McCormick and get your name in this famous column of hers in *The New York Times*. I was greatly impressed. Nobody like the chancellor of Germany ever said to me, 'Do come around and interview me.' "

Told of this episode, James Reston commented, "Daniel was not as nice as she was." Scotty Reston, who could get to important people more easily than almost any other reporter of his era, added that Anne McCormick's ability to gain access was due to her "sheer gift of personality" and her intelligence. "You couldn't throw a ball at her," he said, "without something bouncing back. She was enormously confident in her mind and in her spirit about what was up. She was smarter than the *Times*. But she knew how to use its reputation to get what she wanted."

The last skill surfaced early in Anne McCormick. It was also obvious from the beginning of her career with the *Times* that she knew how to write. Her big stories from Europe, even those from long ago, give the reader of today a thrill of urgency, of immediacy—a sense of being there. In one of her first major pieces, she brought to life two spectacles, the opening of the Italian Parliament and the session of the Papal Consistory in the summer of 1921. It was the first time she had laid eyes on Benito Mussolini.

She described King Victor Emmanuel, showing himself to the people in the streets of Rome on his way to the Chamber of Deputies in "a crystal chariot drawn by white horses with jeweled harnesses, heralded by bugles and gorgeous outriders and all the other glittering circus trappings which monarchies really pay a king to furnish," then coming before the legislators modestly, in the gray uniform of a colonel.

She called Mussolini's first speech to the lawmakers "one of the best political speeches I have ever heard, a little swaggering but caustic, powerful and telling." She declared, "I admire the Fascisti" and their "illimitable energy" in a weary world. Then she added, "But it must be admitted that some of them, that day in Parliament, acted like nothing so much as spoiled children in a howling temper. If they keep up their raging pace, they will either die of physical exhaustion themselves or exhaust and kill the Parliament."

What the Fascists soon did, of course, with Mussolini at their head, was to dissolve the legislature and start Italy down the dark slide into tyranny.

In that early article, she turned from the hullabaloo in the Chamber of Deputies to the "solemn restraints and ancient disciplines" of the Papal Consistory:

The sound of silver trumpets in the distance heralded the approach of the Pope. The sound is rather unearthly, high and piercingly sweet, and its effect was to lay a silence so loud that it shouted upon the whispering throng in the Sala Regia and the crowded corridor outside.

Benedict XV is no more impressive to look at than Victor Emmanuel. In his insignificant figure and rather expressionless face there is no majesty, spiritual or secular. But as he was borne into the consistory chamber in his uplifted golden chair, those ineffable waving fans of white peacock feathers somehow hedged him in and brushed him aside, so that the man inside the Pope did not matter at all. He was lost in something impersonal, perpetual, obliterating. It was the Papacy one saw moving in the hush, swallowing up good Popes, bad Popes, and indifferent Popes, and surviving them all.

As the years went on, Anne McCormick grew even more confident and better at what she was doing, while her husband gradually, inexorably, declined. Instead of the wife trotting at her husband's heels, the husband trotted at hers, arranging travel schedules, reserving hotels, making sure she left dinner parties in time to keep to her schedule. At last, enfeebled mentally and physically, he could do little. She kept up the pretense, and his pride.

No one has described their relationship more sensitively than Cyrus L. Sulzberger, a member of the *Times*'s ruling family and Anne McCormick's successor as the foreign affairs columnist after her death. It was 1940 in Belgrade; she was sixty years old and Sulzberger was half her age, although already a distinguished foreign correspondent. In his memoir, *A Long Row of Candles,* he wrote:

Everyone loved her, and, what was important for a journalist, also confided in her. As always, Anne was accompanied by her elderly husband [he was then sixty-eight], who had suffered a stroke some years past and was but a shadow of his former courtly self; yet she adored him and never traveled without him, pretending to rely upon his counsel. She would not even dictate one of her perceptive articles without Frank standing beside her, often in a tiny telephone booth, gravely turning the pages. . . .

When they arrived at Belgrade's suburban station after a train trip from Romania, Anne descended, embraced me, and began to chatter like a machine gun shooting platinum bullets while poor Frank stood in puzzlement before a mound of luggage, objurgating equally puzzled Serbian porters. When we rescued him and led him to my car he turned with an air of grave knowledge and said: "Aha. Jugoslavakia [*sic*]. Tell me, Cy, who's president now?" Anne chided him affectionately: "Stop teasing the boy, Frank. You know Jugoslavia's a kingdom."

Almost everyone who knew her did seem to love Anne McCormick, but there was at least one exception, one *Times*-man who hated her. He was Frederick T. Birchall, an assistant managing editor to Carr Van Anda, later Van Anda's successor, and finally an outstanding foreign correspondent who won the Pulitzer Prize in 1934 for "unbiased reporting of the news from Germany," including the rise to power of Adolf Hitler.

Birchall was a peppery little Lancashireman with a bald pate, bottle-glass-thick spectacles, and a pointed beard of reddish hue that he plucked constantly when bemused or excited. He went to Berlin in 1932 as the *Times*'s chief European correspondent. From then on, his cables to the home office were studded with complaints about Anne O'Hare McCormick, whom he regarded as a smarmy, amateurish interloper on his turf. To Edwin L. James, the Virginia dandy who had sent terrific news stories from Europe during the twenties and who followed Birchall into the managing editor's chair in New York, he called Mrs. McCormick a "damn nuisance" and worse.

It was Birchall who coined the term "Mistress McCormick"—and it was meant sneeringly. He cabled James from Berlin on October 14, 1933: "AMONG THOSE PRESENT HERE TODAY IS MISTRESS MCCORMICK, WHOM I DON'T WANT AT ANY PRICE." James picked up the nickname and used it frequently, as did some of the other *Times* correspondents. Birchall wrote, "I find her stuff inaccurate superficialities, plus ill-founded opinion," and then added, "both quite well written." He called her big expense accounts "a disaster," said she was "pontificating," "messing up the landscape" for other correspondents, and muddying the waters of clear reporting from Central Europe. He repeatedly expressed the hope that her work for the *Times* would soon come to an end. He was forced to edit her copy, he said, "to conform with facts."

He sent a confidential letter to James: "This Irish b—— knows she has put it over both of us and *isn't* she enjoying it?

You should see her grin at me when she talks of not desiring to interfere with the 'real historians.' To make me feel bad she adopts the feminine trick of pretending to be [the publisher's] special pet. For that reason alone I would like to put a crimp in her."

Meantime, Anne McCormick was mending her fences with the people who really counted around the *Times*—the family that owned it. She and her husband often spent weekends at Hillandale, the Ochs and Sulzberger country estate north of New York City. She wrote captivating letters, full of inside information about a Europe headed for a second world war, to Arthur Hays Sulzberger, Ochs's son-in-law and heir apparent. Sulzberger and his wife, Iphigene, Ochs's only child, loved Anne McCormick. "Anne had the map of Ireland on her face," Iphigene later said, "but what stood out most was her innate charm, her femininity, her dynamic personality."

Some colleagues grumbled that in the twenties and early thirties she was "soft on Mussolini" because he granted her so many interviews, seeming to her as reasonable in private as he was ruthless and arrogant in public. In Germany, soon after Hitler came to power, she got in to see that dictator too; her assessment of the man and his impact provoked a storm of furious letters from readers of the *Times*. A New York lawyer called what she wrote a "stupid and bare-faced attempt to white-wash this arch criminal and pogromist and to present him as a statesman and leader. . . . Miss McCormick evidently became enamored of Herr Hitler because he gallantly kissed her hand in the 'best German manner' and therefore evidently forgets that Hitler is guilty of that most heinous offense against good manners in trampling upon every civilized and humane instinct and plunging Germany into barbarism."

James, the managing editor, was upset. He cabled Mrs. McCormick: "WE CAN USE ANOTHER ARTICLE HITLER'S TREATMENT OF THOSE HE DOESN'T LIKE," and "CONSIDERABLE CRITICISM YOUR GERMAN ARTICLES HERE ON GROUND THAT THEY GIVE ONLY FAVORABLE ASPECTS HITLER BUSINESS." Mrs. McCormick complied. And then, in August 1933, she wrote Arthur Hays Sulzberger one of her long, typically perceptive and ingratiating letters.

"What I tried to do in my German dispatches was to indicate facts as they are in Germany and not as we'd like them to be," she declared. "Nobody can say [as did one outraged reader] that Hitler attained power through 'the defranchisement of a small minority.' What's worse, no one can say now that the majority of the German people don't stand behind him. . . . There's no use blinding ourselves to that fact or its import, national and international, just because we don't like it. . . . I tried my best to discover and suggest why the Germans got that way. There are explanations, one of which is that you can't penalize a nation over a long period without making them dangerous."

She protected her flanks with Sulzberger by contrasting her analyses with those of other foreign correspondents on the scene, who, she said, were "terribly let down" by Hitler's victory and "swore it couldn't happen" because they believed in a democratic, republican Germany "and didn't realize how thin and artificial was the democratic crust." Nothing in the whole situation was worse, she told Sulzberger, than the fact that Hitler and the Nazis were popular. She recounted how the British consul general in Berlin had said to her, "There are only two kinds of Germans, those who like to kick and those who like to be kicked." She added, "But they're the key people of Europe none the less—and we have to deal with them *as they are,* and as they think of themselves. . . . I feel strongly that we must realize how big and dangerous this thing is in Germany. I think the Jews have made a mistake in not making a protest in behalf of all the oppressed. . . . It's so much bigger than an anti-Semitic insanity."

The storm about her articles from Germany soon blew over, and Anne McCormick's star kept rising. She went everywhere in Europe, interviewing Dollfuss and Schuschnigg of Austria, Beneš of Czechoslovakia, Baldwin and Eden of Britain, De

Valera of Ireland, Léon Blum of France, indeed virtually all the men who made the history of their times in Europe. By the mid-thirties, she was feeling the "seismic disturbance" of the coming world war:

"All the rulers of Europe have shriveled or aged during the past few years. On the faces of Mussolini, Hitler, Stanley Baldwin, even the rotating governors of France, strain and worry have etched indelible lines. . . . The face of the world has changed. You walk familiar streets and they are strange. People everywhere are like houses with the shutters down, withdrawn and waiting, as if life were held in suspense; or they are quarreling within their houses, hating one another because long-drawn-out uncertainty has rasped their nerves to the breaking point."

She had learned to write more tightly, so that the mutterings from the copy editors in New York, who called her Verbose Annie, gradually faded away. Raymond McCaw, the night managing editor under Edwin James, scrawled over yet another disgruntled cable from Birchall: "Mr. James—She seems to get in Birch's hair but she sent a damned good piece tonight."

She was also growing bolder about her rights and expressing her views in a stream of letters to her editors and the Sulzbergers. She fussed constantly about her "weekly dole" of $125, which was supposed to cover her retainer fee as a stringer and her travel expenses, spoke of herself as a "stepchild" of the *Times* family, insisted that James change her status in his letters of introduction from "regular contributor" to "special correspondent." She wrote Lester Markel, the fearsome editor of the *Times* Sunday magazine, where most of her writings were printed, that she had seen Mussolini twice on a recent visit and that the dictator, "a curious combination—hypnotist and self-hypnotist," was seeing fewer and fewer people, never the local correspondents and seldom the people in his own foreign office. Then she tooted her own horn: "Increasingly it is true that only 'specials [like herself],' passing through, have the chance to see the statesmen who make news. An important point for a newspaper to consider, I should think, if it's valuable to have any contact with the heads of government." Markel passed the letter on to Sulzberger.

She was fast becoming one of the great political analysts in journalism, along with Walter Lippmann of *The New York Herald Tribune* and Arthur Krock of *The New York Times,* who wrote on the domestic scene, and the flamboyant and enormously influential Dorothy Thompson, also with the *Herald Tribune,* who wrote from abroad. In 1935, Carrie Chapman Catt, the pioneer suffragist, named Anne McCormick one of America's ten outstanding women.

That same year, Arthur Hays Sulzberger was taking out what he called "formal adoption papers which will end the step-child arrangement." They came through in the spring of 1936. Anne McCormick accepted with joy. "It gives me immense satisfaction to break a precedent, and even more to know that the Times at last wants me where I have long felt I belong," she wrote her boss. Then she warned him, "I hope you won't expect me to revert to 'woman's-point-of-view' stuff."

Instead, with her Irish mirth and spunk, the first woman to be appointed to the *Times* editorial board brought laughter as well as prophetic writing to her stuffy colleagues immured in their pseudo-Gothic ivory tower on the newspaper's tenth floor. Scotty Reston, who was soon to know her—he joined the paper in London the day World War II began, a perfect example of Reston's fabled timing—loved her talk and her quiet little pranks.

"She literally twinkled when she talked, and what talk!" he recalled years later. "Everything and everybody interested her, and she illuminated every subject she touched." He remembered her showing up one year at the Republican national convention wearing a white silk dress with tiny Democratic donkeys on it, and appearing the next week at the Democratic convention in another white silk dress printed with small blue Republican elephants.

Anne McCormick contributed unsigned editorials starting in June 1936; she began writing her regular bylined column on foreign affairs on February 1, 1937. She was not the kind to sit on the tenth floor and write what the trade calls thumbsuckers, or think pieces, from her home base. The energetic little body bustled all over Europe on the eve of the Second World War, spending the better part of every year overseas. "Did Walter Lippmann say that nobody can learn anything in Europe?" she wrote Sulzberger from Amsterdam. "I wish I could take in all there is to learn." She told him that it was better that her columns be written on the spot, dismissed the grumbling from the New York office about her prolonged absences, and then ended her long letter: "If I keep on, I'll miss the boat [to England]. It's a bitter, windy night for the Channel crossing."

She had no real home. When in New York, she and her husband lived at Fifth Avenue's dignified Hotel Gotham, and, later, uptown on Madison Avenue at the equally elegant Carlyle, which would become a favorite of Presidents Truman and Kennedy. The McCormicks had given up their home in Dayton, called Hills and Dales, long before. In one typical year, she spent seven months soaking up information in thirteen European countries. She was in Rome when Neville Chamberlain, Britain's prime minister, called on Mussolini. She was in the British Parliament when Chamberlain finally gave up on his policy of appeasement toward the Nazi-Fascist axis. She was in Ruthenia, in eastern Czechoslovakia, cabling dispatches almost hourly, when it declared an independence that lasted only one day, until the Germans authorized the Hungarians to march in and occupy it. When Hitler invaded Poland on September 1, 1939, igniting World War II, she rushed to Romania, which then shared a border with Poland. "It is a story of cracking frontiers and people literally worried to death," she reported. Grigore Gafencu, the Romanian foreign minister, told her: "In the daytime it isn't so bad to be the foreign minister. . . . It is the nights that wear you down, nights when you are tortured by thoughts of the horrors to come." The Nazis soon came. She was with Paul Reynaud, the French premier, when he confessed to her, weeks before the defeat of France, that all was lost. She walked through Berlin during a blackout. "Groping through the tunnel-like streets," she wrote, "you almost never hear a voice. Other gropers are shadows and footsteps."

She was fearless. In France, she insisted on keeping a dinner date with the terrible-tempered General George Patton although to reach his headquarters she had to travel a long pitch-black road, pockmarked with bomb holes and under bombardment, a road where military vehicles were not moving. At the front, she refused to wear a helmet despite Patton's orders, and instead went about in a GI's mustard-colored knitted wool cap. She talked to men in the ranks everywhere, as well as the brass. She wrote of them: "Behind their gay and casual front they are about the angriest army which ever went to war. This anger is general. The prevailing mood . . . is irritation at the waste, the upset, the stupidity, the agony, the destruction, obscenity and arrogance of war."

After it was over, she rode from Berlin to Stuttgart with James F. Byrnes, the American secretary of state, in Hitler's private railroad car, and then went on to Nuremberg to cover the Allied trials of the Nazi war criminals.

She wrote of the women she saw throughout Europe, trying to sweep up the wreckage of the war with their brooms. In Evreux, Normandy, traveling with General Charles de Gaulle, Anne McCormick stopped to talk with a Frenchwoman who was swiping away at the rocks smothering her garden; she asked her what she thought she could accomplish in the wake of two thousand-pound bombs. "Who's to save the cabbages and onions if I don't?" the woman replied fiercely. "They're all that's left of all the work of all my life. And somebody has to begin clearing away this mess."

Mrs. McCormick noted that two wars had left more women than men in Europe—angry women, widows of soldiers, widows of hostages, cleaning up the mess the men had made—and that it was not by chance that women had been named to the San Francisco conference that set up the United Nations. "There should be more of them, for they are in the wars now," she wrote, "and millions of them have nothing much left now but a broom. . . . Certainly it's a sound and self-protective instinct that impels the men to hand over to the women a little of the responsibility for the hardest job in history."

She went on absorbing and reporting into old age, energetic and imperturbable. At sixty-nine she was scrambling up and down the mountains of Greece with guerrillas who could have been her grandsons, as tireless, *Time* magazine said, "as a self-winding watch." She cabled home: "It is easy enough to say that the Greek war is an affair of daily raids, in which armed bands . . . swoop down from the cracks and crevices of a mountain . . . to sack or burn villages and carry off able-bodied men and girls to forced service in their armies. But the imagination cannot picture the desolation that this hit-and-run fighting leaves behind it. . . . Everywhere the atmosphere was heavy with suspense. In such fearful quiet must the early settlers in the West have awaited the descent of the Indians."

On a stormy flight to Athens in a military plane, she was thrown to the floor and hurt her knee. Flora Lewis, who followed her as a *Times* foreign affairs columnist many years later, recalled that on Mrs. McCormick's arrival, "She was very cheerful and clinical about the injury, but so vivid in recounting just what happened that I nearly fainted."

She was rarely snappish, but when she was, her targets were big ones. Anthony Eden, the patrician British foreign secretary, once remarked sniffily to her that American reporters had *also* realized the menace of Germany's and Italy's dictators. "As a matter of fact," she retorted, "they were ahead of the diplomats. After all, Mr. Secretary, diplomats are only badly trained reporters."

And she lit out in public against John Foster Dulles, President Eisenhower's secretary of state. When he threatened to use the atom bomb before the Russians had it, she declared, "I've watched Dulles's performance at a number of international conferences, and in my opinion he's demonstrated a complete lack of sensitivity and understanding." After her death, the *Times* published a eulogy from Dulles, who said that for years, her column was the one he never missed: "She reported with a balance and sanity of judgment and perception which, in my opinion, was unmatched in her profession."

When she died, full of years and honors, in a New York hospital on May 29, 1954, the *Times* printed her obituary and her picture on its front page. Her column space, bordered in black, held a tribute from Robert Duffus, who had long worked with her on the editorial page:

She was a reporter and gloried in the title. She could not understand how anyone could be satisfied with less than the personal observation on the spot. . . . In spite of all her genius for seeing, understanding and reporting, she was also a deeply feminine person and could not help being so and would not have wished not to be so. She had a great compassion for those who suffered. War to her was not something abstract that destroyed nations. . . . War was the thing that wrecked houses in which real people lived, that left children hungry and mothers hopeless. She saw beneath the great striding events of the day. . . . She felt and showed in her writing the great pulses of history and did not deceive herself.

The outpourings—from President Dwight D. Eisenhower, who had known her on the field of war, and members of his government, foreign ministers, ambassadors, mayors, rabbis, publishers—filled the columns of her newspaper for days. Francis Cardinal Spellman of New York offered a mass for her soul at the American College in Rome. Arthur Hays Sulzberger spoke of her as a friend, sharing intimate joys with him and his wife, and mourned the loss of this "agile, facile, profound, happy mind and generous heart."

Lester Markel, the impressive and impossible Sunday editor, who had been her boss during her earliest years of writing for the *Times* (and consistently made her rewrite her copy), said of her that nobody else in the business possessed such an extraordinary ability to be on intimate terms with the people who moved nations. Such praise was rare indeed from the man who for forty years ran an ulcer factory on the eighth floor; Walter Winchell, the acerbic gossip columnist, was fond of saying that the fourth floor of the *Times,* the composing room, was surgery, and the eighth floor was the psychiatric ward.

To Scotty Reston, Anne O'Hare McCormick could not have been such a great reporter had she not been such a great and spiritual woman. Almost forty years after her death he told me, deeply serious, "She is in my mind still."

CHAPTER 3

THE DARK AGES

Anne O'Hare McCormick was the brightest woman star who ever shone upon *The New York Times,* but in her time she was virtually alone among constellations of men on the nation's newspaper of record. She was loved, she was honored, she was rewarded finally with one of the highest salaries on the entire *Times* payroll. By the early 1950s, she was earning $30,624 a year, a princely sum in those days. Only four men on the news staff were paid more than she—the Sunday editor, the managing editor, the head of the editorial board, and Arthur Krock, the national columnist.

But in 1936, the year Mrs. McCormick joined the tenth-floor editorial-page staff, only one woman reporter sat downstairs in the city room, the news center of the paper. "You could have cut the ice with a sword," said that reporter, Kathleen McLaughlin, of her first months on the third floor in 1935. She had been one of the best during a scrappy, exciting decade on the *Chicago Tribune.*

Mrs. McCormick urged women to have careers, but she never worked actively for feminist causes. She once said of herself and other newspaperwomen: "We had tried hard not to act like ladies or to talk as ladies are supposed to talk—meaning too much—but just to sneak toward the city desk and the cable desk, and the editorial sanctum and even the publisher's office with masculine *sang-froid.*"

In 1936, Ishbel Ross, one of the greatest reporters ever to grace the *New York Herald Tribune,* brought out her classic history of women in journalism, *Ladies of the Press.* She noted sadly that even then, there were not enough women in the profession to make any difference. "They have merely established the fact [that they are around], not revolutionized the status of their colleagues," she said. "They are remarkable only because they are exceptions." Mrs. McCormick personified that rarity, the excellent woman making it on her own. Moreover, she had made it on a newspaper that had always been particularly backward in the hiring and promotion of women.

Look back on the landscape of nineteenth- and early-twentieth-century journalism. Nowhere is it emptier of women than on *The New York Times.* While Nellie Bly (the pen name for Elizabeth Cochrane) was whizzing around the planet in seventy-two days or locking herself into insane asylums to do front-page stories for Joseph Pulitzer's New York *World;* while Rheta Childe Dorr was going off to the Russian Revolution for the New York *Mail;* while William Randolph Hearst of the Hearst chain and Roy Howard of the Scripps-Howard chain and Joseph Patterson of the New York *Daily News* and Colonel Robert McCormick of the *Chicago Tribune* were pushing their women stars, *The New York Times* stood fast against what it was sure was the weaker sex. By the 1930s, Helen Rogers Reid, the wife of the publisher and a vigorous vice president of the *New York Herald Tribune,* was naming women to edit the *Trib*'s book review and magazine; she gave Dorothy Thompson her instantly sensational "On the Record" column a year before the *Times* made Anne O'Hare McCormick a columnist and months before she was even put on staff.

"Job seekers knowing the ropes felt it was hopeless to try their luck at the gates of the leading paper in the country," Ishbel Ross wrote. "It was the last citadel. Long after the Associated Press [one of the last holdouts] had welcomed women, the *Times* still regarded them with suspicion."

The number of women who worked as reporters for *The New York Times* from its founding in 1851 until about a century later was pathetically meager. The first woman to write regularly for the paper, beginning in the 1850s, was Sara Jane Clarke. She chose the pen name Grace Greenwood, in the alliterative fashion of the day (Minnie Myrtle and the immensely popular Fanny Fern appeared in other periodicals). Although Clarke never made it to the *Times* city room, she sent many dispatches to the *Times,* one of several newspapers she wrote for simultaneously, from the American West, from Washington, and from Europe. She was born in Pompey, New York, in 1823 and began contributing to newspapers and to *Godey's Lady's Book* by the time she was nineteen. She was a witty, pretty person with a fresh and vivacious style, a militant abolitionist who read proof on *Uncle Tom's Cabin* when she worked for the Washington-based *National Era.* In 1852 she went to Europe for a year, sending back interviews in the form of chatty letters. Clarke dined with Dickens, interviewed Thackeray and Browning, met the pope, struggled up Mount Vesuvius. Her Washington sketches were first published in the New York *Tribune.* She wrote of the Congress: "These saucy serving-men of ours are really becoming disagreeably and uncomfortably quarrelsome." She read and lectured to soldiers during the Civil War; President Abraham Lincoln called her "Grace Greenwood, the Patriot." In 1874, she was listed as an accredited representative of *The New York Times,* along with ten other women reporters, in the overwhelmingly male preserve of the congressional press gallery.

···········

Only one other woman joined the *Times* reportorial staff in the years that preceded Adolph Ochs, who bought and relaunched the dying paper in 1896 and gave it the inimitably *Times*ian stamp it bears to the present.

On a September day in 1869, John Bigelow, the *Times* editor in chief, heard a gallumphing noise and looked up from his desk to see a huge apparition bearing down upon him. The apparition was six feet two inches tall, garbed in rough Irish tweeds, and shod in thick-soled brogues. A whiff of the stables perfumed the air. A deep, melodious voice with an Irish lilt said, "I am Maria Morgan. I want a job." She crushed his hand, shoved a letter of introduction at him, and sat down. Bigelow stammered that the only vacant post he had was that of livestock reporter. "I can fill it," Miss Morgan said. She told him of her background, which included buying six mares for King Victor Emmanuel II ("doubtless the most sporting crowned head of Europe") and transporting them from Ireland over the Alps to Italy. In half an hour, she had a job. She was the first woman reporter ever hired in the city room of *The New York Times*. She took the pen name and nickname of Midy Morgan.

She was born in 1828 to Irish landed gentry near Cork and grew up with horses and with hunting. "I am rather more than three parts crazed on the subject of horseflesh," she said. When her father died in 1865, leaving the family property to his eldest son, she left with her mother and sister for two years in Italy, where she went fox hunting and read Byron, then all the rage. She was presented to the premier, and to the king, Victor Emmanuel, who commissioned her to buy horses in Ireland for his stables. Returning to Italy by steamer and rail with six spirited mares in boxcars, she had thirty-two changes to make, and when she got to Switzerland she was momentarily daunted by the vertical landscape. But remembering that Hannibal had crossed the Alps with horses as well as elephants in his train, she took heart and delivered the mares in splendid condition. The king gave her a hunting watch with his initials encrusted in diamonds. It became her most precious possession. When he died in 1878, she got it out of her safe deposit vault and wore it for a year with a mourning band, and then she put it back in the bank.

Midy covered livestock news, racing, horse shows, and dog shows. She could be forced into service for a cat show, although cats were the only four-footed creatures she could not abide. This great gawk of a woman did her work with a vengeance, stumping around the cattle yards and racetracks in tall laced boots on dry days and hip-high rubber waders when it was stormy. She walked with a limp because a horse had crushed one foot, but she barreled ahead at a tremendous rate anyhow, chewing straws in fierce concentration and practically knocking over anyone in her path. All the horse breeders in the country came to respect her.

General Ulysses S. Grant sought her advice on horses. She was a friend of the man-about-town Chauncey M. Depew, and of the millionaire Commodore Vanderbilt, who invested her money wisely, in New York Central securities. She stomped through the city room to deliver her copy, written in a hand so illegible that it was always sent to the same compositors, who had become used to deciphering it. She rarely spoke to the other reporters. During her years with the *Times* she made three trips to Europe, the first voyage on a cattle boat, where she was outraged at the way the animals were treated. The series of articles she wrote resulted in improved methods of handling cattle at sea, and she continued to battle for more humane treatment of animals on land.

Her domestic life was curious. Soon after coming to the United States, she adopted a German boy. When he decided to marry, Midy threw him out in a rage. During her later years, she lived in a barren room in the railroad station at Robinvale, New Jersey, working part-time selling tickets to supplement her wages. Her rent was free and she got passes on the railroad, perquisites that the thrifty Midy enjoyed. When she was in her fifties she bought some property on Staten Island, and there, over seven years, she had a house built that was as lopsided and eccentric as she was. It was three stories tall, with one giant room on each floor, paneled in exotic woods. The dining annex was covered entirely in thousands of colored seashells. Her sister did the decoration and filled the rooms with furniture from Europe. Midy never retired to her dream house but lived to the end in the Robinvale station. She died on June 1, 1892, at the age of sixty-four, after twenty-three years on *The New York Times,* and was buried from the Little Church around the Corner in New York. She left $100,000 in stocks to her sister. Her good jewelry, including the watch from King Victor Emmanuel II, she bequeathed to the Metropolitan Museum.

....

Four years after Midy Morgan's death, Adolph Ochs became publisher. His reign lasted forty years—years that were the Dark Ages for women at *The New York Times.*

To the end of his life in 1935, Ochs agreed with the outdated views of James Gordon Bennett, the cross-eyed, cross-grained owner of the New York *Herald* from 1835 to 1872. Bennett was probably the worst misogynist among publishers in the nineteenth century: he strode into his office one day and bellowed, "Who are these females? Fire them all!" Ochs, who was a Southern gentleman as well as an autocrat, would never have expressed such an attitude so coarsely. But he carried Bennett's Victorian notions straight into the twentieth century. He believed women belonged at home and certainly not on a newspaper; he fought personally and in his paper's editorials against women's right to vote. Anne McCormick's fifteen-year struggle to get on the *Times* payroll as a salaried employee, a story buried until now in the paper's private archives, is an indicator of Adolph Ochs's unyielding stand against women on his staff. His resistance to a feminine presence on the paper was subtly but unmistakably communicated to his family and to *Times* executives and editors for many a long year after his death.

Adolph Ochs, the oldest of six children of German immigrants, was born in Cincinnati, Ohio, in 1858 and raised in Knoxville, Tennessee. His father was a Micawberish dreamer who clung to the belief that something would turn up to change his ill fortune. That elusive something turned out to be Adolph, who never forgot his family at any point in his triumphal career. At the age of fourteen Adolph signed on as a printer's devil, or apprentice, at the Knoxville *Chronicle*. He was an undersized, serious, observant boy who worked hard and had big visions. He was earnest and he was honest and he had chutzpah. A few years later he was working as a "business solicitor" for a short-lived newspaper in Chattanooga, Tennessee, a rough frontier town with no sidewalks and streets made of mud. When the paper went bust, he decided to use its handpress to print a Chattanooga city directory and business guide, which he compiled himself. It proved a success. By 1878, the Chattanooga *Times* was dying; he wanted to buy it. Adolph Ochs was twenty years old. He purchased a half interest in the newspaper for $250 and ultimately was able to give his own father a job there. The Chattanooga *Times* is still owned by Ochs's heirs, and it is run by one of Ochs's granddaughters, Ruth Sulzberger Holmberg, the only woman in three generations of this extraordinary clan to become a newspaper publisher.

In August of 1896, Ochs bought a controlling interest in *The New York Times,* then on Park Row overlooking City Hall, and moved his family from Chattanooga to Manhattan. The *Times,* at the age of forty-five, was distinguished but dry. It was poorly managed and moribund. Its circulation had sunk from 75,000 at the beginning of the Civil War to a measly

9,000 in 1896, against the 600,000 of Pulitzer's morning and evening editions of the *World*, the 300,000 of Hearst's morning *Journal*, the 140,000 of Bennett's *Herald*.

Adolph Ochs was thirty-eight years old, a man who knew both the editorial and the mechanical aspects of his trade as few publishers ever do. He had borrowed $75,000 from banks and influential friends in Chattanooga and obtained letters of recommendation from men of influence, including President Grover Cleveland. He had studied New York on foot and by rented bicycle. He wanted his newspaper to be impartial and complete, to appeal to businessmen, to be "the newspaper of record" that would, as he said, "not soil the breakfast linen." He purchased new type to make the paper more legible. He sought coverage of government actions, court proceedings, financial news, Wall Street reports, real estate transactions. It was Ochs who thought up "All the News That's Fit to Print," still the *Times* motto. Within weeks of his accession as publisher, he brought out a handsome illustrated Sunday magazine that instantly became popular with readers. By 1901, the *Times* circulation had reached 102,000.

During the four decades that Adolph Ochs held sway, only four women worked as reporters in the *Times* city room. They were Mary Taft, who arrived in the late 1890s; Jane Grant, just before World War I; Rachel McDowell, beginning in 1920; and Nancy Hale, very briefly, in 1934. Their work was carefully compartmentalized. The first two specialized in women's news, such as conventions, society, clubs, and fashion shows. Taft, and then Grant, also covered the rise of the suffrage movement for women—until the movement became front-page material and male reporters were assigned to write the stories. Years after Taft was hired—she had been making $30 a week at space rates and the city editor said she was too expensive and would have to join the staff for $19 a week, which she did—another woman applicant dared to ask Ochs for a job. He told her that the *Times* did not take women on the city staff. "You have Miss Taft," the applicant reminded him. "Oh, yes," a flustered Ochs admitted. "But Miss Taft was practically born here."

Jane Grant, a founder of the feminist Lucy Stone League, married Harold Ross and took an active part in the shaping of *The New Yorker* magazine, of which Ross was the first and greatest editor.

And then came Rachel McDowell. Not since Midy Morgan had there been such an extraordinary eccentric, male or female, on the *Times*. She covered religion. She came to the paper after twelve years of pursuing church news for the New York *Herald,* and she was a tiger of a reporter. Her colleagues called her Miss McDowell to her face, never Rachel, and the Lady Bishop behind her back.

She was born in Newark, New Jersey, in 1880, the same year as Anne O'Hare McCormick. Two of her forebears in the early nineteenth century were moderators of the Presbyterian General Assembly. Her father, a businessman, and all his family went to church three times every Sunday; the seven children, including Rachel, went to Sunday School and belonged to Christian Endeavor. Worldly books were banned on the Sabbath, except, sometimes, the Elsie Dinsmore books, because, Miss McDowell said, one found nothing wicked in the Elsie books. She spent her girlhood vacations at Bible conferences in Indiana and Massachusetts. "I was dark-haired, blue-eyed and vivacious as a girl," she recalled, "and I had many beaux and many honest-to-goodness propositions [of marriage], but I wanted to be an entity, not just a Mrs. Somebody." All her life, she enjoyed nothing so much as a hellfire-and-brimstone sermon.

Meyer Berger, one of the paper's greatest and most-loved reporters, had known her since 1928, the year he joined the *Times*. In 1949, when the Lady Bishop retired, he wrote of her in the *Times* house organ, *Times Talk:*

Two events stand out sharply in Rachel Kollock McDowell's memories of forty years on New York newspapers. She cannot forget how she was accidentally entombed one day many years ago in Princess Anastasia's mausoleum in Woodlawn Cemetery while working on an exclusive story for The Times. Neither can she forget the virginal embarrassment that overwhelmed her when a Times doctor removed her shoe and stocking in a remote corner of the city room and set her left leg after she had broken it on a church assignment.

Within these two events lie the keys to Miss McDowell's character, and journalistic career. The tomb incident points up the fact that she would go anywhere, any time, to get an exclusive for the paper. The other stresses her fear and distrust of laymen [Berger might just as well have said "fear of men," but he was always kind], which decades of newspaper work could not overcome.

From the moment she came to the *Times,* Berger said, "every other religious news reporter in Manhattan blanched at the Lady Bishop's tigerish ferocity when she went after a church story. She haunted churches and cathedrals, presbytery meetings and Bible conferences. She snatched exclusives from under other reporters' eyes. She detested . . . pack reporting. She worked alone. She neither gave, nor asked for, quarter."

She founded the Pure Language League and continued to seek converts for it (in vain) within the newsroom of *The New York Times.* Reporters would provoke her by muttering obscenities whenever she hove into view. She would stop dead in her tracks to pin back the ears of anyone, from executive to copyboy, who swore in her presence. When a speaker told a slightly blue story at the men's Bible class at Riverside Baptist Church, she swept out, never to attend another meeting. Yet she lived just a few yards away from her cherished newspaper in the Hotel Times Square, a raunchy stopover in one of Manhattan's most sordid neighborhoods, presumably oblivious to the sin for sale all around her. When she no longer covered sermons, she spent all day Sunday listening to them in her fourteenth-floor room. Her mind was as unaware of risqué innuendo as a child's. One night a message came to the *Times* telegraph desk from Atlantic City, where she was attending a Methodist convention. "COPY A LITTLE LATE," she wired. "HAVE BEEN ON THE BOARDWALK ALL DAY. AM HUSTLING."

George Dugan, her jolly and very irreverent successor as religion editor, loved to tell of the deadline hour when Miss McDowell thundered up the aisle of the city room to the news desk, waving a sheet of fresh copy and shouting at the top of her lungs, "I've got a hot insert from the bishop!"

She was a freak and a figure of fun to the men on the staff, but she was formidable on her own turf. Perhaps the only time that stout heart quailed was on the assignment involving Princess Anastasia of Greece, the former Mrs. William B. Leeds. The princess died overseas, and Miss McDowell got a tip that the body would be brought home to Woodlawn Cemetery in New York for a secret burial. The gatekeeper repulsed her. She insisted. Finally, with the help of gravediggers and gardeners, she found her way to the family mausoleum just as the funeral cortege drove up. She crouched behind some shrubs while the brief service was said. The mourners departed. Only the undertaker, whom she knew, was left. He invited her smilingly to step inside the mausoleum. She became so totally absorbed in scribbling down the epitaphs on the other tombs that she did not hear the heavy door close behind her. When she turned to leave, she discovered she was trapped. She stood on tiptoe to peer through the glass over the iron grill. She cried out for help. There was no one in sight. She had thoughts of slow starvation. She began to pray, and had just given her soul into Divine keeping when the prankish undertaker reappeared to free her. She bounded past him into the open air without taking the time to tell him off. She was on deadline. "Anyway," she said later, practically smacking her lips, "I got a beat [scoop] on that one."

All through the twenties and into the thirties, Miss McDowell was the only woman reporter in the city room. Eventually she was put in an office of her own down a hall, and then she was removed altogether, to the tenth floor. In 1934, Nancy

Hale, a gifted writer of short stories, fleetingly joined the city staff. Murray Schumach, who was then a rosy-cheeked copyboy, recalled that Hale tried without success to concentrate on her work during the raucous games of jumping-bean that her colleagues played on their desks. "She was very attractive, and some reporters paid a great deal of attention to her," Schumach recalled. "She paid them no attention." She returned to the writing of fiction and less distracting surroundings after only a few months.

....

During these years, Adolph Ochs was going dramatically downhill. In 1933, he suffered his second nervous breakdown, twelve years after his first, and was committed to a psychiatric hospital with acute melancholia. Everything worried him: the Depression, which had prostrated the nation and might shatter his two newspapers; the rise of Hitler and the threat of another world war; the kidnapping of the Lindbergh baby and his fears that his own grandchildren were at risk. He did not snap out of his total isolation—he would not even read his own newspaper—until his last months. By the spring of 1935, he felt well enough to take a trip back to Chattanooga. With him were a nurse and his eldest granddaughter, Marian. On April 8, 1935, he toured the Chattanooga *Times*. He invited the editor and his brother Milton to lunch. The three men chatted and studied their menus. Milton asked, "What do you think you'll order, Adolph?" There was no answer. Ochs was slumped in his chair, unconscious. He died two hours later of a cerebral hemorrhage. He was seventy-seven years old.

His survivors included his wife, Effie, who died two years later; his only child, Iphigene, and Iphigene's husband, Arthur Hays Sulzberger, both in their forties; and their four children, Punch Sulzberger and his three sisters. Adolph Ochs's will gave his entire fortune to his four grandchildren in trust, with Effie and Iphigene to receive the interest for their lifetimes. The inheritance tax, with lawyers' fees, was six million dollars.

THE DARK AGES · 53

By leaving his money in trust to his grandchildren, Ochs avoided paying a far greater inheritance tax to the government. President Franklin D. Roosevelt described it as "a dirty Jewish trick."

Now it was time for the second generation of the Ochs dynasty. But who would be the publisher? Certainly not Iphigene, the daughter, despite all her spirit and intelligence. Her father had discouraged any effort on her part to become involved in the paper, including cutting short her efforts to take a journalism course at Columbia University.

Ochs had let it be known that he wanted his successor to be either his son-in-law, Arthur Hays Sulzberger, or his favorite nephew, Julius Ochs Adler. Adler was a chesty, aggressive, mustachioed war hero whose obvious ambition contrasted with Arthur Hays Sulzberger's elegance and self-deprecating competence. Both men had made their mark working at the *Times*. Ochs had named Iphigene and the two men as trustees of the Ochs Trust. In the end, it was Iphigene who called the tune about who would run the *Times* after her father.

The most detailed account of it, the story that best revealed the right stuff of which Iphigene was made, came from General Edward S. Greenbaum. Greenbaum, the Sulzbergers' legal counsel and dearest friend, told it to the *Times*'s Harrison Salisbury, who put it in a footnote in his book *Without Fear or Favor:*

Greenbaum . . . recalled meeting for four evenings in a row in the house on Eightieth Street where the Sulzbergers then lived to decide what to do. Arthur and Iphigene, holding two of the three trustee votes, controlled the situation. It was a question of tactics. Finally, in Greenbaum's recollection, Iphigene said to the two men, "You are just stupid—both of you. You've been talking for three nights and you haven't decided anything. Now, listen to me! Tomorrow morning we are going down to *The Times* and I am going to sit in Papa's chair and Arthur is going to sit in the room with me. Then the next morning we are going down early and we'll do the same thing. And then the morning after that I'll be a little late and the first thing you know I won't come in at all and Arthur'll just be sitting in the publisher's chair." At first Arthur objected but in the end they did just that.

Iphigene did not remember the incident quite that way—she thought she had suggested that Sulzberger go down alone to her father's office—but she did recall that it was she who had to tell her cousin Julie Adler that Arthur was going to be the only boss. Julius took it like a gentleman and promised to do his part. "[Arthur] was a more able man, less conservative," Iphigene told Salisbury, "and, besides, he was my husband."

It was significant that Arthur Hays Sulzberger's first important act as publisher, encouraged to the hilt by Iphigene, was to put Anne O'Hare McCormick on the staff.

Iphigene Sulzberger, born four years before Ochs bought *The New York Times,* was Adolph's only child, his little princess. She would become the instrument by which a newspaper dynasty has lasted for a hundred years. She lived for ninety-seven years, until 1990.

She represents the first phase of woman power at *The New York Times*—the power behind the throne. Her story is the classic, old-fashioned one of a woman directing by indirection. But to say that she was the daughter, wife, mother-in-law, mother, and grandmother of publishers of *The New York Times,* that she provided a thread of continuity throughout almost the whole life of the *Times,* does not really give this remarkable person her due. She became the liberal and humane conscience of the *Times*'s ruling family. No serious discussion of the women who made a difference at the *Times* could omit Iphigene. It was not just that she influenced the men who owned and ran the paper, prodding them toward more progressive policies. She was the enlightened, free-spirited daughter of a repressive man, making common cause, even as a teenaged girl, against her own father with women fighting for the vote. Born to power, surrounded by males who

THE DARK AGES · 55

upheld the status quo, she was attracted by the politics of change. As she grew older, she seemed to grow more flexible and less afraid to speak her mind. At the age of eighty-five, she expressed indignation in print that women were being paid less than men for doing the same work. She was perfectly aware that at that very moment, a class action suit had been filed on behalf of more than five hundred women on the staff of her family's newspaper, charging the *Times* with sex discrimination. The most serious and provable allegation was unequal pay across the entire range of jobs.

Some of Iphigene's independent attitudes were inherited from grandparents on both sides. Her paternal grandfather was passionately against slavery and fought in the Union army during the Civil War. Her maternal grandfather was Rabbi Isaac M. Wise, a founder of Reform Judaism in the United States. One of his first congregations was in Albany, New York. There he told the men to take off their hats in temple and the women to come down from the balcony, where they were segregated in the Orthodox tradition. "The reaction was so violent," Iphigene recalled with relish, "that he had to leave by the back door."

The Wises next settled in Cincinnati. The rabbi started the *American Israelite,* a newspaper espousing the new religious movement called Reform Judaism, and founded Hebrew Union College, the first Jewish theological seminary in the United States.

Iphigene Bertha Ochs was born to Rabbi Wise's daughter Effie and Adolph Ochs on September 19, 1892. She was robust and full of sparkle from the beginning. A family friend called her the human interrogation point when she was a child because of her irrepressible curiosity, a lifelong trait. She grew up in a series of gloomy apartments stuffed with heavy furniture and hung with thick draperies on New York's Upper West Side. Her mother was a languid and romantic creature who flitted about the rooms at night, moving chairs and tables, leaving crumbs for the mice in the fireplace, and reading books

in bed until lunchtime. Both parents were devoted theatergo-
ers, and Iphigene was taken to Saturday matinees from the age
of five.

When she was eight, she was sent to Dr. Sachs's School for
Girls. She was a terrible student, misspelling words and making mistakes in mathematics, probably because she was not
only unstudious but dyslexic. She was always in trouble. On
one occasion she brought a mechanical mouse to school and
sent it scuttling across the classroom of her German teacher.
"Madame Zeek really let out some shriek," she remembered
with satisfaction. After less than five years there, she tangled
with the great Dr. Sachs himself.

One day, suspecting she had been laughing at him in class,
he hauled her off to his office. After he had shouted at Iphigene
for some time, the little girl said: "I think you have no business
talking to me the way you are." Dr. Sachs went into a rage.
When her governess came to collect her, he "embellished" her
retort, she later recounted. She burst into tears, crying out,
"He's a liar!"

Her father finally convinced Dr. Sachs to let her finish the
two or three weeks until the end of the school year. "And so
it was that I left Dr. Sachs's school," Iphigene said, "expelled
for impertinence at the age of twelve."

Iphigene turned into a handsome, merry young girl, with
big, smoky brown eyes under dramatic eyebrows, a full
mouth, and masses of glossy dark hair. There were Atlantic
crossings and summer-long tours of Europe in the grand manner with her parents. Her father made her memorize the itine-
raries, so that she could recite, in order, the towns they stayed
in, the sights they saw, and by what means they had traveled.
They toured New England in goggles and dusters in a chauf-
feured open Mercedes, saw Yellowstone and Yosemite on
horseback, and cruised by ship along Alaska's coastline.
Theodore Roosevelt, the first of a string of presidents Iphigene
met, gave her a rose from his White House desk. She sipped
tea in Andrew Carnegie's library on Fifth Avenue and shook

hands with Mark Twain and met Thomas Alva Edison. She
had seen the world and the world had come to her father's
door, but Iphigene, bright as she was, needed heavy tutoring
to get into Barnard College in 1910.

Her professors included the eminent historian James Har-
vey Robinson, later a cofounder of the New School for Social
Research. He was fond of saying "I want to show you a perfect
example of the medieval mind" and then reading that morning's lead editorial in *The New York Times*. Iphigene remembered shrinking in her seat with mortification—while agreeing
silently that the editorials were too conservative. Another profound influence at Barnard was Vladimir Simkhovitch, who
taught courses on the history of socialism and on radicalism
and social reform in nineteenth-century literature. Iphigene
declared herself a socialist. There were fights over the dinner
table with Adolph Ochs. He would say, icily, "On what do you
base your opinion?" or "Are you sure of your facts?" He made
her memorize a passage from Benjamin Franklin's autobiog-
raphy about the dangers of being dogmatic—it was on page
95—and in the years to come he would call out "Page 95,
Iphigene!" when he felt she was being opinionated.

She spent every Thursday afternoon at the Henry Street
Settlement on New York's Lower East Side, running a club
for ten-year-old immigrant Jewish girls from Poland and
Russia. She visited their mean tenements. It was her first encounter with poverty.

She also became a passionate suffragist. There were many
heated discussions at home. Ochs, ever the Southern conservative, had fought for years against the idea that women should
vote. Father and daughter held fast to their views. Iphigene
decided not to embarrass Ochs by marching in the suffragists'
parades, but she sneaked her allowance from Ochs to the
women's suffrage committee at Barnard. In 1914 she was
graduated from the college, which would receive a magnificent
bequest upon her death.

Ochs did not like any suitor of whom Iphigene grew too

fond. Nevertheless the daughter, lovely and popular and full of winning ways, continued meeting and enchanting young men. By her own count, she became engaged and disengaged at least twice. She may have chafed at her father's possessiveness but her profound love for Adolph Ochs always won out—until Arthur Hays Sulzberger came into her life.

The two had met casually when she was at Barnard and he was studying just across the street, at Columbia University. The friendship became serious in 1916, when Iphigene's cousin, Julius Ochs, brought Sulzberger to the Ochs's vacation home on Lake George, New York.

Arthur Hays Sulzberger was marvelously good-looking, then and all his life—lean and straight-featured as an Arrow Shirt man, with penetrating blue eyes and an air that was both patrician and romantic. Women found him extremely seductive. He was also a modest, sensitive man who wrote verse, appreciated classical music (but never Mozart), and had some talent as a painter. He liked good Scotch, good company, expensive things. He was hopelessly addicted to puns. His background was as different from that of Adolph Ochs, the self-made tycoon personified, as could be imagined. He came from a privileged New York Jewish family that had settled in America in 1695. He had thought of becoming an architect but instead entered his father's textile-importing firm right after Columbia. Mrs. Ochs liked him immediately. Adolph Ochs told Iphigene, "I don't understand. You've got a good home. Why do you want to get married?" This time his daughter stood her ground.

"My father seemed resigned to the inevitable, though he grumbled up to the time we were pronounced man and wife in my parents' Seventy-fifth Street house," Iphigene remembered. The wedding, on November 17, 1917, was catered by Sherry's; in the wedding photograph, posed against banked palms, Iphigene looks rather wistful in her gown and long, diaphanous train and Arthur Hays is dashing in the uniform of a reserve Army lieutenant. The bride was twenty-five, the groom, twenty-six. At Ochs's insistence, they spent their honeymoon in Washington, as Adolph and Effie had done, and went to the White House to meet President Woodrow Wilson.

One of Ochs's stipulations before his daughter's marriage was that his son-in-law go to work at *The New York Times.* Arthur Hays Sulzberger, like his own son after him, was given an office and the vaguest of duties; he was a minister without portfolio, a man without a mission. He was guided throughout the *Times*'s Forty-third Street plant and its paper mill in Brooklyn; he was put in charge of the *Times*'s annual charity drive, the Hundred Neediest Cases; he became an expert on wood-pulp processing and went on newsprint purchasing trips in Canada and overseas. There were dinners at the Ochs's Manhattan house and summers at Abenia, the Ochs's place on Lake George, in what Iphigene called a "perfectly hideous" Victorian retreat. Later there was the first Hillandale, a palatial white-columned mansion in Westchester County, New York, big enough to have a ballroom, big enough to include the Sulzbergers and their children and the phalanxes of other relatives.

The Sulzbergers' first child, Marian, the beauty of the family, was born on New Year's Eve in 1918. Ruth came next, in 1921, on March 12, Adolph Ochs's birthday; Judith, the third daughter, was born on December 27, 1923. And then there was a son, Arthur Ochs Sulzberger, born on February 5, 1926, a bouncing, spaniel-eyed, genial baby who, his father said, had "come to play the Punch to Judy's endless show." Therefore his nickname ever after.

···········

The Dark Ages for women at the *Times* did not end until after Ochs's death, in 1935. The first woman reporter hired under the regime of Arthur Hays Sulzberger—even before Anne O'Hare McCormick—was Kathleen McLaughlin, who went on general assignment in the city room in May 1935. She had been recommended to the new publisher by Edwin L. James, the managing editor.

Kathleen had been struck early, as I had, with a hopeless infatuation for the newspaper business. When she was a little girl, growing up in Atchison, Kansas, she would sprawl on her stomach on the living-room floor, poring over the articles in the Atchison *Daily Globe.* She asked her mother, "Who finds out what happened?" Her mother said, "They're called reporters." Kathleen announced, "When I grow up I want to be a reporter." She never changed her mind.

Straight out of St. Scholastica's Benedictine Convent in Atchison, she marched into the office of the *Daily Globe* to ask for a job. She got it, and became the only woman reporter then at the *Globe,* which had been rated the best small-town daily in the country. A year later, in 1925, she was hired by the *Chicago Tribune.* According to Kathleen, the editors at the *Tribune* didn't care about their reporters' gender as long as their stories were good, and women were often sent out on top assignments. The newspaper's star of that era was Genevieve Forbes Herrick, called Geno. She was a graduate of Northwestern University, where my mother had gone, and I after her, and Mother spoke of Geno to me with awe when I was growing up in Chicago. She was Kathleen's heroine too.

Kathleen's first big scoop for the *Tribune* was an interview in jail with Olgivanna Milanoff, a Montenegrin Lolita who had been arrested under the Mann Act with the great architect Frank Lloyd Wright when they crossed the Mississippi one day into Minneapolis. Chicago readers lapped up the details. From this enterprising start Kathleen was swept into crime reporting. "I covered a wake a week at times," she later said. When Big Tim Murphy had finished his jail term at Leavenworth for robbing a mail train at Chicago's Dearborn Street Station, she traveled to the prison by train with his wife, Florence, and they became great friends. Kathleen remembered Big Tim as "one of the most loving and tenderest husbands I have ever known." She visited them often at their bungalow. One day, opposition mobsters with machine guns rubbed out Big Tim on his own front lawn. Kathleen wrote the funeral story. A year later she had a clean scoop when Florence married gorgeous John (Dingbat) Oberta. As was often the case, he died an untimely death too, his life outside the law cut short by three erstwhile pals in a liquor deal. It was a lovely funeral, with hearts made out of roses and crosses of lilies. That night the widow broke down and told Kathleen who had done it. In her story Kathleen described the man, Polack Joe Saltis, as he stood in the light of flickering candles, staring down at Dingbat Oberta in his coffin.

Kathleen covered every criminal, freak, and celebrity of the period. She reported on national political conventions and on numerous trials. She did a series on maids, going out herself to apply for housekeeping jobs. She started a popular column and for eighteen months edited the women's page. In ten years, she had made herself one of the most versatile performers on the *Chicago Tribune*. Edwin James of *The New York Times* had been watching her byline, and hired her away.

Many years later, Kathleen told a young interviewer from the Columbia University Oral History Project what it was like in the *Times* city room in 1935: "At the time that I arrived I was the only woman in the newsroom. And if I may say so, and I will say so, you could have cut the ice with a sword. I can remember only one reporter on the staff, whose name was Marshall Newton, who was nice enough to come over to me and say, 'We're delighted you're here and welcome.' Because for the rest of them, I just wasn't there, for months on months."

The ice melted slowly, and she went on to better days, in New York and in Washington, where she covered that liveliest of first ladies, Eleanor Roosevelt, and became a trusted friend. The *Times* finally responded to her pleas to go overseas. She was assigned to Europe as World War II was ending, reporting mostly from Germany for six years. In 1951, Kathleen was transferred to the *Times* bureau at the United Nations, where she spent much of the rest of her career. She met many an important name, but nobody was as riveting as those gangsters she had hobnobbed with while on the *Chicago Tribune*.

CHAPTER 4

ROSIE
THE REPORTER

When the Japanese bombed Pearl Harbor on December 7, 1941, finally catapulting the United States into World War II, an entire generation of American men—ultimately sixteen million of them—volunteered or were drafted into the armed forces. They left their jobs behind, and American women streamed by the millions into the vacuum. Many worked in the war factories and were immortalized in "Rosie the Riveter," one of the catchiest, most popular tunes of the time. The war transformed their lives. They discovered that they could do every kind of work once thought to be the province of men only. They could be welders, pipefitters, plumbers, electricians, truck drivers, stevedores. They could be reporters. A whole generation of women entered the newspaper business during the 1940s; they filled the city rooms—

but not at *The New York Times*. Women were never hired there en masse, as they were elsewhere. Not that they were made welcome elsewhere either, but at least editors at other papers bowed, however grumpily, to necessity. When possible, however, they hired males—those too old or too young for the draft, functional alcoholics, semi-incompetents, or men who been judged not physically fit for the military.

Arthur Gelb was in the "limited service quota" because of his bad eyes. "Where I lived in the Bronx, many boys had bad eyes," Gelb remembered. "We were called 'four-eyes,' because of our thick glasses; we were 'bookworms.' My other friends were all going off to the war, and I was very depressed." Artie's mother, a designer and the owner of a high-class children's dress shop, told her towering, awkward son to stop mooning around the house and get a job on a newspaper. He came to the city room at the age of twenty in 1944 as a tall, eager, nearsighted copyboy. He spent the rest of his working life there, rising to the post of managing editor.

Nobody who entered the city room of the *Times* during the war years could doubt for a second that it was a man's world. There were spittoons everywhere on the floor in a filthy litter of cigars and cigarettes and crumpled papers; the old oak desks set in rows were battered and scarred with burns and topped with huge, clunky Underwood typewriters. The reporters wore their press passes in the bands of their snap-brimmed fedoras, barked into stand-up telephones, and spat into their cuspidors. The copyreaders, hunched over the rims of semicircular copy desks, wore green eyeshades and drank beer on the job; some seemed old beyond counting. Other employees made periodic trips to the locker room to drink the hard stuff.

About three o'clock every afternoon, Edwin James, the managing editor, would emerge from his office in the south-west corner of the city room, having consulted that day's racing form. Chomping a cigar, natty in striped shirt, broad suspenders, and a cravat with a stickpin, he would place his bets with the two clerks who doubled as bookies. Occasionally, a wife would appear on the third floor, claiming piteously that her husband was drinking and gambling his salary away. Gelb was at the *Times* only two days before he lost his first weekly paycheck on a horse. Bridge games, poker, pinochle, and gin rummy were played all night long, sometimes for high stakes. Kibitzers clustered around. The reporters would play a hand and then write a few lines. Then they would play another hand and write a few more. Their cries of "Copy!" and "Boy!" echoed through a fog of smoke. (There was not a single copygirl at the *Times* until 1962; other papers began hiring copygirls during World War II. The first *Times* copygirl was Elaine Potter, such a celebrity for her singularity that Gay Talese wrote about her for the house organ.)

Summers were hell. There was no air-conditioning, and people dripped with sweat, dragging in from assignments or pounding their heavy typewriters. Salt tablets were dispensed at the watercoolers. The only windows were spaced along the southern wall overlooking Forty-third Street, where the editors sat in Olympian isolation behind a low wooden fence. The city room, about a third the size of the current one, was presided over by David Joseph, the fuddy-duddy city editor, who wore his Phi Beta Kappa key dangling prominently over his vest. A bachelor, he lived with his unmarried sister. According to men and women alike, David Joseph was terrified of females.

"Not only that—no one at the *Times* ever believed back then that women had true reportorial skills," said Arthur Gelb.

World war or no world war, almost the only way women seemed to be able to get onto David Joseph's staff was through pull or as campus correspondents for *The New York Times*. Among those who made it were Doris Greenberg, Lucy Greenbaum, and Kathleen Teltsch.

Doris Greenberg came to the paper in 1942 by the second route, as a *Times* campus correspondent at New York University. She had transferred that fall from Goucher, then a prissy girls' school in Baltimore. At NYU she found that the last of an unbroken line of boys who had reported for the *Times* had marched off to war. Eighteen years old but, Doris recalled, "looking like twelve," she presented herself as an applicant for the job to Mr. Joseph. The man muttered a few questions through a nimbus of smoke, leaned far back in his wooden swivel chair, and stared at the ceiling while Doris stumbled through the answers. Finally he said, "All right! Let's give the girl reporter a chance," and turned away to his typewriter.

The male reporters were kind to Doris, most of all Meyer Berger, who teased her and made her feel like an adorable mascot. That was what women hoped for then at the *Times*— that, or the compliment "You write like a man."

Man or woman, if you were young and scared and had no idea how things worked at the *Times,* Mike Berger would show you the way. Bald and graceful and thin, with a long, lugubrious face and shiny, buttonlike brown eyes, he befriended every underdog, all copyboys and secretaries and new reporters. From time to time, just to liven up the place, he would stand on his hands until the coins fell out of his pockets, or emit a piercing whistle between his thumbs, or leap from desk to desk around the room, while nobody batted an eye. Kitty Teltsch remembered how he would make a little slit in a peanut shell and wear it raffishly on his earlobe. When on rewrite, he would badger legmen on the telephone in his soft, persistent voice until they coughed up the last niggling detail about a crime scene. Manny Perlmutter, a superb police reporter, would hear Berger, who was writing the story, saying on the other end of the line, "How many pictures are there in the room?" and Manny would say, "How the fuck do I know?" and then Mike would ask, "And what kinds of pictures are on the wall, Manny? Would you mind going back and letting me know?" and as Manny told it later, "Anybody but Mike Berger, I would have hung up."

Doris Greenberg thought Berger was a saint. His kindnesses

and the spirit of fun he personified in the city room solidified her desire to be a full-fledged reporter. She spent all her spare moments covering campus news for the *Times,* pasting her clippings end to end and then bringing them in to be measured by the auditing department. The going rate was eight dollars a column. Young aspirants also wrote up sermons for three dollars apiece. After graduation, Doris was hired as a regular member of the *Times* staff—and was immediately sent upstairs to the women's page under Eleanor Darnton.

Mrs. Darnton was a lively, imaginative woman, the widow of Barney Darnton, the first American correspondent killed in the Pacific war, and the mother of John Darnton, who became a Pulitzer Prize–winning foreign correspondent and metropolitan editor of the *Times.* The men downstairs thwarted Mrs. Darnton's every effort to introduce fresh ideas. The women's page, according to Doris, "was noted for pedestrian writing, publicity and puffery, and that was all the editors wanted. The copy desks treated us like dirt."

Shortly after the war ended, Doris, after much pleading, was transferred down to the city room for good. "I was surrounded—literally surrounded—by all these handsome young men who had come back from the war," she recalled. She dated one and then another of the eligible veterans. And then along came Harold Faber. Hal had gone through World War II unscathed, except for breaking a leg in a baseball game. In 1950 he was sent as a *Times* correspondent to the Korean War. He was injured once by shrapnel and quickly recovered. Within weeks his luck ran out. On October 12, 1950, Faber was returning from Korea to Tokyo for a breather when his Flying Boxcar crashed in fog on landing. There were terrible burns. His right leg was amputated above the knee. On June 21, 1951, the day of his discharge from Walter Reed Hospital in Washington, Hal and Doris were married. Faber came back to the *Times* to a sedentary job as an editor on the national desk. Doris handed in her press pass "with a pang," but she had chosen to be a free-lance writer, working from home and raising a family. She went on to write more than forty books, mainly for children. One of the most popular dealt with a great American feminist. It was *Oh, Lizzie! The Life of Elizabeth Cady Stanton.*

Lucy Greenbaum came to the *Times* during the war years by the first route—connections—and stayed longer than most of the women of that era. Her uncle, Edward Greenbaum, was the Sulzberger family's lawyer. Her father, Lawrence, was a boyhood chum of Arthur Hays Sulzberger's: they had grown up in adjacent townhouses in Manhattan. "I want to be a reporter," said Lucy, fresh out of Bennington College, to her father. "I might be able to arrange something," said Lawrence Greenbaum. The next thing Lucy knew, she had received a call from Bruce Rae, the *Times*'s assistant managing editor and husband of Ishbel Ross of *The New York Herald Tribune.* Rae said there were no openings but counseled patience and told Lucy not to give up. "Call me every four months," he said. For a year, Lucy learned the ropes on the Mamaroneck *Daily Times* in suburban Westchester County. Finally, in the fall of 1940, Rae had a job for her. She described the scene in characteristic prose in a recent book, *The Beloved Prison:*

The city room lay in front of me as I entered a masculine domain. I found myself the lone female in a sea of male reporters. . . .

I hardly dared savor the glory. All those men. I had always looked up to a man as far more valuable than my inferior self. Suddenly I was placed in equal position with a man in a profession I believed hallowed. I also dared the fleeting thought that among all these masculine forms perhaps I would find a husband.

The masculine forms straightened from their habitual slouches, electrified. Lucy Greenbaum personified the Yiddish word "zaftig"—alluringly plump. She specialized in low-cut dresses and spike-heeled shoes with puffs on the toes. Her eyes were blue and round and trusting, her lips a perfect cupid's bow. Her voice was low and whispery. Jimmy James, never long on tact, called her Sadie Thompson and became unusually attentive when she bent over the water fountain.

Lucy's first assignment was to cover a tea party given by a Cairn terrier in honor of a poodle. She comforted herself with the thought that the party was to raise money for hungry children in Nazi-occupied France. Her biggest story came in 1947, when she was pulled off a women's convention in Texas to help a *Times* team cover a catastrophe in Texas City: two ships in which ammunition had been stored in Galveston Bay blew sky-high, setting off further explosions and fires in a chemical plant and in the town, killing hundreds and injuring thousands. She flew there in a Navy plane that was bearing plasma, and she remained to report in the midst of chaos for five days. On the first night, after filing her story to New York page by page, Lucy bolted upright from an exhausted sleep at two in the morning to check her copy. She reread it with horror. Sure enough, she had written, "In the shadow of the raging fires, a cow munched away at scrubby grass, no one around to milk him." It was too late to file a correction: the last edition had gone to press. She crawled dejectedly back to bed.

When Lucy returned to the city room, a young copy editor, Bill Freeman, approached her. He complimented her on her stories from Texas City, shoved all her clippings into her hand, and said, "I also fixed the sex of the cow. Your story made the front page and I wanted it to be correct." Bill Freeman and Lucy were married soon thereafter in the ballroom of Fifth Avenue's swanky Hotel Gotham, with a big *Times* contingent on hand. Naturally, Arthur Hays and Iphigene Sulzberger were there. So was the irascible Sunday editor, Lester Markel. Jimmy James sent a vase.

Lucy Greenbaum Freeman, who spent twenty years in and out of psychoanalysis, created the paper's mental health beat in 1949. Her first and most popular book, *Fight Against Fears,* was one of many she wrote on the subject of psychoanalysis. Kathleen Teltsch, known as Kitty, was another of the women war babies at *The New York Times*. She was the *Times*'s campus correspondent at Hunter College, which prepared legions of intelligent women for the world beyond. She joined the *Times* staff in 1944. Kitty was to gain a melancholy kind of fame within the newspaper. She went to its United Nations bureau in 1946, when she was twenty-three years old. She became an excellent reporter and in time learned more than anyone else on the paper about the Byzantine workings of the UN. Nonetheless, Kitty watched as man after man was appointed to head the bureau. She waited for her own moment for thirty-one years. In 1977, at the age of fifty-four, she became bureau chief. Of those decades of waiting she said, "It is too painful to talk about."

Only the most dedicated women of that wartime generation, those who had lost their hearts to journalism and were persistent as well as talented, stayed on in newspaper work. The reason was that in the fall of 1945 the men began coming home in their millions. In almost all cases, employers had guaranteed that GIs could have their jobs back when they returned. Most people thought that was right. Men were being discharged from the military at the rate of 70,000 a month. The newsreels were full of smiling, happy women, ostensibly eager to turn their tools over to the veterans. "What are you going to do after the war?" the booming announcer for *The March of Time* asks a female war worker. "When my husband comes back, I'm going to be busy at home," she replies, visions of feather dusters dancing in her eyes. There were news stories about women who refused to leave jobs, abandoning their "eight-hour orphans" to a baby-sitter. "Why doesn't Mommy stay home anymore?" was the caption under a newspaper photograph of a forlorn little girl.

I was nineteen years old and at Northwestern University when World War II ended: not quite old enough to be one of those who got her job because all the men were away at war. I did not have visions of feather dusters dancing in my eyes. I was determined to be a newspaperwoman, and I became one in a most implausible way.

CHAPTER 5

THE ROAD TO TIMES SQUARE

If Grandpa had not come to live at our house when I was four, God knows what line of work I might have gotten into.

Grandpa was the first man I ever loved. He was my first intellectual. He brought books into my life. He was the key that unlocked the door of our gray stucco house on Chicago's far North Side and set me free, to soar through worlds of imagination then and forever.

Grandpa Morrish, my mother's father, had lost all in the Crash of 1929. He and my grandmother came to us, dead broke, the following year. The moving men carried in crates of books, hundreds and hundreds of them, from Grandpa's library, mostly nineteenth-century English, French, and American classics, which filled our living-room bookcases from floor to ceiling. Dickens, Thackeray, Sir Walter Scott, Victor Hugo,

Balzac, Edgar Allan Poe, Hawthorne, Melville—they came to live with me for good when Grandpa and Grandma Morrish joined our household.

Richard Hamilton Morrish was then seventy years old. He looked like Somebody, and so did Grandma. He had a noble brow and the nose of a Roman senator, a jaunty way of tilting his head up and back that reminded me of Franklin D. Roosevelt. (Though I never would have dreamed of comparing the two aloud; to my rockbound Republican parents, President Roosevelt was "That Man in the White House.")

My grandfather's realm was the back sun parlor, and here took place our endless conversations on literature and the Meaning of Life and Is There a God and, in time, the Meaning of Love. He was my mentor and best friend, a man comfortable with Greek and Latin and stimulating talk about ideas. He was a Victorian gentleman who gave me a lifelong taste for doomed romantic heroes such as Dickens's Sydney Carton and Hugo's Jean Valjean.

He worshiped my grandmother, Margaret, a stately beauty, cool-eyed and somewhat mysterious, who never came down in the morning unless her dress was freshly ironed and her hair perfectly waved. I remember their diamond wedding anniversary banquet at the Edgewater Beach Hotel in 1942. Grandpa's touching, flowery, and somewhat bibulous tribute to his wife of sixty years was cut short as Grandma tugged at his elbow and hissed, "Richard, sit *down!*"

Grandpa made a bookworm out of me. I spent a large chunk of my childhood in a deep chair by the living-room fireplace, lost in a book while my family's life went on around me. In summer, I lay on my back on the garage roof, reading and plucking cherries from the tree whose branches drooped over me. I became the heroes of my books. I organized the kids on the block into Robin Hood and his Merry Men, and you may be sure I played Robin Hood, not Maid Marian or the men. I went through a medieval period and suddenly every child on Hood Avenue was jousting with broomsticks, and metal ashcan covers used as shields.

When I was eleven, a girl I shall call Dorothy Grant joined my sixth-grade class at the Hayt Elementary School. She was the first truly bookish and brainy friend of my own age I had ever known. We instantly became hearts' companions. After school, we would walk miles to the library, choosing one branch, then another, savoring the selection and leaving with as many books as our arms would hold. We must have looked a funny pair. I was short and skinny, with round brown eyes and a dark Dutch-boy bob; she was tall and blond and elegant in a cool Scandinavian way, with cheekbones I would have died for and a radiant white smile.

Dorothy and her family lived very close to poverty. Her parents owned Grant's Café on a run-down street on the North Side, and lived with their three daughters in two rooms overhead. I recognized that storefront café many years later, in the somber city scenes that Edward Hopper painted. Inside was a horseshoe counter, with a glass case in the middle that contained the day's desserts, always the same—tapioca, rice pudding, baked apple, and Jell-O. Mr. Grant was the cook, but it was Mrs. Grant—raw-boned and rough-spoken and taller even than her eldest daughter, Dorothy—who ran that show.

One day I turned to Dorothy and said, "You know what I want to be when I grow up? A reporter." That was Dorothy's dream too. She loved words as much as I did—loved to study the meanings and nuances and power of words—and besides, newspaper work seemed like a lot of fun, and you got to meet all sorts of interesting people. I remember saying that I thought I had the right personality for it: I was friendly and unafraid and curious. I did not know that I possessed another quality that can make a good reporter: I was savagely competitive. Year after year, I beat every boy on my block in wrestling, running, swimming, and tree-climbing. I was a terrible loser, so awful, in fact, that when I was nine, Mother sat me down and gently told me why it was that nobody ever liked a bad sport. From then on, I tried to mask my anger when I lost.

In 1940, when I was almost fourteen, my father died of a heart attack. My mother, at the age of forty-eight, had abruptly become the sole support of my grandparents, my sister, and me. Devastated by grief though she was, she took over my father's Robertson Tool Sales Company. She made a success of it during the war, but she never overcame the hostility of the men who were her competitors.

I wanted to earn money for her. The Grants, in their kindness, gave me a job. I worked at the café after school, first as dishwasher and then as waitress. Dorothy and I remained close friends all through Senn High School, where I had only one teacher who stands out in my mind. Henrietta Haefmann, a blob of a woman who teetered about on legs as skinny as a sandpiper's, ignited in all of us her passion for foreign news. I first saw *The New York Times* in her classroom. Nothing ever gave me a more vivid sense of the "great striding events" that the likes of Anne O'Hare McCormick covered than those magnificent wartime front pages did, with their eight-column, three-deck banner headlines.

My path in life began to diverge from Dorothy's when I went to college. I chose Northwestern, because it was my mother's university and because the Medill School of Journalism was there. Professor Roland Wolseley was teaching a class called Journalistic Writing. He was the toughest of all the professors, and one of the very best. He demanded plain language and descriptive detail. He insisted we use all our senses. He wanted real-life reporting for the articles we wrote.

And so I assigned myself to do a piece for Wolseley on a day at Grant's Café. Dorothy was still there, helping out, because the family could not afford to send its brightest, most studious daughter to college. I sat the whole day long near the horseshoe counter, observing the customers and the family and writing it all down in my steno pad. I focused on the figure of Mrs. Grant, with her forceful, even brutal, manner, the varicose veins in her powerful legs, the torn slip straggling below the hem of her skirt.

Late in the afternoon, I went out through the kitchen to the bathroom. I left my notebook on the counter. I was gone perhaps ten minutes. Meantime, Ruth, the second Grant daughter, the imp of the family, had scooped up the notebook and showed the contents to her mother.

Mrs. Grant was waiting for me, a butcher knife in hand, hoarsely shouting her hurt and anger. I fled. I arrived home stunned and grief-stricken. Dorothy was on the phone, sobbing. "My mother says she's going to kill you," Dorothy said. "She says she'll kill me if I see you. I don't blame you, but you see, she doesn't understand what you were trying to do."

I had betrayed Dorothy and her family. I could not forgive myself. For the first time, I had felt that tug between the impulse to write down reality as I saw it and the wish to spare people's feelings. I never let go of my reporter's pad again in a subject's presence.

More than forty years would pass before I saw Dorothy Grant again. She and Grandpa had been the most important friends of my childhood, the friends who had summoned up the very best in me and drawn me with them into the world of books and writing. I lost them both in the same year. Grandfather died when I was nineteen.

By then I thought I might have a chance in my chosen profession. Professor Wolseley had told me at the end of a year in his class: "You are good enough. You will be a writer."

It was Wolseley's habit at each class session to read aloud one or two of our articles, without giving the name of the author. At the end, he would tell us what grade he had conferred, and why. My first effort, in the descriptive writing series, was about the Union Stock Yards in Chicago. It was this piece that Mr. Wolseley read to kick off the semester. I sat high up near the last row of banked seats, rigid with apprehension, praying it would soon be over. He read it all in a cold monotone. From time to time, students would gasp or utter expressions of disgust, for what I had described was a factory of blood, violent death, and disembowelment. I remember little of that piece except its most dramatic scene: a bloody black giant, stripped to the waist and glistening with sweat, legs astride for balance on a high platform, clutching a huge knife. Above him on an assembly line came the pigs dangling head downwards, their rear trotters chained to hooks, their snouts open in piercing squeals. As each one swung by he raised the knife and slashed its throat. The squeal stopped abruptly and the blood spurted out in dark cascades.

Mr. Wolseley finished the piece and paused. "It will come as a surprise to you, perhaps, that the reporter is a *girl,*" he began. More gasps; amazement in the ranks. "She has used all her senses, not just her eyes, to convey the smell and feel of the stockyards. She chose a difficult subject, an offensive subject. Her imagery was strong enough to revolt you." Pause. "I have given this piece an A-minus."

It was the best grade I ever got from him. The article on Grant's Café, written after the shattering rupture with Dorothy, got a B.

I remember one other incident in Professor Wolseley's class. We were analyzing newspapers, and at that point in my life, I knew of no other so fresh and witty and well-written as *The New York Herald Tribune.* That is where all the really good writers went, I thought. There is where I wanted to be. Another student was on his feet, raving about *The New York Times.* I stood up and asked bellicosely: "What has *The New York Times* got, except accuracy and complete news coverage?" There was a storm of laughter and jeers. I sat down, mortified.

I sailed for Europe after graduation in 1948, there to learn the journalist's trade. Two years later, only recently married, I and my husband, Allyn Baum, a news photographer, moved from Paris to Berlin. I soon met Kathleen McLaughlin, the

Berlin correspondent of *The New York Times* and my first friend on the paper.

McLaughlin was fifty-two and I a callow but gung ho girl of twenty-four, struggling to further my career in newspapers as a stringer in Germany for *The Milwaukee Journal* and the Gary, Indiana, *Post-Tribune*. Kathleen was a perfect lady. She had a wide, flat, Irish face, enormous pale blue eyes, and a manner so placid and seemingly full of trust and goodwill that a nun's wimple would have looked quite natural around her pretty face. She was a Catholic and the soul of piety. Yet she had learned her trade in the most hard-boiled city of the twenties and thirties, my hometown, Chicago. I would listen open-mouthed while this cozy soul spun out her memories of Al Capone and Dingbat Oberta and Big Tim Murphy (her favorite) and Greasy Thumb Guzik (my favorite) and other infamous hoodlums of long ago. Kathleen punctuated her bloodthirsty anecdotes with a merry, infectious chuckle I can hear to this day. This was real life, I thought. This was the newspaper business, right out of *The Front Page*.

By the time I came back to New York in 1955, I had reported for five newspapers—among them the Paris *Herald Tribune*—and had also done some free-lance writing for the *Times*. I had seen enough *Times* foreign correspondents at work to know why they and their newspaper were so respected. The *Times* was, quite simply, in a class by itself.

Turner Catledge, then the managing editor, had gotten a letter of recommendation about me from Drew Middleton, the *Times*'s London bureau chief, who had known me for years. The day I went to see Turner's stuffy assistant in charge of hiring, Richard Burritt, I decided to wear a glen plaid suit, custom-tailored on London's Savile Row, bought in those days for peanuts. It was sober and understated, superbly cut but not too fashionable, faintly dowdy, even. It was just like my picture of the *Times*.

Burritt sighed heavily as he began the interview. "We have

no job openings," he said. He proceeded to question me for an hour, delving into my résumé, testing my psychological soundness, and winding up with the question I had been warned he would ask. "And just why," he said, "do you want to work for *The New York Times*?" Friends on the staff had briefed me on how to answer.

My eyes gleamed with sincerity, with enthusiasm. "Because, Mr. Burritt," I gushed, "it's the best newspaper in the world."

Burritt smiled. I added, "*Vogue* magazine offered me a job yesterday, but oh, Mr. Burritt, I don't want to work for a magazine. I want to work for a newspaper."

"Maybe we can find something for you," he said.

I dogged Burritt for ten days, phoning him at least twice a day. Finally, he offered me a six-week temporary job for $100 a week as a news assistant in the women's news department, to work on a special fashion section. I reminded him of my years in Europe as a general assignment reporter for other excellent American newspapers. I reminded him that *Vogue* was offering me $150 a week. Burritt stood fast. "I'm sure the temporary job will turn into a permanent one," he said with a touch of rue. "I can't begin to count the people who came to the *Times* as temporaries and are still here twenty-five years later. People *never* leave *The New York Times*."

I was twenty-eight years old. I was thrilled every time I entered the beige marble lobby on West Forty-third Street, just off Times Square. Straight ahead, tucked into the curve of a marble staircase rising to the second floor, was a bronze bust of Adolph Ochs, set on a pedestal. On the wall behind him in bronze letters was an excerpt from his first statement upon becoming publisher in 1896: "To give the news impartially, without fear or favor, regardless of any party, sect or interest involved." I believed it. High on the wall to the left of the entrance doors was a mural in bright colors showing a sunrise. "Every day is a fresh beginning," it said. "Every morn is the world made new." I believed that, too.

The women's news department was then on the ninth floor,

six floors above the city room, where I longed to be. I had gotten a glimpse of the intimidating dimensions of the city room, which then stretched through an entire block from Forty-third Street to Forty-fourth, where the lights of the Shubert Theatre flashed through the windows, and Sardi's restaurant was just to the west of the *Times*'s back door. Redone and enlarged to three times its former size after the war, the city room of the mid-fifties displayed row after row of gray metal desks, all facing the entrance, with heavy Royal typewriters sunk into their wells. The reporters were seated according to importance, with stars such as Mike Berger in the front. Toward the middle of this enormous room, in which the city editor summoned reporters by a loudspeaker, I could discern only four women, seated side by side, with the doughty Edith Evans Asbury on the aisle. The rest of the room was just as it had been in Lucy Greenbaum's day fifteen years earlier—"a sea of male reporters."

My home for the next five years, however, was to be upstairs in women's news in an almost entirely female setting. Those years would prove to be among my happiest on the *Times*. We were all young and gifted and full of the devil, and the friendships I made there have endured for a lifetime. Most of us were put on the permanent staff by Elizabeth Penrose Howkins, who knew absolutely nothing about the way newspapers worked, but had an incredible eye for talent.

Mrs. Howkins had been the editor of *Glamour* magazine and British *Vogue,* and she often wore a hat indoors, as lady editors did in those days. She had a kind of faded prettiness, with big hazel eyes set off by turquoise eye shadow. I loved her laugh, which was silvery and girlish and tinkled forth frequently from her glass-enclosed office at the center of the floor. In fact, I loved Mrs. Howkins, who displayed a touching faith in me. She asked me questions about how newspapers were run. When I became the union's shop steward for the women's department about twelve months after coming to the *Times* and started enthusiastically signing everybody up, she asked if she could join the Guild. "No, Mrs. Howkins," I told her. "You are the management and we are the employees. We are basically adversaries. The management cannot join the union." She seemed rather hurt.

It was already natural for me to be a liberal activist. For years in Paris, Berlin, Frankfurt, and London, I had sat at the feet of older American reporters who had suffered through the Depression—underpaid, unprotected by a union, or unemployed. Some of them, desperately seeking jobs, had "ridden the rods" across the country, clinging with other tramps to the undersides of boxcars to escape the police. They had helped to organize the Newspaper Guild in the mid-thirties. Howard Katzander, a dear friend and mentor, told me a Depression-era tale I never forgot: The publisher of a paper he had worked on assembled his staff in the city room, drew a line with a piece of chalk across the floor and said, "Everybody on that side of the line is fired." Such stories severed me forever from my family's conservative political point of view. I became a liberal Democrat and a "union maid" for life.

Mrs. Howkins did not understand about unions. She appeared not to understand much about the craft of newspaper writing, either. She thought, and said, God forgive her, that "anybody who can write a letter can write a newspaper article." No one ever convinced her otherwise. She divided her world into two unequal classes of women—the "taste ladies," who had an eye for styles and pictures, and the writers, like myself, who ghostwrote the Sunday fashion spreads for the taste ladies, as well as doing their own bylined work. We were the nerds. The irony was that Mrs. Howkins often hired wonderful writers. She did understand pictures and type and layout, and she broke the women's page out of its stiffly corseted image and made it the boldest and most visually exciting page on the paper.

Mrs. Howkins hired Betsy Wade, and Gloria Emerson, who went on to report brilliantly from Vietnam and Africa and Paris; she hired Marylin Bender, a memorable writer on business and finance who became the Sunday business section editor; she hired Phyllis Levin, who would write a definitive biography of Abigail Adams, and Agnes McCarty Ash, who wound up publishing the Palm Beach *Daily News.* She hired Carrie Donovan and promoted the beautiful Dorothy Hawkins to fashion editor; neither Dorothy nor Carrie could write at that early stage in their careers, but both were sensational at spotting trends, picking styles, and staging photographs. Carrie later made waves at *Harper's Bazaar, Vogue,* and Bloomingdale's and ultimately returned to the *Times* Sunday magazine. Betty Howkins hired Martin Tolchin to write on the parent and child beat; after he was transferred to the Washington bureau he became one of the most knowledgeable reporters ever to cover the United States Congress. She also hired Charlotte Curtis, a celebrated modern byline on the *Times,* who transformed society reporting into sociological satire; Curtis then succeeded her as women's editor. But the best day's work Mrs. Howkins ever did, she was fond of saying, was the day she hired Craig Claiborne as her food editor. It was a grand leap of faith.

Craig, then in his mid-thirties, was definitely down on his luck, spending weekends with friends at Fire Island and eking out a living by publicizing Fluffo, the golden shortening. He had left *Gourmet* magazine in 1957. Mild of manner and mien, raised in his mother's Mississippi boarding house, he was a graduate of the great school for hoteliers and chefs in Lausanne, Switzerland. Craig had never written for a newspaper before. He did not know what a "lead"—the beginning sentence or paragraph of a story—was. The thought of a daily deadline terrified him. No matter. Mrs. Howkins somehow saw something ineffable in Craig, who repaid her gamble by becoming world famous as a food and restaurant critic and writer of classic cookbooks.

I learned a great deal on the women's page. I already knew something of fashion—I had been a publicist for Christian Dior in Paris in 1950, shortly after he sprang the New Look on the world and made every woman in the West clean out her closet; I had later done free-lance fashion reporting and women's news from London for *The New York Times.* I remember the lead under my first byline on the women's page. It was: "It's easy to buy a Paris dress. All you need is time and money." Well, at least it was short and punchy, although I never liked it much. I learned how to write features on the women's page, sometimes weaving my tapestries out of what seemed thin air. I wrote about chinchillas ("the only rodents that can make any woman shriek with pleasure"), Miss Subways ("Meet Miss Subways—a queen whose realm is a hole in the ground"), fashion piracy, male models, Tiffany's windows, how Seventh Avenue set its prices by calculating the labor cost of every part of a garment, including buttonholes and hooks. I learned twenty different words for shades of red and tried to analyze the magic of Mainbocher, a designer of such quality and subtlety that women could wear his evening dresses for thirty years and never look one stitch out of style. I was lucky in my competition. While writing, I would look out my window on the ninth floor to the back of a tall, narrow building only two blocks south of the *Times.* I would wonder, What is Eugenia Sheppard writing now? Eugenia was the tiny, tireless women's features editor and chief fashion writer of the *Herald Tribune,* and she was the best in the business; sharp, fresh, witty, she made high fashion, and the people who designed and wore it, come to life. She made me try my damnedest, and I improved by studying her. I can't say I ever caught up.

I learned something else on the women's page—that all the pious utterances by *Times* editors and publishers about the separation of news and advertising did not hold true for the coverage of fashion. Fashion was New York City's most important manufacturing industry. We were never allowed to forget it.

Each fashion writer was assigned a group of department and specialty stores. We were required to come up every month with articles whose total column-inches reflected the relative advertising strength of every store. Mrs. Howkins kept tabs. I had the good fortune to be assigned to some of the quality emporia, such as Bergdorf Goodman, Bonwit Teller, and Henri Bendel, and it was easy to write about them. We all groaned if we had to dredge up a story on Lane Bryant, which catered to unfortunates—women who were too fat, too thin, too tall, too short, or pregnant. The monitor of all this was Monroe Green, the advertising director of *The New York Times,* who had been a powerful executive for many years at Macy's. There was hell to pay from Green every time an advertiser was not adequately represented in the "news" columns of the women's page: periodically, he would barge into Mrs. Howkins's office to demand why Bloomingdale's or Gimbels or Macy's had been slighted that month, and periodically she would plead with us to come up with a story idea about Bloomingdale's or Gimbels or Macy's.

The *Times* prided itself that whole pages of ads would be ripped out of the paper to make way for important breaking news. No other newspaper in America did that. The women's department was the *Times*'s dirty little secret, tucked away by itself far above the city room; it provided the sop to the people who bought space in a newspaper that elsewhere in its columns gave the news "impartially, without fear or favor, regardless of any party, sect or interest involved." After some months on the women's page, I would read that statement of Adolph Ochs in the *Times* lobby, repeated endlessly by generations of the paper's executives, with a certain measure of cynicism.

My first Christmas on the *Times* arrived. I was introduced to Christmas loot, another shock. Throughout December, messengers came all day long into the women's news department, burdened like camels with elaborate gifts from stores, designers, manufacturers, publicists: handbags, coats, dresses, crystal, silver, costume jewelry, crates of vintage wine, and liquor. I could not see how I could report on these people fairly and accept their gifts. Three little words kept occurring

to me—"conflict of interest." I sent the presents back, un-
opened, with a courteous note. Just once, curiosity almost got
the better of me. A small box came from Van Cleef & Arpels,
one of the Big Three of Fifth Avenue jewelers along with
Cartier and Tiffany. I never found out what was in it. I sent it
back to Van Cleef's publicity director by messenger. An hour
later she was on the phone. "I received your gift back," she
began, in what seemed to be icy tones. There was a pause.
Then she said, "And I couldn't agree with you more."

This corrupt side of the women's page distressed me. It did
not embitter me; I was having too much fun with the lively,
talented bunch of women who were turning that page into the
brightest on the paper.

Among the important friends I made there was Betsy Wade.
Reserved and dignified on the surface, charged with emotion
underneath, virtually unknown to readers of the *Times,*
known to few within its walls, she would shake the newspaper
to its roots.

Betsy arrived on the *Times* the year after I did. She was the
first woman copyreader hired by *The New York Times* in all its
history. Before being packed upstairs to Mrs. Howkins in
women's news, she spent four weeks training on the third
floor's city copy desk.

More than anything else those first weeks, Betsy wanted to
look unsexy. First she cut her long black hair. Then she
shopped for a wardrobe. The clothes she had were not austere
enough—the necks too low, the arms too bare. "But how does
one ask the lady at Saks: 'Please, a suit in which I can sit in the
middle of an ocean of men and not be noticed?' " she commented later. "Saks functions by the opposite precept."

She bought a navy blue dress with a demure white collar
and a gray dress, both of which covered her from here to there.
She wore the blue and the gray on alternate nights and cleaned
them on weekends. "The copy desk did not put a screen
around me," she said of those first weeks in the city room.

"But they took the cuspidors out of the city room the first week. And a copyboy got some deep ruffling and put it around my paste pot. He meant well. I smiled wanly." There is a photograph of Betsy with her petticoated paste pot in that month's issue of *Times Talk,* the paper's house organ. She is bent seriously over a piece of paper, thick copy-pencil in hand. She did not want her picture taken. She did not want attention called to her in any way.

She did her work doggedly. She developed calluses copying her errors and corrections into the back of her style book. She learned how to spell "vichyssoise," and that a defendant is held "in" bail but is released "on" bail, and that "attest" is not followed by "to." She said later of this time: "In the eyes of the rest of the desk, I was an amusing mascot, an amiable freak that, fortunately, would go away. My destiny at that time was reading copy in the women's department, and my colleagues hurriedly explained this to anyone who asked what a woman was doing editing the budget, a murder, and a rape. Then I disappeared into the women's department."

On the women's page she was quiet, private, dauntingly intelligent, and very good at her work. Howkins had hired her after Burritt's initial screening, but she could not pigeonhole Betsy. She was not a taste lady. She was not a writer. Finally, in pretty confusion, Mrs. Howkins asked her, "What exactly do you do?" Betsy showed her.

In the spring of 1958, after repeated requests, Betsy was transferred to the city room for good. Years later she recalled that the men on the copy desk fell into three categories. The first mumbled, just loud enough to be heard, "Damn, hell, nonsense, place is getting to be a bloody tea party, not like the old days." The second group was too kind. She could not struggle twenty seconds with a headline before someone would present her with his version, all done up with alternate word choices. The third just toiled away and ignored her. Once in a while, someone would tell a clean joke "to make me feel less like a temperance worker at a brewery picnic." She was grateful to the third group of copy editors. Soon, she remembered, "I began to feel not so much in the way."

Very quickly, the editors of the *Times* were sizing up Betsy Wade for another reason—for her obvious excellence. It was obvious from the beginning how talented she was. She rose through the ranks, making good copy better and bad copy competent, cool in crisis, a superb judge of what news was important and what was not. There are some very respected people at the *Times* who believe she had all the stuff in her to make a great managing editor. But somewhere that upward trajectory flattened out, and Betsy Wade kept hitting her head against a glass ceiling.

············

The earliest friends in Betsy Wade's life, as she was growing up in Bronxville, New York, were the little girls she met in books. In every one of her favorites, a little girl was the center, the one to whom things happened. There were the child heroines of Ruth Sawyer's *Roller Skates* and Carol Brink's *Caddie Woodlawn,* of Frances Hodgson Burnett's *Little Princess,* Elizabeth Enright's *Thimble Summer,* and Dorothy Canfield Fisher's *Understood Betsy.* In the last, a sickly orphan, raised in the city by a febrile aunt, finally thrives among loving folk at Putney Farm. In these books, Betsy Wade entered into an interior life that became part of her forever. "I think the reason that I turned out to be an independent being at all I can trace to these little girls," she says. "They were the role models for my outside life." That outside life, in her family and in Bronxville, gradually became painful, chaotic, and unclear.

Born in Manhattan on July 18, 1929, she was the elder daughter of Sidney and Elizabeth Manning Wade, a handsome and ultimately mismatched pair. When she was five and her sister, Ellen, was one year old, the Wades moved to Bronxville, a prosperous suburb north of New York City, in search of better public schools. Betsy's parents came from radically different backgrounds, the mother's genteel and even distinguished, the father's lowly. Her mother, Elizabeth, was the first and central tragedy in Betsy Wade's life. She was a manic-depressive. She was regularly hospitalized, in cycles of about seven years, when her mood swings became uncontrollable. By the time Betsy was ten, she also knew her mother had become an alcoholic.

When Betsy was in fifth grade at the Bronxville Elementary School, Sidney Wade started her on her lifelong obsession with the precise meaning of words. He had read that the key to success in business was a big vocabulary. He bought *The Johnson-O'Connor Vocabulary Builder* and with this tome instructed his obviously intelligent and bookish elder daughter.

The first chapter contained "words unknown to 5 percent of the population" and the last contained "words unknown to 99 percent of the population." Sidney and Betsy went through it page by page. "Every time I missed a word, he would put a tick against it and test me on it the next day," Betsy recalls. "I learned about the specialness of words. The word 'terminal' gave me a great deal of trouble. I would say 'Grand Central Station' and he would say, 'No. Grand Central Terminal—the tracks end there.' The fact that in college I specialized in Samuel Johnson [creator of one of the great dictionaries in the English language] could not possibly have come as any surprise." To this day, her conversation is sprinkled with curious, unusual, sometimes old-fashioned words, such as "dogsbody" for a drudge.

By seventh grade, Betsy had decided that what she "really, really, really wanted" was to be in journalism. She was editor of *The Wallpaper* at Bronxville Junior High. "Two copies were printed every week and put on the bulletin boards," she says. "You could really *see* your readership, looking up to where the newspaper was tacked on the wall." She went on to edit the weekly high school newspaper.

At home, her parents' marriage was deteriorating in elegant surroundings. Elizabeth had inherited some Manning money,

Sidney had risen to the vice presidency of the welding-torch division of Union Carbide, and the family had moved out of a garden apartment into an enormous fieldstone house. There were walkouts at the dinner table, verbal explosions between the two. The mother was becoming ever more erratic and strange, periodically retreating to her bed with crippling hangovers. There were hospitalizations. Betsy still has her mother's diary from one such time, with excerpts from poems and newspaper columns sandwiched between broken cries from the abyss. One entry reads "1:40 A.M. This is it. If you ever cared about the human heart and soul . . ." and trails off in rapidly disintegrating handwriting.

Betsy spent the month of August in 1942 at Camp Manumit, whose name means "to set free." She was thirteen years old. It was there that her political coloration began to emerge, and her lifelong affinity with the downtrodden and the disenfranchised. Manumit attracted the kind of pupil who went to the Little Red School House in Greenwich Village, a school that was not literally red but was politically left. "I was immensely happy there, at Manumit," Betsy recalls. "It was a place I had been living in, in books. Now I was in that place myself." She painted a picture of a "Hooverville," the generic nickname for the shantytowns of the Depression. The task of campers that summer was to dramatize *The Grapes of Wrath* by John Steinbeck, the story of one poor migrant family among tens of thousands driven out of farms, jobs, and homes in the Southwest by the catastrophic droughts and dust storms of the thirties. The campers went to a neighboring straw-hat theater to see Lillian Hellman's *Watch on the Rhine,* a powerful play about the Nazi menace. Political awareness was the hallmark of Camp Manumit. The next summer Betsy was sent to a camp for rich kids in Maine, where she made leather belts.

"I don't know where I got my beliefs, but I had them," Betsy says of herself as an adolescent. "When we were visiting my mother's people in South Carolina, every time I came to a sign that said Whites Only I told my mother, 'I'm not going in there.' "

The rich, snobbish Bronxville of the 1940s was no more to Betsy's taste—it was a John Cheever nightmare, sodden and decadent. "The Bronxville Field Club, the local tennis club, was a repository of all things bad and ugly, starting with anti-everything," she says. "A Jew couldn't buy a house in Bronxville, no matter what he did. There were kids I went to high school with who were Jewish, but they commuted from Hartsdale, just over the line." She was not wildly popular. She did not have dates and went to few parties, which greatly pained her mother.

In 1945, Elizabeth and Sidney Wade were divorced. Betsy was sixteen and her sister nearly twelve. "It was hideous, just hideous," she says. "There are probably good divorces, but this was not one of them." Betsy could barely wait to go to college, to be far away in every sense from neurotic Bronxville and the mess at home.

She chose Carleton College in Northfield, Minnesota. The signs at the approach to the pretty little midwestern town in 1947 read "Cows, Colleges, and Contentment." They made Maltomeal Breakfast Cereal there. "I thought it was so wonderful to be in this normal place," Betsy says. "It was just staggering after Bronxville."

She made lifelong friends at Carleton. The closest was Tom Morgan, older than she, who involved Betsy in Democratic politics, civil rights, and the student newspaper. Morgan was graduated and went on to New York and a life of writing and editing.

Betsy came back to New York herself to enter Barnard College in 1949. "I began at Barnard to find something out about the life of the mind," she says. She studied Samuel Johnson and James Boswell in eighteenth-century literature classes under Professor James L. Clifford, whose scholarship and enthusiasm ignited her own. Two years later, she was graduated from Barnard. She proceeded right across the street to Columbia's Graduate School of Journalism for a year of learning her chosen trade.

At Columbia, she came into contact with some of the biggest names on *The New York Times,* which in those years had a lock on adjunct teaching positions in the journalism school—particularly on classes in copy editing. Among the eight or so authority figures from the Gray Lady were Frank Adams, the city editor; Lewis Jordan, the news editor; and Nat Gerstenzang, the assistant foreign editor. Betsy floundered badly in news writing under Frank Adams, a red balloon of a man, brusque and shy, who had been one of the fastest, clearest reporters on the staff. "But the men who taught copy editing just thought I was the berries," Betsy says. "They just fell out of their chairs with joy. I was a good editor and I wrote wonderful headlines. I would find messy copy and clean it up. All that reading of dictionaries, all that force-feeding of vocabulary from my father—it had peculiarly fitted me for this trade. I could see the other shore. I could see a job at the *Times.* I could see where I was going. It didn't really worry me that I wouldn't be Nellie Bly, star reporter. Then began a relatively long drag to get there, to get to *The New York Times.*"

She received her master's degree in journalism from Columbia in June 1952, standing at the top of her class of sixty in copy editing. The next month, she took a job, at $52.50 a week, on the women's page of *The New York Herald Tribune,* editing articles for the Sunday supplement. On her first day at work, a women's news reporter, Joan Cook, showed Betsy around the premises. They became instant friends. The women there were a close-knit group, eating lunch in the paper's test kitchen to save lunch money, and playing endless games of canasta.

On December 27, Betsy married James Boylan, an Iowan she had met through a Carleton friend, whose pale and innocent good looks concealed a tough, exacting intellect. It was a meeting of minds. Jim, a 1951 graduate of the Columbia journalism school, was working on *This Week* magazine, a magnet at the time for first-class talent. "Oh, he was bright, he was very, very bright," Betsy says. "He was a very successful journalist, very solid. He came from Iowa—a suitable place." They would go out Saturday nights and spend Sunday mornings at Betsy's snuggery in Greenwich Village, doing the *Times* crossword puzzle together.

On the Friday before Labor Day weekend in 1953, Betsy was fired from the *Herald Tribune.*

She remembers the scene perfectly. "Eugenia Sheppard had just come back from the fashion collections in Europe. The first thing she said was, 'Is there anything anybody wants to tell me? Anybody get married? Anybody run away?' " Betsy cleared her throat and spoke up. "I said, 'Well, yes—I'm pregnant.' Eugenia said, 'Oh, dear—this is dreadful. I'll have to talk to the managing editor.' The last person hired was the first person fired, and I went. You couldn't get unemployment insurance in those days if you were pregnant. We were living up the Hudson River at Fort Lee, New Jersey. I was in a state of terror and confusion, sewing a layette. My career was washed up. I didn't know if I'd ever get another job."

Betsy found secretarial work at the Columbia journalism school at $37 a week, for a professor she describes as "a bully and a blowhard." Richard, the Boylans' first son, was born in March 1954. In July she connected with the Newspaper Enterprise Association, which syndicated columnists. Betsy wrote what she calls "the kind of stuff that holds apart the ads in newspapers—five beauty columns a week, June brides, back to school, outdoor living, fix up your house."

One day in 1956, Turner Catledge, the managing editor of *The New York Times,* spoke to the alumni of the Columbia journalism school. He told them there was a terrible shortage of copy editors at his paper. Betsy was in the audience. She went home and said to Jim: "I'll write another letter," one of many applications for a job. She told Catledge: "If you're really, truly looking for copy editors, why not me?"

Richard Burritt called her for an interview. "I knew enough," says Betsy, "not to wear my Bohemian dress and my Raymond Duncan sandals laced up to mid-calf." Burritt inquired if her parents had been happy together—that was the kind of pop-psych question he liked to ask of men and women alike. She fudged that one, and impressed him. On October 1, 1956, twenty-seven-year-old Betsy Wade arrived at last on what she had called "the other shore."

....

The week I came to work at *The New York Times* in 1955, I met Joan Cook on an assignment; she was the woman who had shown Betsy Wade the ropes on the *Herald Tribune*. Ostensibly Joan was my direct competitor—after all, she was then covering fashion and women's features for the *Trib*. But straight off, she performed an act of mercy for me that made us friends. In contrast to Mark Twain, I was an innocent at home. I had never lived in New York before. I had been spoiled by the logic of the subway systems in London and Paris, networks that any stranger can quickly decipher. I was baffled by the BMT and the IRT and the IND; which was the Eighth Avenue and which the Seventh and where on earth did they go? The direction signs in these mysterious tunnels seemed to be cunningly tucked away behind pillars, or pointing every which way, or of minuscule size, or simply not there. Joan Cook took me by the hand and explained it all to me, leading me around the subways from one assignment to another and chuckling away the while. The woman really chuckled; she was kind and motherly, four years older than I, with an open face and big, luminous eyes and an amused view of the work we did—not the kind of tough bird I had supposed I would run into in the world of big-city reporting.

Joan looked, and was, as comfortable as an old sofa. I soon

learned that behind her placid exterior, she was enduring the kind of strain that would have broken a lesser person. Gerald Cook, her second husband and the love of her life, had long been a target of the government's hunt for Americans suspected of being Communists or in sympathy with Communism. Gerry's own life and its lessons were the central, shaping events that made Joan into the woman she became. Her political philosophy, her compassion for the underdog, her deep involvement in the Newspaper Guild and the women's cause at *The New York Times,* were all crystallized by the long travail she endured with Gerry Cook.

Gerry—whose tough-guy Irish good looks reminded me of the young James Cagney—lost his magazine job in the early fifties because of his politics, and for many years thereafter he was blacklisted from every editorial job in New York. When Joan introduced Gerry to me, he was working as a bartender. The FBI kept watch on them, bugging their phone, summoning Gerry to Washington to disclose the names of his political friends—which he would not do. There were three children to raise. There never was enough money. I never heard Joan or Gerry complain.

···········

Joan Riddell Cook, born January 5, 1922, had a protected and happy childhood. Her father, John Riddell, had been a cavalry officer in the regular army in World War I; after the war, Riddell left the army and moved to Los Angeles to go into the construction business. It was boomtime in boomtown. The Riddells, Ethel and John and their two girls, lived in a big pseudo-Tudor ranch house, and there were two cars. The only shadow on the household was that Patricia, the older daughter, had been born with a harelip and cleft palate. She had endured fourteen operations by the time she was fourteen years old, and the surgery never helped. One surgeon removed the bone in her nose, which ruined her face. Joan loved her sister. "She was funny and bright—and unhappy," she says. "I was always guilt-ridden about being the attractive one. I had to let her win at games."

Joan saw her mother's parents every weekend. She adored them. Grandfather Frederick Malpas had been a prosperous banker and businessman until the Great Crash of 1929. Like my own grandfather, he lost almost everything in the stock market collapse, and brought a wonderful library and the love of books into his granddaughter's life.

In the Riddell household, Joan's mother, Ethel, "sat and did her needlework and ran the railroad," her daughter says. "She didn't do anything as vulgar as working for a living; she worked for the Episcopal church. Her fondest wish for my sister and myself was that we be educated and able to support ourselves—or preferably, marry ambassadors and pour a superb cup of tea into fine porcelain cups."

The Riddell children were kept from the reality of the Depression. The family had a nice house at a time when people all over America were losing theirs. They had two cars, a luxury even though one was falling apart. Joan went to a fine private school, where the classes were small and the teachers good. "The only time the lack of money ever mattered to me," Joan says, "was when it kept me from going to Stanford University after I had worked my ass off at the Marlborough School for Girls." She entered the University of California at Los Angeles but left after her sophomore year to join her parents, who had moved to Minneapolis. John Riddell didn't think that women needed a higher education. So she got her first newspaper job on the *Minneapolis Star* as a classified-ad saleswoman. The managing editor would not hire women as reporters: "When you yell at them, they cry," he said.

In 1942, Joan married George Barlow, known as Geeb. There followed a typical wartime odyssey, with Joan going ahead of her husband from one military posting to another to find a place to live, "hanging the curtains and putting a candle in the window." They ricocheted all over the country. In San Francisco, Joan became pregnant with her first son. "Geeb was posted to Hawaii," she says, "where he spent the rest of the war living on the fat of the land, while I dined on canned tamales and seethed on the opposite shore."

After the war, Geeb and Joan settled in New York. While their son was still small, she stayed at home, decorating wastebaskets for the Women's Exchange and free-lancing for magazines now long gone, such as *Coronet* and *Today's Woman*. She met Gerry Cook at a party, and her life was irrevocably changed. Both divorced their spouses. When they were married on October 28, 1950, she was twenty-eight and he was thirty-three. She was working on the *Herald Tribune* and he was on the staff of *Everywoman's* magazine. The world was their oyster—until Gerry's boss received an anonymous letter accusing Gerry of being a Communist. It blasted his career and their carefree existence forever.

Joan Cook and Betsy Wade had begun their friendship on the *Herald Tribune,* and very quickly the two women and their husbands forged a lasting bond, one of the most significant in their lives. In 1959, Joan joined *The New York Times* as a reporter on the women's page. She and Betsy became inseparable, sharing political views, facing every joy and tribulation together. Joan never made the professional mark on the *Times* that Betsy did, but she was a leader in other ways, and her steadiness was a kind of safety net under Betsy, an emotional highflier.

···········

Late in 1959, shortly after Joan's arrival on the *Times* women's page, I was transferred to the city room as a general assignment reporter. I had eagerly looked forward to it for almost five years, because the city room is the core of every newspaper—the place where the fundamentals of the trade are learned. What I did not know was that I would find the love of my own life in the city room of *The New York Times.*

I had been powerfully attracted to Stan Levey, a *Times* labor reporter, for a long time. But I felt an affair would be impossible, sure to hurt people, sure to cause a scandal. Stan was married and had two teenaged sons. I had been married since 1950 to Allyn Baum, who had become a close friend in college and had come to the *Times* as a photographer several years after I arrived there. Despite my misgivings, I found myself frequently wandering down from the women's department to Stan's desk in the city room to chat with him on one pretext or another. Shortly after I joined the city staff, we declared ourselves. It was the beginning of the central event of our lives.

One day in August 1961, Frank Adams, the city editor, summoned Stan to his swivel chair at the front of the room. "I want you to go to Pittsburgh this weekend," he said. "There's a steelworkers' story to cover." Stan said, "I can't go to Pittsburgh, Frank. I have an important personal commitment." Adams turned purple with anger. In those days, it was almost unthinkable to refuse an assignment. "I order you to go to Pittsburgh," the city editor said. Stan returned to his desk, fuming. Within five minutes, he was standing in front of Adams again. "The reason I can't go to Pittsburgh this weekend, Frank," he said evenly, "is that I'm marrying Nan Robertson on Sunday." Adams sputtered in shock and blurted out that he understood, that of course Stan could take the weekend off. We were married in the Victorian Suite of the Carlyle Hotel, with only ten friends who had known of our secret in attendance.

In the spring of 1963, following a four-month-long newspaper strike that blacked out all regular news outlets in New York City except television and radio, CBS offered Stan the job of national labor correspondent. For most of the strike, which threw both of us out of work at the *Times,* he had been reporting on the labor scene for CBS. The network was impressed. Stan accepted its offer and decided, after nineteen years on the *Times* in New York, that Washington, D.C., was the place where he had to be. I had had four years on general assignment, covering courts, crime, storms, parades, fires, air crashes, many features and human interest stories, and two national political conventions. I knew this would cut no ice with Scotty Reston when I asked him for a job in the *Times*'s Washington bureau. There were three reasons: First, he did not like to take on New York reporters from his own newspaper, preferring to hire his protégés from elsewhere. Second, I was a woman, and as everybody in the business knew, Scotty was uncomfortable with professional women. The third strike against me was that I had divorced one *Times* man to marry another, which probably scandalized him.

Nobody has summed up his attitude toward women better than Gay Talese in *The Kingdom and the Power:* "His attitude toward women was, like Ochs's, both romantic and puritanical. . . . The heroines in Reston's world did not work in offices—they were mothers and wives who excelled in their roles, who inspired their husbands as his wife had always inspired him."

Nonetheless, I went down to the capital to ask Scotty Reston for a job. He was hardly a fearsome figure, despite his legendary status. He was shortish, with an appealing, open face and a way of looking straight into your eyes with grave attentiveness that was flattering and reassuring. I told him I knew nothing about national politics and therefore would bring a fresh eye to the Washington scene. He listened. He smiled. He puffed his pipe. He did not say no. He never said no. But when he brought me down the aisle of the bureau's newsroom after an hour's chat, Russell Baker, the *Times*'s resident philosopher-king, sauntered up to say "Do I encourage her or discourage her, Scotty?" Scotty said, "Discourage her." Russell, at that time dissatisfied with his own career at the *Times,* took me to lunch and gave me an unrelievedly gloomy report about the way things were going on the paper. It was almost impossible, he said, to write colorful stories from Washington. Ted Bernstein and his copy-desk minions up in

New York were death on good writers. I wound up on a bench in Lafayette Park across from the White House, sobbing on Stan's shoulder. I would have to leave the *Times*.

Back in New York, I wrote a short, heartbroken letter of resignation to Clifton Daniel, who was acting managing editor while Turner Catledge was out of town. Within five minutes, he summoned me to his office. He waved my note at me. "Nan, we love you personally and professionally," he said. "We will not let you go. Let me talk with Scotty."

I do not know how Clifton convinced Scotty to take me. He does not remember what he said. A fortnight passed without a word. And then, on a sunny day in May, I was standing in a crowd of *Times* colleagues outside Temple Emanu-El on the Upper East Side, where Reston had just delivered a magnificent eulogy at the funeral of Orvil Dryfoos. Dryfoos, the *Times* publisher for only eighteen months, had died of a heart ailment at the age of fifty, killed, people said, by the cruelly stressful newspaper strike. Suddenly I was face to face with Scotty. "I think we can work something out," he said, and turned away. I was jubilant. Washington! I thought. With the *Times*!

CHAPTER 6

THE GIRLS IN THE BALCONY

No woman who was a reporter in Washington during the 1950s and 1960s could forget the balcony at the National Press Club. I remember it well. To this day, Marjorie Hunter and Eileen Shanahan and I, colleagues during those years in *The New York Times*'s Washington bureau, look up and think of that vanished balcony every time we enter the new ballroom of the refurbished press club, which finally allowed women as members in 1971. The men had fought fiercely over the female invasion in vote after vote at the club; finally, the pro-women forces within the membership triumphed. Until then, a time still close to our own, the balcony was one of the ugliest symbols of discrimination against women to be found in the world of journalism. It was a metaphor for what working women everywhere faced.

After World War II, every man of consequence on the globe who wanted to deliver an important speech in the capital preferred to do so at the club. What these leaders said was carried that night on radio and television and the next day on the front pages of newspapers across the country. Prime ministers of Britain and France, presidents of the United States, spoke there. It was almost as prestigious as appearing before a joint session of Congress. Women reporters never covered such speeches. They were not allowed even to set foot inside the press club doors for any reporting events. The women protested that they didn't want to be members, all they wanted was equal access to the news. They were not believed. The State Department colluded in the arrangement. It continued to route foreign chiefs of state and other high government officials to the club.

And then in 1955, after years of pressure from the Women's National Press Club, the men thought of a solution. They would put the women reporters in the balcony of the ballroom. Of course they would get nothing to eat during the speeches, which were usually delivered at lunch. And there would be no place to sit up there—it was too narrow for chairs if there was any kind of crowd. But by God, no woman would be able to say that the club didn't let her in to cover the assignment. The National Press Club's officers congratulated themselves, and the bureau chiefs began sending their women reporters off to speeches and press conferences there. It was humiliating.

During the balcony days, Bonnie Angelo, ninety-eight pounds of pepper out of North Carolina, was chief of the *Newsday* bureau in Washington and then became a star reporter for *Time* magazine. Decades later she could barely contain her outrage as she described the scene:

"I remember being in that damned balcony crowded up against Pulitzer Prize winners like Miriam Ottenberg of *The Evening Star* and Marguerite Higgins [who won her Pulitzer on the *New York Herald Tribune* during the Korean War], and I was in the middle of it. I stood and looked down at all those lobbyists and patent lawyers and doctors and dentists—the male reporters loved bringing their doctors and dentists to hear the bigwigs, and the patent lawyers had their offices in the building—sitting there on the ballroom floor and luxuriating over their crummy National Press Club apple pie. They were people who had never written a line of a newspaper story in their lives. In professional terms, it couldn't have been meaner, it couldn't have been pettier. God, it was mean.

"Here were the people in the balcony, distinguished journalists treated like second-class citizens. I *had* to cover the stories there. Some people equated the balcony with the back of the bus, but at least the bus got everybody to the same destinations just as well. We could not ask questions of the speakers. Most of the questions were written and passed along the tables up to the dais. When the speakers left with their security guards, there was no way to gather around as the men on the floor did to shoot questions at them.

"It was so hot, it was so hot in that balcony. All those bodies up there, jammed under the eaves. There were camera crews up there. Television equipment was much bulkier then, and the TV lights were hotter than they are now. It was hard to hear. It was hard to see. People would come early to try to get to the front of the balcony. All this standing—it was like a cattle car. And all the time you were really boiling inside. You entered and left through a back door, and you'd be glowered at as you went through the club quarters. It was discrimination at its rawest."

Maggie Hunter recalled the day she started a little mutiny at the *New York Times* bureau because of the balcony. Scotty Reston, then the bureau chief, had sent her off to the club to cover a speech by Madame Nhu, the beautiful and sinister female leader of South Vietnam, the wife of Ngo Dinh Nhu.

Now, Maggie, a Southern lady and a thorough professional, was no feminist firebrand. That day, however, "I stood on a rolled-up carpet in the back of the balcony and I couldn't hear a goddamned word going on down there—I couldn't hear a word." Afterwards, she marched, fuming, into Reston's office. She blurted out, "Scotty, don't you ever send me to that damned National Press Club ever again."

Reston turned to Wallace Carroll, the bureau's news editor, who had befriended Maggie at the Winston-Salem *Journal* in North Carolina and had brought her to the *Times.* "Wally," said Reston slowly, with an air of innocent wonderment, "what's wrong with Maggie?"

"I don't think," she said years later, "that Scotty ever understood why I was so mad."

Eileen Shanahan and I joined her boycott, refusing to cover any event at the club from then on. Reston, the most venerated newspaperman of his time in Washington, was not only baffled by the fuss, he was quietly furious. He dropped any effort to assign us to the National Press Club.

Scotty belonged to the "What Do Women *Want*?" school of thought. There is a story about him and Mary McGrory, one of the most beloved, as well as one of the most literary and intuitive, political journalists, which was widely circulated in the Washington of my day. Gay Talese put it into print: ". . . when one of the best reporters in the country, Mary McGrory, appeared for a job on his Washington staff [Reston] said she could have it if she would work part-time on the telephone switchboard, which she refused to do."

I often wondered if it had really happened as Talese had reported it. In 1990, when I asked Mary point-blank about the anecdote, she answered simply: "It's true." As Mary remembered it, the job interview took place in 1954, following her coverage of the Army-McCarthy hearings that brought about the downfall of the Red-baiting Senator Joseph McCarthy. Eileen Shanahan, who has superb recall, talked to Mary about it much closer to the time of the event, probably in the same year. The way Eileen remembers it, McGrory told her: "Scotty made me feel as though he wanted me to work the telephone switchboard part-time." Whichever version is accurate, the story says something important about how Reston's views on professional women were perceived.

McGrory never joined the *Times.* She won a long-deserved Pulitzer Prize in 1975 for her work on the Washington *Evening Star.* When the *Star* folded in 1981 she went to *The Washington Post.* Now in her early seventies, she is still a columnist on the *Post,* still hitting home runs every week.

When I came to the Washington bureau in 1963, I discovered immediately that Scotty ran it like a men's club. There were only two other women reporters there, along with Nona Brown, for many years the Sunday department representative, and Barbara Dubivsky, her assistant. The reporters were Maggie, who had been hired in 1961, and Eileen, who came in 1962.

The men lunched with the men. The women ate with each other. Every day this went on. Hunter would frequently try to throw a grappling hook over the wall by going down the aisle of the newsroom and asking plaintively, "Anybody for lunch?" The men invariably begged off or bent their heads silently over their work. It was the men Scotty called to his councils in his office, and the men who were invited to lunch or dinner at the Metropolitan Club. The club excluded women.

When Punch Sulzberger, the new publisher in 1963, came down to Washington to meet the staff, off went Scotty and Reston's Rangers, as they were called, to the Metropolitan Club while the women reporters stayed behind, mortified. I figured there was little I could do alone to desegregate the Metropolitan, but there must be some way I could tear down the barrier between the men and women at lunchtime. It was ludicrous. After the easy camaraderie of the city room, I wasn't going to stand for it. So I went around the bureau, asking several men each day, lightly and with assurance, to join me and one or two of the other women for lunch. Maybe by now they were ready. It worked at once. The wall simply melted away. The men obviously liked the new openness. Of course, so did we.

Scotty Reston had hired Hunter because he needed a woman to cover the first lady, although Maggie was by instinct and training a first-class legislative reporter. He had taken on Shanahan as an economics reporter because she was too able and experienced to pass over, and because Richard Mooney and Edwin Dale, both bureau members specializing in economics, had repeatedly assured Scotty that Eileen was the tops—and neither a bitch nor a troublemaker. "We practically had to tie Scotty down to get him to hire her," Mooney recalled. She arrived to take Mooney's place when he was transferred to London.

According to Eileen, I had been the first person in the *Times* city room to make her feel welcome when she was in New York for her month-long training period. She did the same for me when I came down to the Washington bureau.

On my first day in the office, she burst out of the elevator and made straight for my desk with her long, loping stride. Her eyes were ablaze with excitement. "The Federal Reserve is split!" she cried, and paused hopefully for my response. I was stunned speechless and could only reward her with a nervous giggle. She never lost patience with me. Tony Lewis, then in the bureau, used to crack up many a cocktail party with a takeoff on the daily dialogue between Eileen and Ed Dale, another high-decibel enthusiast. One spoof began this way: Eileen, rushing up to Ed: "Did you hear? Did you hear? Australian shorts are long today!" (This had something to do with money, I think.)

Eileen and Ed sat near me in the bureau, and so I, too, was regaled with such fascinating tidbits as this:

Ed: "Is Joe Schlunk a liberal or a conservative on the Federal Reserve Board?"

Eileen, snapping her usual wad of gum: "What, on liquidity?"

She made an immediate impact, frequently getting out on page one with such fluffy topics as John Kennedy's tax program, the debt ceiling, the balance of payments, and the trade tariff war. Typical headlines over her stories read: "U.S. TO RETALIATE AGAINST EUROPE WITH TARIFF RISE" and "STUDY FOR S.E.C. CHARGES CONTRACT MUTUAL FUNDS WITH VICTIMIZING BUYERS." In one extraordinary column she discussed the problem of the national debt ceiling in household terms, with the man representing Congress and his wife the Kennedy administration.

Washington and its labyrinthian politics were no mystery to Eileen. She had been born and raised in the capital and had spent her entire working life there. The will to work hard, to be first and best, had been drummed into her from her earliest years.

She was the younger daughter of an Irish Socialist and militant atheist, Thomas Shanahan, and a Jewish hausfrau, Malvena Karpeles. The family lived one step ahead of the rent collector, within brushing distance of poverty, in a series of homes all over the District of Columbia and its blue-collar suburbs. Eileen's father, the son of immigrants, was handsome, clean-cut, bald, courtly with women. Because of a boyhood accident, he was blind in one eye. He was rejected for military service in World War I and turned to a job in the U.S. government. His wife, Malvena, called Vena, the daughter of Austrian Jews, was plain to the point of homeliness, with a large nose and hair skinned back into a bun. She did not seem to know how to make herself more attractive, or care to try. Her large green heavy-lidded eyes were her most striking feature, which Eileen inherited.

"I don't feel that my mother had a very happy life," Eileen says. "She did her duty. She made it her business to learn about nutrition. She was a good, plain, all-American cook. She made pot roast from a recipe I still use, fricasseed chicken with dumplings, liver and onions, spareribs with sauerkraut, and the best soup out of chicken feet. I used to love the little tiny bones. At almost every meal, Daddy would say, 'Mother, you've outdone yourself!' It was a running gag."

During the 1920s, Tom Shanahan left a job at the Internal Revenue Service to go with a private law firm, earning his law degree at night school. Eighteen months after the Great Crash of 1929, they fired him. Tom Shanahan was unemployed for two and one-half years.

Eileen remembers coming home from school the day it happened; she was seven years old and had spilled ink on her dress. "It is one of those mental snapshots I will always have with me," she says, "like what I was doing when I heard about Pearl Harbor or John Kennedy's being shot." Her mother met her in the back hall of the house and in the gentlest tone said, "Dear, you must be more careful with your dresses. Your father has lost his job." Eileen can still summon up the clutch of fear she felt. "I was never ashamed," she says, "because other people's fathers had lost their jobs too. I remember Daddy—a Socialist all his days—explaining that 'the system' had failed, that he, Tom Shanahan, hadn't failed. But what was so terrible was that this was a man *destroyed* by the Depression."

Often, the parents dined on crackers and milk. Tom would break the crackers into the bowl and say, "Oh, Mother, crackers and milk—oh, I'd hoped we'd have crackers and milk tonight."

In 1933, Tom Shanahan finally got another job, with the Federal Emergency Relief Administration. He clung to government posts, safe and secure but all of them far below his skills, for the rest of his days. It was only through his daughters that Tom Shanahan was ultimately able to satisfy his yearning for intellectual excellence. (Eileen's older sister, Kay, was also a successful woman in a field long monopolized by men—she became a psychiatrist.)

"My father was very good at sticking *your* neck out," Eileen says. "We were told: achieve, achieve, achieve; achieve, achieve, achieve. He would say: 'You're Eileen Shanahan, you're Tom Shanahan's daughter, you get all A's.' We're talking *grade* school here.

"When you got your report card, you would go home and show it to Mother. It was put beside Father's plate at the dinner table. In 1940, my senior year in high school—I remember it as though it were yesterday—Father looked at my report card and saw I had gotten a B in solid geometry. I am terrible at spatial concepts—I never could figure out what was on the other side of a polyhedron. Father picked up my report card and tossed it away with disdain and said, 'Not so hot in geometry, I see.' I had worked hard. I felt a combination of anger and shame."

Still, when graduation time came around, Eileen won the history and Latin prizes and ranked third in the class. "So I stood up three times, and my father was proud of me."

Mrs. Shanahan, Jewish though she was, for years sent her daughters to the neighborhood Presbyterian church so they wouldn't grow up "heathen." She gave each of them a dime, big money for the family, every week for the Sunday school; she contributed in other ways to church events. Eileen dropped out when she was twelve, but her sister continued to go. When Eileen was fourteen, her mother was told she had cancer—which would kill her after three traumatic years. In her final months, Vena would say to Eileen, with hurt in her eyes, "I wonder why Mr. Custis [the Presbyterian minister] doesn't come to call."

The day after Vena died, Eileen was at home alone when she saw Mr. Custis coming up the front steps. Eileen stood inside the screen door to bar his entrance. She said: "Why didn't you come when my mother was alive?" and the minister replied smoothly, "I understand she was not of our faith." Eileen blew up. "She was enough of your faith," she yelled, "to cook a casserole for every church supper and bake cakes for the cake sales and give us money for Sunday school when we had no money and you, sir, can go to hell!"

In 1940, at the age of sixteen, Eileen had entered George

Washington University in the District of Columbia on a full four-year scholarship. During that first college year, she had come face to face with a more brutal form of prejudice. She never forgave herself for how she handled it. But it was, she says, "the single most important thing that happened to me that made me what I am, other than my parents and my skills. I had been a very unchallenging, unskeptical person until then."

In her time, and in the poor neighborhoods where she had grown up, "a mixed marriage was when an Irish Catholic girl married an Italian Catholic boy and both the mothers rent their garments at the wedding." Irish-Jewish marriages were almost unheard of. Tom Shanahan, despite his own choice of a Jewish wife, was a bigot. In his eyes, there were few "good Jews" other than Malvena and her family. Eileen ingested her father's biases and became ashamed of being half Jewish.

She came to college "dying to be beautiful and popular and to get into a sorority, where they would show me how to be beautiful and popular and make me better-looking than I knew how to make myself." Boys had avoided this brainy, superenergetic girl in high school. She had had a total of four dates in four years.

At George Washington University, she went through sorority "rush," the screening ritual for social acceptability, and was pledged by "not the nerdiest sorority; it was about third from the bottom." The night of pledge initiation, the chapter president came down a line of the newly anointed with some questions for each. Eileen was standing in the middle. She heard the president ask the first pledge, "Is there any Jewish, Negro, or Oriental blood in your family?" and the girl almost shrieked, "No, of course not!" By the time the president reached Eileen, she had decided to lie. "I wanted so desperately to be in a sorority," she says.

A few months later, a national officer of the sorority came to the campus. By then, some of the group's gloss had rubbed off on Eileen—she had learned a bit about dress and makeup and was enjoying more dates than she had ever dreamed of.

The officer summoned Eileen to an appointment. "We understand," she said, "that your mother is Jewish. Is that true?"

"And I knew the jig was up," Shanahan recalls. "And she held out her hand and said, 'I must ask you for your pin,' and I gave her the pin and walked out and I didn't cry until I got out the door. I thought my life was over."

But the incident caused her to think about her own behavior, and about prejudice. It led her to take an interest in her heritage. She began a serious romance with a Jewish boyfriend. They went to temple on Friday nights. She learned about the great culture and history of the Jews. "Nobody had ever told me there was anything to be proud of. Joe Epstein told me," Eileen remembers. She went to a rabbi, a distant relative by marriage, "to learn who I was."

She had joined the student newspaper, *The Hatchet,* in her first week as a freshman, urged on by a new friend. And there she found her first real home at any school, among other students who were accepting, fun to be with, intellectually stimulating, engaged with life. For the first time, she was meeting people her own age who were even brighter than she. She rose through the ranks to become *The Hatchet*'s editor.

When Eileen Shanahan walked into the city room of *The Washington Post* for a summer job in 1942 at the end of her sophomore year, she was eighteen years old and, she says, "so innocent that it is fair to say that I had barely been properly kissed."

It was wartime; all the copyboys had enlisted or been drafted. Eileen was the second copygirl ever hired at *The Washington Post.* When the reporters wanted their copy run up to the city desk, they still yelled "Boy!" "Boy!" "Boy!" "Copy!" "Copy!" "Copy!" and Shanahan leaped from the copyboys' bench at the front of the room. She fetched coffee and cleaned paste pots, she sharpened pencils, she ripped dispatches from the chattering Teletypes. At deadline hour, the din of manual typewriters rose to a pounding crescendo, and Eileen rushed hither and yon, snatching the sheets of paper from urgent outstretched hands. Before the week was out, Shanahan was a goner. She thought the people in the city room were the most interesting, friendly, exciting bunch of people she had ever met, even though there seemed to be quite a few boozehounds and womanizers among them.

By the time she had finished her second summer as a copy-girl at *The Washington Post,* she knew a career in journalism was for her. It was 1943; the United States was deep into the war and beginning to win; the news was exciting every day. Even Eileen, compiling college football scores and covering high school football games, with a *Post* byline of "E. J. Shana-han" so readers wouldn't know she was a female, felt part of the larger picture.

One stormy night that summer, Shanahan was sent over to the *Washington Evening Star* to pick up some wirephotos. There was a cloudburst, and Eileen, who is five feet six inches tall, borrowed a raincoat from the *Post*'s assistant night city editor, who was six feet four inches tall. Coming back, she bounded up the stairs to the city room, huaraches squelching, dark hair sopping, past a tall, calm young man named John Waits, a clerk in the advertising department, who was attend-ing George Washington University part-time. "I've got to meet this woman," Waits said to himself. He managed an introduction that very night and they began dating. They were married fifteen months later, in September 1944, three months after Shanahan got her college degree.

Eileen applied for her first full-time job at the United Press. Those were the days when hard-bitten newsmen thought the business was going to hell, what with all the women, and even worse, *college graduates,* begging to witness life as it was really lived. But editors were desperate because the men were away in the military; they would take anybody. "Can you spell, college girl?" asked the night wire editor. "Yessir!" said Ei-leen. She was hired as a telephone dictationist, typing thou-sands of words night after night as U.P. correspondents dictated their stories to her by phone from all over the nation.

"One time I spelled 'recommend' with two *c*'s and one *m*, and Harry Sharpe, my boss, came over and waggled the copy in front of my nose and said, 'I thought you could spell, college girl—you're fired!' I was concentrating on only one thing—not crying. I walked to my locker at the end of that long room, and Sharpe followed me and clapped me on the shoulder and said, 'Aw, you're not fired, college girl. Come on back.' "

Soon thereafter, Eileen took dictation from a reporter who phoned in two and one-half tedious pages about the wartime Office of Price Administration setting new, increased prices on canned sour pitted cherries. Sharpe said, "Rewrite it for what it's worth." Eileen was scared to death.

This was what she carved out of that two and one-half pages, remembered decades later word-for-word, the way reporters often remember their first real story: "The Office of Price Administration announced today higher prices for sixteen different grades and sizes of canned sour pitted cherries. The increases ranged from one and one-half cents a can on lower grades and smaller can sizes to six cents on higher grades and larger can sizes." Period. The end. It was not poetry, but it was an early example of the clarity with which Shanahan thinks and talks and writes.

"A few minutes later," Eileen recalls, "Sharpe jumped out of his chair and pointed at me and said, 'You'll do, college girl!' and he never called me college girl again."

In the winter of 1946, with the war over and the demobilization of the gigantic American armed forces accelerating, United Press, reflecting what was happening all over the country, fired all but three women in its Washington bureau. The holdovers were Eileen Shanahan; Helen Thomas, who rose over decades of tenacious reporting to become the first woman dean of the White House press corps; and Charlotte Moulton, who covered the Supreme Court and humiliated generations of her news competitors by always getting it right. She was so good that, according to Eileen, U.P. "was afraid to fire her."

As for Thomas and Shanahan, "one might think, given our successful subsequent careers, that we, too, were kept on because of our perceived excellence," she says. "Not so. Helen and I were kept on because nobody else wanted those crummy jobs rewriting the news from the local papers for the radio wire."

A year later, Shanahan left United Press to have her first child. After eighteen months at home alone with Mary Beth, however, she went through a frightening emotional deterioration, becoming so depressed she would leave dishes in the sink for days. Finally her husband said, "Go get a job. You've got to get out of here. You've got to go back to work."

"Well," she recalls, "it was pariah city out there." She heard the same lines that women would hear into the 1960s: "Your husband has a good job and you're leaving your baby at home?" The man at CBS radio said, "What on earth makes you think I'd hire a woman?" The man at ABC said he already had one woman on the staff. She worked her way down from the top floor of the National Press Building, where the Washington bureaus of almost every news organization in the nation were then located. On the eighth floor, she rapped on yet another frosted-glass door. Inside sat Walter Cronkite, aged thirty-two. He had covered the war for United Press and was then the Washington correspondent for a string of midwestern radio stations. It was February 28, 1949, Eileen's twenty-fifth birthday. Cronkite hired her that very day. In less than two years, he taught her as much about the news business as any mentor ever did. To her distress, he then moved on to CBS and fame.

Eileen's second child, Kathleen, was born. Soon there was war again—this time in Korea. Eileen joined the Research Institute of America, a newsletter publisher. There were full-scale wage and price controls during the Korean War and many industrial materials were rationed. She found that covering price controls was a way to understand the anatomy and physiology of the economy and how industries worked. When the war in Korea was over, she started covering bills in Congress and Supreme Court decisions that affected business. Her course was already set. She would be an economics reporter.

The most prestigious business newsletter of the era was the *Kiplinger Letter*. She wangled an appointment with its founder, Willard Kiplinger. Her friends told her it was hopeless. Kiplinger opened the interview by saying, "You wanted to see me?" and then said not another word, Eileen recounts. "I talk of my qualifications and interests. He says nothing. I talk some more. Still nothing. Finally, desperately, I ask, 'Do you have some questions that I'm not answering?'

"He replied that he wanted to see what kind of woman would apply for a job doing the kind of reporting the *Kiplinger Letter* required—inside information. 'A respectable woman, the only kind of woman we would want here, just couldn't do it,' he said. I didn't ask him what kind of favors his male colleagues gave in return for the inside information *they* got."

A *Washington Post* editor told her that he liked her work, but that an economics story under a woman's byline would not have any credibility. Eileen kept looking. The stodgy but widely respected *Journal of Commerce* hired her in 1956.

In 1961, the *Journal* printed her ten-part, ten-thousand-word series, "The Kennedy Administration and Business." Secretary of the Treasury Douglas Dillon called it "the only accurate interpretation of the whole economic policy of the Kennedy administration." Dillon asked her to become his spokesman for the tax side of the Treasury. She decided to stay only a year. She stayed a year and three days, and then she joined the Washington bureau of the *Times*. She was thirty-nine years old. It had taken her twenty-one years to rise from her copygirl's job on *The Washington Post* to star economics reporter at *The New York Times*.

CHAPTER 7

THE BRIDE OF THE NEW YORK TIMES

On the night of January 4, 1970, Leonard Bernstein, the conductor of the New York Philharmonic, and his wife, Felicia, gave a glamorous cocktail party in their thirteen-room Park Avenue duplex penthouse for the Black Panther Defense Fund. The invited—besides a number of militants in fuzzed-out Afros, black turtlenecks, and Cuban shades—were people who in those days were called limousine liberals; they listened approvingly and nibbled Roquefort balls rolled in crushed nuts while the guests of honor told off the world of white money and privilege. Among those present was a thin, intense little woman, neatly and discreetly packaged in basic black from Saks, not a hair out of place in her strawberry blond coiffure. She was taking it all down in her notebook in a backward-leaning, girls'-school handwriting. At one point during a strident presentation, Donald Cox, a Panther field marshal, said, "If business won't give us full employment, then we must take the means of production and put them in the hands of the people."

"I dig absolutely," Bernstein said.

The exchange showed up the next morning in *The New York Times* under the byline of Charlotte Curtis. Bernstein was crushed. He felt he had been shown up as a self-flagellating fool. Tom Wolfe, who wrote about the same party much more devastatingly in his book *Radical Chic & Mau-Mauing the Flak Catchers,* said of the fuss Charlotte caused: "It wasn't anything she wrote that infuriated them. It was that she put down exactly what they said—that's always what seems cruelest of all, to hold up a mirror to people that way. Her political leanings were probably *with* the Bernsteins, who she later wrote had done a lot of good, but she approached their party the same way she did those of people whom it was fashionable to ridicule. It wasn't at all fashionable, intellectually, to ridicule people like the Bernsteins." But Charlotte, he said, "never let her own sympathies get in the way of the job of reporting."

Charlotte Curtis, like Wolfe, had perfect pitch for the way the rich and often infamous spoke and a wonderful eye for detail. She did her homework obsessively. She revolutionized the manner in which society was covered and diversified the topics that appeared on the *Times*'s women's page. She was imitated by women's news editors across the country and by the reporters on her own newspaper who were her protégés. She was the *Times*'s first woman media celebrity, profiled by *Newsweek* and *Time, Cosmopolitan* and *New York* magazine, *Women's Wear Daily* and the television networks. The *Times* itself extolled her in house ads, as it had paraded Anne O'Hare McCormick, the foreign affairs columnist, during the 1940s and early 1950s. McCormick was celebrated long before the advent of the term "media celebrity" or Andy Warhol's concept that everybody in America would be famous for fifteen minutes. She shrank from the limelight; Charlotte did not.

Charlotte was the only *Times* woman other than the dynasty's matriarch, Iphigene Sulzberger, to be given more than a few lines in Gay Talese's exhaustive study of the paper, *The Kingdom and the Power*. In 1967, in a letter to his best buddy Talese, David Halberstam, who had won a Pulitzer for the *Times* in 1964 for his reporting from Vietnam, said Charlotte was "now one of the most powerful men [*sic*] on the paper." She was the first woman ever to make the masthead of the *Times,* as an associate editor and the editor of the Op-Ed page. Her work was her life. The newspaper was her life. She was never off duty. She was the bride of *The New York Times.*

Sydney Gruson, who became the paper's vice chairman and Punch Sulzberger's close friend, and who knew every twist and turn of the *Times*'s internal politics, said this of her: "It was the paper on which she lavished her love, her hopes, her attention. She cared about the paper, almost desperately. And I think her first desire, above everything else in her working life, was to try to make it better. To do that she always wanted to be more deeply involved. If she couldn't be involved openly, well, you know how she operated."

Charlotte often said that Clifton Daniel had invented her. She invented herself, but Daniel certainly set her feet on the path to fame. In 1963, after she had languished for two years as a fashion reporter under Elizabeth Howkins, who told her, in an appalling lack of judgment, that she could not write, Daniel, then the assistant managing editor, took her in hand. "Write about society as news and treat it as sociology," he told her. Daniel had always been fascinated by society. Elegant and courtly, although capable of being freezingly cutting, he had been the toast of London drawing rooms during and after World War II, when he was a *Times* correspondent and a most seductive bachelor. "It has been alleged, with some justification, that I was partial to rich and celebrated ladies," he wrote in *Lords, Ladies and Gentlemen,* a memoir. "And why not? As a rule they lived in grander houses, served better food and drink, wore prettier clothes and bigger pearls, were more sophisticated and amusing, had more glittering friends and did wonders for my ego." In the end, he married President Harry Truman's daughter, Margaret.

Daniel and Curtis were made for each other. He had noticed, if Mrs. Howkins had not, how keen an observer, how sharp a listener, how good a writer, she was. Little escaped her pale blue eye. "I had been nagging at Russell Edwards, the society editor, to get something on the society pages besides those damn routine wedding and engagement stories," Daniel told me. Edwards replied that he had a tiny staff. Daniel gave him Charlotte. The society editor was flabbergasted—she was overpowering, overqualified for the job. "Just assign her some stories and kick her out the front door and when she comes back, print what she writes," Daniel said.

"She was an overnight sensation," Daniel remembered with relish. "The next day, people said, 'More! More!' Everyone turned instantly to her page to see what she had written. For quite a time, she was the talk of New York society." It was not just New York, either. Daniel sent her around the United States, around the world. She perfected a witty, irreverent descriptive style that could be merciless, but except for the Bernsteins, the people she skewered usually lapped up what Charlotte Curtis wrote. She was invited everywhere.

The Maharanee of Baroda told Charlotte of a typical day: "I wake at 2, sometimes 3. First is my massage. Afterwards, I answer my phone calls and see my bankers, racing managers and lawyers—the usual daily chores."

This is how she reported on George Plimpton's wedding, which she crashed: "Mr. Plimpton was married here last night, not to Mrs. John F. Kennedy, Queen Elizabeth II, Jean Seberg, Ava Gardner, Jane Fonda, Princess Stanislas Radziwill or Candy Bergen, all of whom he has escorted at one time or another, but to Freddy Medora Espy, a wisp of a photographer's assistant."

She told the world that proper Bostonians sweat. "Bostonians are an elegantly athletic lot," her story began. "They prove it periodically by swirling, twirling and swooping about in graceful dance patterns until beads of perspiration materialize on their aristocratic brows." The article noted that these genteel exertions caused the temperature in the ballroom during that Waltz Evening at the Sheraton-Plaza Hotel to rise from 59 degrees to 64 degrees. Whether Charlotte simply checked a thermostat or interviewed the janitor, you could be sure she was dead accurate.

Before descending on Boston, she had, typically, boned up as if she were preparing for an exam. She combed the libraries. She browsed through Standard & Poor's listings of corporations and executives and a classic Works Progress Administration history of Boston. She scanned *The Education of Henry Adams.* She checked out the genealogies of the city's first families. She was being, in short, a good reporter.

She described Miami as a "youthful city of indeterminate social standing" with the "third largest Jewish population in the world," then got to her point: "However, there are no Jewish members in the Surf Club, the Bath Club or the Indian Creek and La Gorce clubs."

In a profile of Los Angeles society, she showed in one line how some Angelenos viewed the rest of the country. When the host at a party she attended was told that the young native at his elbow had just entered Harvard, he said, "What's the matter? Couldn't you get into Stanford?"

There were bulletins from Charlotte from everywhere in the haut monde: Princess Grace of Monaco eats peanut butter; the Begum Aga Khan wears perhaps five pounds of pearls; Princess Caroline learned to wolf-whistle at camp in America; the Count of Paris milks cows; "Princey" Baroda adores his mother's Cherry Mousse nail polish; Count Giovanni Volpi climbs a tree at a Côte d'Azur party to pelt the Ford family with vanilla ice cream and raspberries; Henry Ford spritzes the count with Perrier; the radically chic at a Southampton lawn party are asked to close their eyes and imagine they are migrant grape pickers. Charlotte spotted the black alligator shoes on Jerry Ohrbach's butler, the gaping zipper on "Bunny" Mellon's Balenciaga, Norman Mailer stirring his gin and tonic with his left index finger, the thirty-five-cent mask taped to Alice Roosevelt Longworth's temples at Truman Capote's Black and White Ball. She heard Ethel Scull say, "I've never been so bored in my life" at a $15,000,000 art auction. Even at the International Sporting Club in Monaco, Princess Youka Troubetzkoy could not escape her origins as "the Toledo, Ohio, spark-plug heiress" with Charlotte on the scene. The staid copy editors back on West Forty-third Street almost died at what Charlotte was writing and how she was writing it. But they seldom trimmed her copy. Clifton Daniel had become managing editor in 1964, and he was watching.

In 1965, when Mrs. Howkins retired because of ill health, he appointed Charlotte as her successor. David Halberstam said that Daniel valued Curtis's "opinions on everything." He read the women's page every morning with the most finicky attention. Daniel did not gush over her—in fact, when they squabbled, neither one would give an inch. Talese tells of one such quarrel, in which Charlotte insisted that the nickname of Prince Stanislas Radziwill, Jacqueline Kennedy's brother-in-law, was both pronounced and spelled "Stash," and Daniel argued that although it was pronounced "Stash," it was spelled "Stas." The absurd argument went on for months. Daniel won after tracking down the prince, an old acquaintance, in Europe.

Not all of Charlotte's assignments in her peak writing years were about the rich. She was sent to help cover the moon shot, presidential campaigns and inaugurations, and national political conventions, including the violent Democratic National Convention in Chicago in 1968. Just two months earlier she had been aboard the train that carried the body of Robert Kennedy, assassinated during his campaign for president, from New York to his grave in Arlington National Cemetery. She described Bobby's eldest son, Joe, then fifteen years old:

Down the swaying train he went, putting out his hand in 19 of the other 20 cars saying, "I'm Joe Kennedy," while outside in the early afternoon sun, the old men of Linden, N.J., stood silently in their undershirts and the women held handkerchiefs to their faces.

"I'm Joe Kennedy," he said to strangers, his pin-stripe black suit not yet a shambles from the failing air-conditioning, his PT boat tie clip neatly in place. "Thanks for coming, thanks for coming."

When the train arrived at Union Station in Washington, a five-foot-tall figure sprinted up to Steve Smith, Bobby's brother-in-law, panting, "Where's the goddamned telephone?" so she could dictate her story back to the *Times* faster than anybody else in the press corps.

Charlotte was certainly no Dresden doll in Clifton Daniel's eyes; she was pretty in a cool way, but not made of porcelain. She was one tough little character: "Intellectually she was made of cast iron. She had an iron will, an iron determination, an iron integrity."

She came from a remarkable family. She was born in Winnetka, Illinois, a wealthy North Shore suburb of Chicago, on December 19, 1928; when she was ten, the Curtises moved to Columbus, Ohio. Her mother, Lucile Atcherson Curtis, was the only child of a very rich man in Columbus who had amassed a fortune from hotels, real estate, and streetcars. Lucile was graduated from Smith College at the age of fourteen. After further study, she went into the diplomatic corps, becoming the first woman field officer in the United States Foreign Service, holding posts in American legations in Switzerland, Panama, and Haiti. Charlotte's father, George Morris Curtis, the son of a minister, met Lucile in Berne, Switzerland, while doing advanced medical training there; he became a distinguished surgeon and chief of research surgery at Ohio State University. Charlotte's was hardly a conventional childhood: she and her younger sister, Mary, were made to learn all the stars, all the trees, all the birds. By the time Charlotte was ten she could recognize and draw pictures of every part of the body, and when she was forty-six, she told an interviewer, "To this day, I could draw you a pituitary." The sisters grew up in an affluent Columbus suburb and went to the best schools: Charlotte described her own background as "overprivileged." Privileged they may have been; pampered they were not. Charlotte and her kid sister were not allowed to give a poor performance at the piano, or on the tennis court, or at school, according to Mary Curtis Davey, who went on to become a social worker and deputy mayor of Los Altos, California. When the Curtis parents did not wish their daughters to understand what they were saying at dinner, they spoke in French, Spanish, or German. Charlotte and Mary retaliated by developing their own secret sign language.

Charlotte went to the Columbus School for Girls, and made her debut. In 1946, she entered Vassar College, where she majored in American history. Jacqueline Bouvier, later Kennedy and then Onassis, roomed down the hall, and the Vicomtesse de Rosière was Charlotte's roommate. The summer after her freshman year, Charlotte presented herself at the *Columbus Citizen,* gave her age as nineteen instead of seventeen, and entered the scuzzy world of newspapers. When editors needed a reporter, they would yell out, "Hey, Vassar!" "There wasn't anyone like me when I went to the *Citizen* to work," Charlotte said. She was "a rich girl from a rich suburb—the suburb was Bexley—and going to what was considered to be a rich women's college."

She worked at the *Citizen* every summer during her college years and then joined the staff full-time after graduation in 1950. Don Easter was her first editor. He turned her first story back with every word underlined in red and the note, "Otherwise, this is excellent." He would bark, "Curtis, you didn't get your clothes off fast enough!" meaning that she had not gotten to the point of her story as quickly as she should. It was terrific training.

Meanwhile, she kept up her genteel side. She joined the Junior League. She married the boy next door, who had grown up to become a lawyer. She wrote a daily "Mostly About Women" column, a Sunday "Charlotte's Ruse" column, and covered assignments ranging from Richard Nixon to a monkey who preferred peanut butter to the original nuts. Her husband wanted Charlotte at home, fussing over hors d'oeuvre in a frilly apron. They were divorced after less than three years, in 1953. "I turned out to like newspapering more," Charlotte said. "Fortunately, we didn't have children, so our parting was easy."

A colleague on the *Columbus Citizen* during the ten years that Charlotte spent there said of her: "She had the disposition of a thoroughbred—overtrained, overbred and tense. She had a pride in being able to cope. She was against copelessness."

In April 1961, Charlotte Curtis joined *The New York Times*. In a speech years later, Marylin Bender described her entrance: "A miniature whirlwind blew in from Columbus and took possession of the desk adjacent to mine in the women's news ghetto, which was then six floors above the city room. I remember the distinctive manner in which she wrote her first story and every story thereafter. This Nellie Bly would pull up her right foot and sit on it, with the weight of course of a tiny little body, and then she would pound away at the Royal upright typewriter, an exquisite canary diamond ring blinking from the third finger of her right hand, and dabbings of Joy, then the world's most expensive perfume, wafting from underneath her auburn pageboy hairdo."

Charlotte's greatest years at the *Times* were the sixties and early seventies, first as a reporter at the pinnacle of her powers, and then as women's news editor. Julie Baumgold of *New York* magazine described the change on the page: "Along came Charlotte in 1965 [as the women's editor], when the women's universe was lifting its face. She simply opened the doors, and there were urban affairs, black models, politics, new lifestyles—a whole interracial interclass flood. . . . One had only to look at the pictures. Along with Junior Leaguers flapping their puppets in the faces of the hospitalized, there was a grinning Mark Rudd [a leader of the student revolt at Columbia in 1968] being bussed on the cheek by his Jewish Mommy. . . . [and] 'Mr. Cool,' young super spade in shiny green-gold-lemon-purple alpaca pants."

This was the Anything Goes Decade, and no topic was taboo. Abortion, lesbians, unwed fathers and mothers, alcoholism, drug abuse, incest, peace marches, and love-ins all made their appearance—with heavy helpings of radical chic, to be sure—on the women's page in the last half of the decade and into the seventies. At times, Iphigene Sulzberger and her son, Punch, the publisher, thought Charlotte had gone too far. An article on the women's page described how young women and men at New York City's universities were living together outside the bonds of matrimony. One of them, a sophomore at Barnard College, Iphigene's beloved alma mater, had had an abortion and now was trying to conceive, but still thought marriage was "too serious a step," more serious than having a baby. The authorities located the student and sought to expel her; student protests erupted; the *Times* kept on covering it, to Mrs. Sulzberger's dismay. She said to her son, "Why not put sex in perspective?" and added: "It went on in my day too."

Punch blurted out to one of his executives: "My God! You can't get a piece about anybody on the women's page these days unless she's a black lesbian mother!"

But Charlotte Curtis was riding high, and there was really no one during that period who was ready or willing to unhorse her. She had become a personal and social friend of Punch and his wife, Carol. She was a visitor to the second Hillandale, the Sulzberger family estate near Stamford, Connecticut. She did not hesitate to use her clout.

Sydney Gruson, who was very fond of Charlotte, talked in a speech in the 1980s about a side of her that few people saw—"Charlotte the conspirator." "Behind that lovely little lady, turned out in the pretty skirt and beautifully done hair, was a conspirator of worldwide order," he said. "She was always trying to figure out ways of bending things to her will. I never thought she'd try to break things, just to bend them."

Gruson described how Curtis would telephone him and then come up to the fourteenth floor, the publisher's floor, where Sydney polished his languid Scarlet Pimpernel image while actually getting a great deal done. Charlotte's visits were usually about what she considered some outrage or other within the paper, such as a staff transfer or assignment. "I can hear her now," Gruson said, "sitting opposite me with one leg tucked beneath her, smoke forming a halo above her, and her sharp voice saying, 'Sydney, you just can't let this happen.' " Gruson added, drily, "It usually happened."

···········

Only one other woman on *The New York Times* during the sixties and seventies was as visible, as powerful, as admired, as feared, as Charlotte Curtis. She was Ada Louise Huxtable, and she made her way in a field where few women had trod before—architecture criticism.

Ada Louise Huxtable came onto the staff in 1963 as the first full-time architecture critic on an American newspaper. It was two years after Curtis had arrived, and the year she made her sensational debut as society's sociologist. In some ways, the two women seemed alike. Both were small, dainty, well born, well dressed, well coiffed, ambitious, fiercely competitive. Each brought an unmistakable zing to her writing. One was fair (Charlotte), one dark (Ada Louise). In terms of honors, Ada Louise (*never* just "Ada") scaled the heights. She became the second woman, after Anne McCormick, to win the Pulitzer for the *Times*. It was the first Pulitzer given for any kind of criticism, in 1970. She was the second woman, again after McCormick, to be elevated to the *Times* editorial board, in 1974. Her list of awards goes on and on: thirty honorary degrees from colleges and universities, member of the American Academy and Institute of Arts and Letters, Fellow of the American Academy of Arts and Sciences, Honorary Fellow of the Royal Institute of British Architects, grants and board memberships almost beyond counting.

Ada Louise Huxtable was no bride of *The New York Times,* however. She considered herself an outsider and said so. She came late to the *Times,* at the age of forty-two. She was already a seasoned architectural historian. "Did I think of a journalism career?" she said. "Never, not for a moment." Although she plunged with zest into the daily struggle to get on the front page and could crunch her opposition like a Sherman tank, she rarely involved herself, as Curtis did, in the internal politics of the newspaper—unless, that is, the politics impinged on her own path. Her copy packed a tremendous wallop—it was slangy, energetic, angry, amusing, at times overblown, and always opinionated.

One article began: "New York's longest-run show, the Architectural Follies, goes on. Performances as usual." It ended:

Watch an architectural landmark demolished piece by piece. Be present while a splendid building is reduced to rubble. See the wrecking bars gouge out the fine chateau-style stonework. Hear the gas-powered saws bite into the great beams and rafters. Thrill to destruction. Take home samples. Hurry to the show.

On second thought, don't hurry. There will be many more performances. Good demolitions could outrun *Abie's Irish Rose.* Free demolition-watchings will be offered in all of New York's best styles and periods: High Victorian, Early Skyscraper, Cast-Iron Commercial in the path of the Lower Manhattan expressway, Greek Revival on the waterfront. If this isn't going to be faced as a public responsibility, it might as well be taken as a public spectacle. Anyone coming from City Hall?

Some of her book titles were equally punchy, including the delightful *Kicked a Building Lately?* and *Will They Ever Finish Bruckner Boulevard?* She demolished Washington's Kennedy Center for the Performing Arts in one phrase: "a cross between a concrete candy box and a marble sarcophagus in which the art of architecture lies buried." As if that were not enough to send her friend the architect Edward Durell Stone to the nearest goblet of hemlock, Huxtable described his creation as a "superbunker" of which Albert Speer, the Nazis' architect, would have been proud. She was kinder to the capital's Hirshhorn Museum, calling it only "the biggest marble doughnut in the world."

At times Ada Louise became so intoxicated with her own vocabulary that she would spin almost out of control. Discussing Eero Saarinen's great black CBS skycraper in midtown Manhattan, she wrote: "It is not, like so much of today's large-scale construction, a handy commercial package, a shiny wraparound envelope, a packing case, a box of cards, a trick with mirrors. It does not look like a cigar lighter, a vending machine, a nutmeg grater." Then she got to her point: "It is a building in the true, classic sense: a complete design in which technology, function and esthetics are conceived and executed integrally for its purpose. As its architect, Eero Saarinen, wanted, this is a building to be looked at above the bottom fifty feet, to be comprehended as a whole."

She cared very much about the way any building affected the people who used it or lived near it or simply gazed at it. She influenced other critics and city planners, attacked the greed and vulgarity of developers, managed to save many threatened structures, and helped to establish New York City's Landmarks Preservation Commission in a metropolis obsessed with tearing itself down and obliterating its physical history.

The New York Times got an architecture critic because Iphigene Sulzberger, who was interested in all aspects of the urban landscape, wanted one. The task fell once more to Clifton Daniel, then the assistant managing editor, and once more, he picked a winner who was a woman. He had noticed Ada Louise's occasional articles in the *Times* Sunday magazine. Additional impetus came from Aline Bernstein, a friend of Ada Louise's and an assistant art critic on the *Times,* who was leaving the paper to marry Eero Saarinen and felt she could no longer cover architecture without a conflict of interest. She recommended Huxtable. Daniel called her in. At first she turned him down, saying daily journalism would disrupt her private life. Daniel looked elsewhere, assiduously, but in his own words, "I couldn't find anyone better than she was." The second time he asked her, she said yes. Daniel was one of Ada Louise's three significant mentors. The others were Lester Markel, who was furious that Daniel had snatched Ada Louise away from the Sunday magazine, and John Oakes, a member of the *Times* family dynasty and ultimately her boss on the editorial board. Of Daniel, Huxtable said, "He gave me confidence. He trusted me. He said from the beginning, 'Go to it!' just as he had done with Charlotte Curtis. I think he liked women."

There was no precedent for Ada Louise. "There was no way to fit me into the journalistic framework," she commented later. "I was *sui generis.* I was like a creature from the moon. I had been trained as an historian, I had worked mostly for museums and specialized magazines. But I gained respect on the *Times* very quickly. I very quickly learned the trade. I had an excellent nose for news." She also discovered, very quickly, that "*The New York Times* was one of the last great male chauvinist institutions. It amused me. It infuriated me." Nevertheless, Ada Louise charged straight ahead. Self-doubt and low self-esteem do not figure in her psychological makeup.

And she is totally at home in New York. Charlotte Curtis always spoke of herself as "100 percent midwestern." Ada Louise Huxtable is a self-described "child of New York." She was born on March 14, 1921, in Manhattan, and was named Ada after two grandmothers and Louise after her father, Michael Louis Landman, a physician specializing in internal medicine and immunology. Her mother, Leah Rosenthal, was a Bostonian and a beauty—John Canaday, a *Times* art critic and connoisseur of feminine esthetics, always imagined Leah reclining languidly on a chaise longue, nibbling bonbons. "She was a walking candy box," Canaday once recalled. She was also, according to her daughter, "an intensely visual woman with an impeccable eye and an abhorrence of anything fake."

Ada Louise Landman was an only child and a solitary, self-sufficient one. She grew up in one of those massive old apartment buildings on Central Park West that were the bastions of the cultivated, socially conservative, and politically liberal German Jewish families who set the tone of much of New York's cultural and civic life. Iphigene Sulzberger was a perfect example of the genre, which Stephen Birmingham profiled in his book *Our Crowd.*

Ada Louise was a product of New York City public schools and of its great art museums. As a little girl, she would roller-skate across Central Park to spend whole days at the Metropolitan Museum of Art. Her father, Leah's second husband, loved art and wrote plays in his spare time; his first, called *Pride of Race,* was about interracial marriage and shocked audiences in pre-1920 New York. Doctor Landman died when his daughter was eleven. Ada Louise went to the High School of Music and Art, where she edited the school newspaper, and then to Hunter College, a part of the New York City college system that was famous for its brainy women. At Hunter, a professor told her to give up because she refused to follow strict models for short-story structure. She was graduated magna cum laude in 1941 at the age of twenty with a major in art. "I was trained to teach art, but I did have to support my mother," Ada Louise recalled, so off she went to Bloomingdale's. "I've just won your interior decorating contest and I need a job," said she.

One day in the autumn of 1941, while she was demonstrating model rooms, a slender young man with a narrow face and bony features asked her if she would help him furnish his bachelor apartment. She sold him a chest of drawers for $49.95. He invited her to dine with him. First she took him home to meet her mother. Ada Louise Landman and Leonard Garth Huxtable, then thirty years old and well launched on his career as an industrial designer, were engaged within a month.

They were married early in March 1942, just before Ada Louise's twenty-first birthday. Her mother signed the marriage application, Ada Louise not having quite reached the age of consent. The next year, Leah married for the third time.

Ada Louise had chosen art as her vocation and studied for a master's degree in art and architectural history at New York University's Institute of Fine Arts. She left without graduating when her thesis proposal on nineteenth- and twentieth-century Italian architecture was rejected. Out of that research grew a Fulbright scholarship in Italy in the early 1950s and then, in 1960, her first book, *Pier Luigi Nervi,* on the Italian architect-engineer. From 1946 to 1950, she was the assistant curator of architecture and design at the Museum of Modern Art in New York. After her return from Italy in 1952, she became a freelance writer, contributing to art and architectural periodicals. In 1958, she received a Guggenheim fellowship for the study of design and structural advances in American architecture. And then Aline Bernstein introduced Ada Louise to Lester Markel, the editor who had been making strong men tremble since the twenties at *The New York Times Magazine.*

"I knew his reputation," Ada Louise said. "He was the king and the terror of the *Times.* I walked into his office, which appeared to be ninety feet long, with his desk at the other end." Now, Ada Louise may be small, but she has two fierce black eyes in that head of hers. Markel took one look at her and said, "What are you planning to do—hit me over the head with your book or your umbrella?" Round one for Ada Louise and the beginning of her career at the *Times.*

Her husband, L. Garth Huxtable, who had studied with Raymond Loewy and Henry Dreyfus—both pioneer industrial designers—won distinction in his own field for a wide range of products, from tools for Sears to a café for the Metropolitan Opera to the china, glass, and flatware still used at the Four Seasons, a ritzy restaurant frequented by high-powered book editors and literary agents in the magnificent Seagram's skyscraper on Park Avenue. There were no children of the marriage. It lasted for forty-seven years, until Garth Huxtable's death in 1989.

....

Both Curtis and Huxtable were in the tradition of Anne O'Hare McCormick—so good they could not be ignored by the men who ran the establishment, and so personally assertive that they *would* not be ignored. As Iphigene Sulzberger, with her undocumented but real influence behind the scenes, personified the first form of woman power at *The New York Times,* so McCormick and Curtis and Huxtable represented the second form of woman power: outstanding individual talent and determination. Their mentors on the staff were male, because there were no female role models above them at the *Times* to bring them along. McCormick and Curtis also had the ear and the friendship of the publisher.

What none of these women had was the direct executive and corporate power given as a matter of course only to men since the paper's beginnings.

But by the early 1970s, the social climate for women was changing dramatically. In 1964, Congress had enacted Title VII of the Civil Rights Act, the principal modern federal law against job discrimination. In 1971, the Supreme Court gave the statute more life and force by declaring that Title VII prohibited "not only overt discrimination but also practices that are fair in form, but discriminatory in operation."

As women poured into the labor force, more and more of them discovered, among other things, that they were making, on the average, only fifty-nine cents to every dollar earned by men doing similar jobs. They were discovering, in thousands of newly formed consciousness-raising groups, that the discrimination each woman thought she was unique in experiencing was the lot of every other working woman. The National Organization for Women and the National Women's Political Caucus had been founded, *Ms.* magazine had been launched. Even the *Times* family/style page had changed beyond recognition from its cozy domestic concerns of yesteryear as its staff reported on every aspect of what was then called the women's liberation movement. The momentum everywhere in the country was irresistible. And finally, slowly, the women of *The New York Times* began to move with it—to demand, together, equal rights on their own home ground.

CHAPTER 8

THE OTHER SHOE

Grace Glueck stood in a thick knot of people staring up at the bulletin board in the city room of *The New York Times*. The reporters and editors, copyboys and clerks and secretaries who clustered there on the last day of July in 1969 were reading an important announcement couched in *Times*speak, the colorless, opaque, and self-congratulatory language the management always used when telling the troops about internal upheaval and change. The same language would appear in the *Times* the next morning. Few on the outside would be the wiser. That was the result the *Times* desired. But those inside were like Kremlinologists poring over the photographs of Soviet leaders atop Lenin's tomb on May Day—Who's standing next to whom? Who's missing?—and by such portents trying to read the future of an enigmatic bureaucracy. There was buzzing and chattering around the bulletin board. This was a big one.

The publisher, Arthur Ochs Sulzberger, was announcing that four men in the uppermost ranks of the newspaper were going to new jobs. James Reston, fifty-nine years old, who had been executive editor in New York for just over one year, had been elected a vice president and would go back to Washington, there to continue to write his column three times a week. Clifton Daniel, fifty-six, the managing editor, would become an associate editor with a group of new duties designed "to develop improved methods of news presentation." A. M. Rosenthal, forty-seven, had been named managing editor in Daniel's place. Seymour Topping, the foreign editor, also forty-seven, was promoted to assistant managing editor.

"The New York Times has never had such a wealth of young talent on which to build its present and future growth," Sulzberger's announcement said. "Nearly two years ago, we began seriously to plan the transition to the next generation. . . . We will retain the skills and experience of our present senior executives at the top levels of our operations but will at the same time increase the load of younger men who have demonstrated their capacity to carry it."

The announcement droned on. It told the staff that Reston had taken the post of executive editor "with the understanding that it would be for a limited period, his principal mission to be, as he put it, to facilitate 'the changing of the guard.' " The publisher added, "That mission has been accomplished."

What all of this pap boiled down to, the people around the bulletin board knew, was that in the game of power politics within the *Times,* Abe Rosenthal had come out on top. Rosenthal, the tough little New York street fighter, was king of the hill, knocking out of his path to absolute power Daniel and Reston, two of the most adroit politicians ever to work on *The New York Times.*

Grace Glueck was having other thoughts. Where are the women? she asked herself. Where are the women when there is any movement at the top in this place? What's all this stuff about the wealth of young talent and the next generation? She remembered a memo Punch Sulzberger had sent to the entire staff only four months before, in April 1969. Sulzberger's message to his employees began: "The New York Times believes in equal opportunity employment because it is morally, economically and socially right." The language of the memo made it clear that the paper was aiming at the hiring, promotion, and training of blacks and Hispanics—to enable "those who have been held back by prejudice and poverty to earn and enjoy a decent life."

The publisher's memo concluded, "As a Government contractor, the Times and its subsidiaries are bound by legal requirements on non-discriminatory employment. But if there were not a single regulation, I would still want it to be the Times's policy to help overcome what I believe to be one of the most urgent tasks facing our country: to enable all Americans to share in the abundance of our economy."

Grace had thought then, too: What about us women? We're half the population, we've got the education, there isn't any cultural gap, and still *we* aren't getting anywhere on this newspaper either—it is totally dominated by white men. On that Thursday in July 1969, as she read the news from the top in Sulzberger's latest communiqué, Grace found herself becoming very upset. Now, she is not a woman who wears her soul on her sleeve. The persona she has invented for herself is brittle, sophisticated, toujours gai. Her heart may be cracking; she will hide it with a wisecrack, flashing a brilliant smile.

This day, Grace was furious. She left the crowd at the bulletin board and went at a fast trot back to her desk in "Culture Gulch"—past row after unbroken row of identical gray metal desks in the block-long city room to the cultural news department, where she was an art reporter writing the "Art People" column. She rolled a sheet of paper into her clunky manual typewriter. "Dear Punch," she tapped. Punch was forty-three years old, born the same year as Grace, and an accessible man. She could not have imagined ripping off a memo to his elegant and somewhat remote father, Arthur Hays Sulzberger, when the elder Sulzberger was publisher. Her memo to Punch was only several sentences long. It was polite. She congratulated him on the splendid team that had been promoted. She asked, "Why were no women included?" She rushed the note upstairs, to the publisher's floor.

To her intense surprise, Sulzberger's answer was in Grace's hands the next day. Point well taken, he said. I will consult with "key management executives" when they return from their August vacations and we will see what can be done. Grace showed her note and the reply to some of the culture department's old-timers: the kosher philosopher Dick Shepard, the great *Herald Tribune* alumnus Joe Herzberg, tiny Abe Weiler, the manic wag. What do you think about this? she asked them. "They laughed," she recounts. "They thought it was cute. In effect, they patted me on the head." She waited for some kind of follow-up from Punch. "I never heard another word," Grace adds.

But all-unknowing, she had jolted the publisher. A worried Sulzberger spoke to Sydney Gruson, then his special assistant and closest friend on the paper, a former foreign editor and correspondent. Punch wondered if the women were organizing. He and Gruson waited for Glueck to "drop the other shoe," as Sydney was to put it later. Instead there was silence.

Two and one-half years would go by before the women of *The New York Times* got together to complain about their starkly unequal lot at the newspaper. Grace was destined to be one of the leaders—and the resident wit—of the Women's Caucus. More than any other, she leavened its serious purpose and lightened its darkest crises.

Everything about Glueck was and is crisp, immaculate, polished, right to the top of her clipped, perfectly coiffed head. She enunciates clearly and speaks in finished sentences. She is small and thin, with a dare-anything smile and large, slightly protuberant blue eyes fringed by black, curly lashes. John

Canaday, a *Times* art critic, loved those lashes and her race-horse ankles (when he mentioned them, Grace got furious) and said she reminded him of Rosalind Russell "in one of those movies in the 1940s where she played a brisk business executive who always turns out to be a real softy for Cary Grant beneath the surface polish."

The jest is all. Her humor is sharp and self-mocking and she summons it to her aid in every situation. Once, when I was trying to delve into her childhood, asking her about her parents, she interrupted me. "Haven't I ever told you about my Primal Scene?" she said, her eyes sparkling wickedly. I was all agog. "Well, one early morning when I was very little, I was pattering toward the bathroom past my parents' bedroom when I heard my mother moaning and sobbing and my father shouting. . . . He was shouting, 'I *told* you to go to four no-trump!' "

Despite her wall of aplomb and chic, Grace's insecurities are legend. She bleeds when she writes, and rewrites, and re-rewrites. When she is not laughing, her brow is knitted with worry. Her desk is a high-rise slum—she throws nothing away, for fear she might find a particular scrap of paper useful one day. Her apartments are never finished. She is a hypochondriac. When she was ordered to go to a Guatemalan jungle to cover the unearthing of an important Mayan tomb, "visions of malaria, filariasis, psittacosis and heartworm, to say nothing of ordinary snake and spider bites, danced in my head," she told *Times Talk.*

She went, of course, arming herself first with crackers, baby food, string, bottles of soda, mosquito netting, and toilet paper—and three new designer jungle outfits that she was anxious to try out on the parrots. One of her traveling companions crushed a spider the size of a dinner plate in her hotel room, and the rutted jeep track to the archeological dig was strewn with rocks, fallen branches, and potholes and blocked by men with guns, but Grace was determined to get her story—and fast. "I had a hairdresser's appointment in New

York on Saturday," she explained airily. She wound up with a world scoop on the front page.

··········

Grace Glueck's childhood might have been idyllic, but like Betsy Wade's, it was made painful by one tragic family figure. She was born in Manhattan on July 24, 1926, to Mignon Schwarz and Ernest Glueck—the name is pronounced "Glewk," but few at the *Times* ever got it right, settling for "Glick," "Gluck," or "Glook." Grace and her older brother, Charles, grew up in Rockville Centre, Long Island, which she remembers as a wonderful small town, "the kind of town where your kids were out playing sixteen hours a day and the parents never worried."

Throughout the 1920s, Ernest Glueck was a salesman of municipal bonds. The Crash of 1929 wiped him out. Like Eileen Shanahan's father, Ernest was out of work for two years, from 1931 to 1933, and like Tom Shanahan, he spent the rest of his life in a safe job, as an insurance broker. During those years of unemployment, the Gluecks did not have enough money for charge accounts, or for the mortgage, or for keeping a car. The bank would send a man around to collect the delinquent mortgage payment, and while Grace watched, her mother would be reduced to tears of humiliation.

The Depression's effect on the Gluecks was not the worst of it by any means. The tragedy of Charles, five years older than Grace, haunted all the family, but for years and years the parents refused to admit that anything was wrong with their darling son.

Charles's head was crushed by forceps at birth. The doctor would concede nothing, but there was frontal lobe damage. Grace described him to me as retarded from his earliest years, "an emotional basket case" with autistic tendencies, who would bang his head all night long against his bedroom walls. Small and puny, he took his frustrations out on his sister, hitting her frequently. The parents blamed Grace, saying she teased him. "As a child, I hated him," Grace said. "The first thing I remember about my brother is his gripping me from behind and giving me these painful bear hugs. 'Just stay out of his way,' my mother would say. 'Don't provoke him.' " The Gluecks insisted that Charles go to the public school, where he was cruelly treated by the other children. "He would come home in these towering rages and strike out," Grace recalled. "Somehow, he managed to learn to read and write, clumsily, and make it through eighth grade."

The parents did not face up to reality until Mignon Glueck had a stroke; Charles was then twenty-seven years old. Grace told her father: "You have *got* to put him somewhere or his problems are going to kill Mother." Remembering the scene, Grace said: "Father still thought Charles was going to become a neurosurgeon or a Harvard professor, when all he could work at was a simple job in the supermarket. He should have been sent away when he was five." Ernest and Grace finally found a special school in New Jersey. Charles is still institutionalized. His sister visits him regularly. "I didn't realize for years how angry I was at my parents," Grace told me, "and it doesn't get any better."

In junior high school, Grace compensated for her shyness and her inability to express her feelings to her mother and father by becoming the class clown. She would do anything, say anything, to get attention. The teachers thought her loud and vulgar. Her classmates thought she was terrific. "I was doing what they all wanted to do," she said. When Mignon, who was so genteel that she would say to her daughter, "Do you have to attend to your wants?" instead of "Do you want to go to the bathroom?" visited school, the teachers could hardly believe that this was the mother of outrageous little Grace. Outrageous Grace she is to this day.

She entered New York University, and for the first time in her life she came up against real intellectual competition. "It scared the bejesus out of me," she said. She had not gone out with boys in high school—they frightened her, as her brother frightened her. College liberated Grace. She dated, her grades improved dramatically, she majored in English literature and became editor of *The Apprentice,* the literary magazine. She got her degree in 1948.

Grace came to *The New York Times* in 1951, when she was twenty-five years old. Her previous jobs had included a stint at the Metro-Goldwyn-Mayer studios in Hollywood as a star-struck gofer, and several years of writing promotional copy for a fashion magazine publisher in Manhattan. Unlike Betsy Wade and Eileen Shanahan, she did not make her mark on the paper right away; hers was a long and winding path to prominence. "I clawed my way to the bottom" is the way she puts it.

She first landed on the men's fashion section of the *Times* magazine, booking models and logging in clothes. Then she became a floater, serving as typist and receptionist in women's news, working in the letters-to-the-editor department—she wrote some of the letters and signed her mother's maiden name—and "just drifting around being useful." Her first great mentor was Seymour Peck, a soft-spoken, sensitive, scholarly man who was then editing the Sunday drama section. Sy was much beloved, a gentleman in the profoundest sense of the word.

After two years, Grace got a job as a picture researcher for the Sunday book review. She stayed there for ten years. "It was a nest, a refuge," she said. "It was routine. It was closed. It was a family—better than the one I had." Sometimes, however, she dreamed of breaking out, of becoming a full-fledged writer for the *Times.* She was not given much encouragement along the way. When she told Daniel Schwarz, the assistant Sunday editor, that she wanted a writer's job, he replied, "Why don't you go home and get married?" Grace did not go home and she did not get married. She spoke of her writing aspirations to Theodore Bernstein, the assistant managing editor, then the most important hands-on editor. Ted was the house grammarian and enforcer of rules of style; he wrote

Winners & Sinners, a little bulletin that pointed out the good and the bad in recent issues of the paper. When Grace approached him about becoming a reporter, he replied, "Do you think you can write *really well*? Because a woman needs something *special* to make it on *The New York Times.*"

Grace's quiet decade as a picture researcher for the Sunday book review came to an end in the early 1960s. In 1962 and 1963 the pop art world exploded. Lester Markel, the Sunday editor, noted, "We have all these critics, but no news coverage of the art world." A column called "News of the Rialto" had covered the Broadway scene for some time. Seymour Peck suggested that Grace Glueck write a new weekly art column, to be called "Art People." On November 22, 1963, the day John Fitzgerald Kennedy was assassinated, Grace got the job.

Soon she found herself also going out on art assignments for the daily paper. It threw her into a panic—she had never worked on a daily deadline before. And then she found another mentor, a Vassar graduate who was covering society as nobody else had ever covered it for *The New York Times*. She was supportive and helpful. She would look over Grace's pieces and she would say briskly, "Now look—this is the way your lead should go." Her name was Charlotte Curtis.

••••••••••••

Fast forward, as Grace would say, fast forward to a day in January 1972. After Punch Sulzberger's brief reply to her 1969 memo about management's failure to give women some power around the *Times,* there had been no further communication between them on the subject. And then, that January day, Grace Lichtenstein, a young and fiery reporter in the city room, was talking with Glueck about the *Times* management's incredibly old-fashioned ways.

Lichtenstein was already gaining a reputation as a bit of a bomb-thrower, always begging her editors for assignments to what they called women's libber stories and bristling when she thought she was being patronized. She was practically sizzling with pique that the *Times* editors refused to use "Ms." as an honorific, although most publications of note had agreed that it was unfair to specify the marital status of every woman whose name appeared in print. Glueck's response was "Oh, come on—that's the least of it. What are they doing to us in terms of jobs and money?" She pointed out that newswomen elsewhere were organizing for more equitable treatment. "At the *Times,*" Glueck said scornfully, "we're all hiding behind the door."

"You're absolutely right," said Lichtenstein. "Let's get some other people interested. Let's sit down and talk about it."

One obvious possible recruit was Betsy Wade. More than almost anyone else the two Graces could think of, she would lend heft to such a meeting. She was solid, respected, liberal, a union activist. She held the highest position ever achieved by a woman in the city room, having just been named head of the foreign copy desk, yet she was not part of management. She had been the first woman copyreader hired by the *Times,* in 1956. By 1972, Wade was ready to organize.

"Even when I was first hired, you could see there was something wrong," she said. "There were no women ahead of me. There were no women doing what I was doing. There were no women alongside me. There were no women, except for [the women of the Sulzberger family, who were on the *Times*'s board] in any position of authority at the paper."

At Christmastime in 1971, Betsy's husband, Jim Boylan, had jotted down a revealing entry in his diary. It was right after a holiday party given at the home of James Greenfield, the foreign editor and Betsy's boss. "It was a pleasant enough party," Jim wrote, "almost 100 percent *Times* men and their wives, showing again how isolated B. is in her department even after all these years."

Still, in 1972, Betsy Wade was not a disaffected person. She loved her job, and the *Times*. But she was also an idealist, convinced that there are moments when a person must stand up and speak her mind. This was one of them.

Betsy was among the small group of women present at the founding luncheon of the Women's Caucus of *The New York Times* on February 1, 1972. "It was just us chicks from the newsroom," said Glueck. They were joined by Judy Klemesrud, an Iowan with a mass of creative insecurities, the brightest and most prolific writer on the family/style page. The setting was Act I, a neglected restaurant of dubious cuisine high up in what had been the Times Tower, the famous wedge-shaped skyscraper at the southern end of Times Square, which had been sold to Allied Chemical.

"We wanted to meet in a place where nobody would see us," Lichtenstein recalled. "So we picked a restaurant none of our group would normally choose, like Sardi's [out the *Times*'s back door], or Gough's [a seedy, smelly, but, to some, beloved bar across Forty-third Street] or the Greek's [the Pantheon, on Eighth Avenue]. We were nervous."

Out of the luncheon came the idea of a letter to Punch Sulzberger and his family of women. Punch's mother, Iphigene, and his three older sisters were all directors of the *Times*. The letter would set forth the unenviable status of women employed by the paper in 1972. Women were second-class citizens at the *Times*, the most respected newspaper in the nation, the paper its readers looked to for moral leadership. It was like Israel—somehow, you expected more of the *Times*, something finer, nobler.

But before accusing this esteemed institution, the group had to do their homework, to back the complaints with statistics. Then as many women as possible had to be convinced that they should sign the letter. There were between five hundred and six hundred female employees at the *Times*—of a total work force of six thousand—including cleaning women, secretaries, classified-ad takers, reporters. In this initial stage, almost all the activists were writers, researchers, or editors.

In the meantime, some of them were beginning to hear distant thunder from the office of the managing editor, Abe Rosenthal. Like Punch Sulzberger, Abe was the only male, and the youngest child, in a family made up of doting sisters—five, in Rosenthal's family. Again like Punch, he believed that he understood women, that he was at home in a woman's world. But Abe did not have a sunny disposition, and he almost welcomed confrontation. The first to feel his wrath was Grace Lichtenstein.

One day in the winter of 1972, a crew from Channel 13, New York's public television station, was shooting a documentary in the city room of *The New York Times*. They put the thirty-year-old Lichtenstein, who assumed she had been singled out as the "token young woman on general assignment," on camera. They asked, "How would you make this place better?" As usual, she spoke her mind. It was a great paper, she said, but it was entirely run by white middle-aged, middle-class men. It would be even greater if there were more women. "There aren't enough women, there aren't enough blacks, there aren't enough Chicanos," she said. "There aren't enough American Indians," she added for good measure. The program was broadcast several weeks after the luncheon at Act I. The next morning she was told the minute she entered the newsroom, "Abe wants to see you."

The managing editor was "beside himself," according to Lichtenstein. He had seen the telecast. She was disloyal and traitorous. He raged on for what seemed an endless time. Lichtenstein was stunned into silence. "It was the worst chewing-out of my life," she said later. "I walked out of there in shock." It was a foretaste of worse scenes to come.

From the very beginning, Betsy Wade and Joan Cook, the two Earth Mothers, and Grace Glueck, in the wisecracking Myrna Loy role, were the troika that pulled the Women's Caucus. They learned that the Newspaper Guild, like all unions, was compelled by law to give payroll data to any employees banding together to improve their lot, provided individual names were erased. It was then that they discovered that the average salary of male *Times* reporters was $59 a week higher than the average salary of the women reporters. They also found that 23 percent of the women were working at the minimum union salary for reporters' jobs, while only 6.8 percent of the men reporters were working for the minimum salary. Right there were two patterns of discrimination.

Nineteen male reporters were earning more than the most senior woman reporter, who had been at the *Times* more years than half of those men. She was no drone—her stories repeatedly hit page one.

The Caucus leaders turned to the pension plan to get a buildingwide picture of the salaries of men and women. The information thus uncovered sobered and angered the members. Since no two salaries were exactly alike, each could find her own ranking on the Newspaper Guild lists. "When we saw the inequities in pay, that's when we really hit the ceiling," Lichtenstein said. Betsy's reaction to the revelations went deeper.

"It required us to look at what it was that we had hoped for and what it was that we had wanted when we went to work there," she said. "It required us to look at what we wanted for the paper. I think this was finally what had the greatest impact on us—we all wanted the paper to be better than it was." The problem was much more than the inequalities in salary, the fact that women came cheaper and were kept more cheaply; the problem was a newspaper, she said, that spoke with a "white male voice," seldom reflecting America's diversity or the emerging voices of women—except on the women's page.

There were meetings in Caucus members' apartments, draft after draft of the letter to the publisher, and finally the important grievances were documented. The letter was headed "From: Women on the News Staff of The New York Times." The final draft began:

The voices of women are being heard in greater number in this country. As a result of this pressure, some improvement has taken place in the status of women in the professions. In other cases, as in the academic world, women are being compelled to take remedial action to assert their rights.

At The Times, we note little change in the basic situation of women. While we acknowledge improvement in the hiring of women reporters and critics, we feel that The Times is and always has been remiss in seeing that women employees reach positions in the vital decision-making areas of the paper.

Then the letter got down to specifics:

We call your attention to the 21 names on the masthead—both editorial and business executives. Not one is a woman. Of the 10 vice-presidents of The Times, one comes from the Industrial Relations department, two from the business area, two from the Legal department, two from the News department, one from the Production department, one from the Promotion department, and one from a subsidiary corporation. In all those Times departments named, there is not one woman even in a position to aspire to a vice-presidency.

The letter went inexorably on, citing numbers and gaping omissions throughout the building. Near the end, it said:

A . . . breakdown of women's and men's salaries in the Guild-covered areas of The Times shows compellingly that women are paid less than men at all ages.* The primary cause of this inequity is the lower-paying jobs to which women are confined. Even when men and women have jobs in the same classification, and their education, ability and length of service are comparable, the latter are generally paid less.

Of even greater concern is the fact that in the area of job expectations, men are encouraged to think in terms of larger goals by virtue

*The Newspaper Guild, a vertical union representing employees from cafeteria busboys to reporters, is unlike the newspaper craft unions, which represent members in a single specialty, such as stereotypers, pressmen, typographers, or deliverers.

of the better assignments and promises of promotion given to many. We feel that few executives seriously entertain the idea that women should have access to the varied experiences that would equip them for executive responsibilities.

The letter closed with the reminder that *The New York Times,* like other businesses subject to the Civil Rights Act of 1964, should adopt an affirmative action plan for women: "We look forward to receiving from you a timetable for the achievement of such an affirmative action program, to be discussed at a general meeting."

The letter ran almost five double-spaced typewritten pages. It was to go to the publisher, his three sisters, and his mother, as directors of the New York Times Company. Copies were to be sent to Abe Rosenthal as managing editor, Daniel Schwarz as Sunday editor, and John Oakes, the editorial page editor and a first cousin of Iphigene Sulzberger.

Damning as the statistics were, the tone of the letter was dignified, even stuffy. It was a truly *Times*ian epistle. Nonetheless, the task of getting signatures on the letter took weeks. Some signed eagerly. Many did not. "There was fear—and there was almost an inbred, white-gloved reluctance," Joan Cook remembers. "Ladies didn't do that sort of thing." There were also quite a few loners, those focused on their own careers.

Betsy had long admired the reporting and writing of Gloria Emerson, a coltish and dazzlingly original eccentric who, through sheer talent and dogged perseverance, had at last been assigned to cover Vietnam during the late 1960s. And so, as her copy chief on the foreign desk, knowing how hard it had been for Gloria to get out of the women's news ghetto and overseas, Betsy Wade approached her to sign. "Oh, dear," said Emerson, "they've let me ride my water buffalo, why should I get involved in this?" Betsy told her why. Emerson signed.

One of Grace Glueck's primary targets in the culture department was Ada Louise Huxtable. Huxtable had already told Edith Evans Asbury, the most venerable of the newsroom stars, that she did not want to sign. The architecture critic was very visible on the paper and she was feared and courted by those in the field. With the exception of Charlotte Curtis, the family/style editor, she was the most successful woman at the *Times.* She had won the Pulitzer Prize two years before. It was important to have her name on the letter to the publisher.

So Glueck got to work on her. As Grace recalls it, "Ada Louise was disdainful about the whole idea of women getting together to seek a fair deal. She said to me, 'You know very well, Grace, that you and I can go in to Abe [Rosenthal] anytime to negotiate and get anything we want.' " Glueck also quotes her as saying that if the women made a fuss in a group, the management would "just hire a lot of younger women at a higher salary than we're getting, and then they'll promote Charlotte Curtis," whose path in 1972 seemed to point only onward and upward in management.

According to Grace, Huxtable appeared to waver. Let me take the letter home and study it, she said. "I'm not letting this letter out of the office," Grace said sternly. "It's not going to the publisher until the end of May." And then, against her better instincts, she gave a copy to Ada Louise. (Years later, Huxtable remembered none of this. "If I had ever seen that letter I would have signed," she told me. "If anyone says I did see it, I cannot recollect seeing it. I feel very strongly about these things but I wouldn't be the leader. I would have been part of it if anybody had shown me that material.")

The day following Glueck's exchange with Huxtable, on Thursday, May 18, 1972, eleven women, all gifted members of the news staff, received a curious and urgent invitation from Abe Rosenthal. The memo was odd because there seemed to be no reason for a hastily called meeting with the managing editor and because vagueness, rambling, even unease, rose off the page—most uncharacteristic of Rosenthal's swift, punchy communiqués.

"I know there has been discussion about the whole question of women and the newspaper business in general and women and The New York Times in particular," he began.

I think it would be worthwhile if we met to see what ideas and suggestions were in people's minds.

I would appreciate it if you would meet with me tomorrow in my office at 11:00 a.m. Please forgive the short notice but I will be away after tomorrow through Memorial Day at a Times management meeting and I do think a discussion has been overdue. Tomorrow's meeting will give me some thoughts to turn over in my own mind during the next week and also perhaps to discuss with other Times editors and executives during the week.

To answer an obvious question that might be in your mind, this list [of eleven women] is not meant to be all-inclusive or representative or selective or anything of the sort. It is simply that a meeting large enough to include all of the women in the news department would be too large for any real discussion so I have simply picked some reporters and editors more or less at random. I hope we will have discussions later on that will include people not on this list. A.M.R.

The list at the top of his memo included Charlotte Curtis, Ada Louise Huxtable, the two Graces, Glueck and Lichtenstein, Betsy Wade, Judy Klemesrud, and Edith Asbury, among others. Joan Cook decided to invite herself along as a substitute for Wade, who was going out of town. Ruth Block, a picture editor and researcher and one of the Sunday department's most conscientious supporters of the Women's Caucus, also asked to come.

Paranoid, Wade and Glueck conferred. "Abe is trying to head us off at the pass," said Betsy, "trying to get to us before we send the letter to Punch."

Charlotte Curtis confided to Marylin Bender, a close friend and one of those invited, that Rosenthal had gotten wind of something brewing among the Times women. "He asked me and Ada Louise to get together a list of women to talk about

THE PIONEERS

In 1859, Maria (Midy) Morgan became the first woman reporter on *The New York Times*'s staff. She was six feet two inches tall and covered racing and livestock news. A king, a president, and millionaires sought her advice on horseflesh.

She had poetry in her, and the gift of prophecy. Anne O'Hare McCormick, the foreign affairs columnist and first woman on the editorial board, was the paper's first woman Pulitzer Prize winner. There would not be another for thirty-three years.

"A sea of men." The city room of the *Times* in 1948. The paper was called the last citadel of male reporters and editors in the country and had a long tradition of viewing women as interlopers.

THE LONE STARS

In the 1960s and 1970s, Charlotte Curtis wittily wrote about society as sociology and opened the door of the women's page to unheard-of subjects. The newspaper was her life, she was the "Bride of *The New York Times*," but she would not join or support its Women's Caucus.

Ada Louise Huxtable was the first full-time architecture critic on an American newspaper. Her copy packed a tremendous wallop, she was the second *Times* woman to win a Pulitzer, but, like Curtis, she did not lend her clout to the women's struggle.

THE MEN

© *The New York Times*

Arthur Ochs (Punch) Sulzberger, publisher of the *Times* from 1963 to the present, affable, friendly, with three sisters and a strong-willed mother. When his women employees complained, he said, "Holy crow! I thought this was a good place to work!"

© *The New York Times*

"You're suing *me*? Me, Abe Rosenthal, who likes women?" He was the all-powerful editor whose meteoric rise and rule during two decades dazzled and burned those in his way.

© *The New York Times*

The heroines in Scotty Reston's world, Gay Talese wrote, "did not work in offices—they were mothers and wives who inspired their husbands as his wife had always inspired him." Reston, an idolized Washington reporter and bureau chief, never fully understood the aspirations of career women.

© *The New York Times*

Clifton Daniel, who gave a new depth of meaning to the word "suave," was a mentor of talented women, among them Curtis and Huxtable. Curtis often said that Daniel had invented her.

THE WOMEN

© *The New York Times*

© Photo by Sara Krulwich

Her first week in the city room, they banished spittoons and put a petticoat around her paste pot. Called "one of the glories of the newsroom," Betsy Wade was head copy editor of the foreign news desk. She became the chief named plaintiff of the sex-discrimination suit against the *Times*.

Joan Cook, a reporter and activist, was Wade's alter ego and close friend. Her steadiness was a safety net under Wade, an emotional highflier.

© *The New York Times*

© *The New York Times*

A friend pictured Grace Glueck, an art news reporter, as the sophisticated, wisecracking Myrna Loy character in the "Thin Man" movies. Her humor masked a more serious intent: She was the first to tax the publisher with the lack of women in high places.

Washington correspondents with steel egos quailed when Eileen Shanahan was on a story in a field monopolized by men—economics, big money, taxes. Her public criticisms of the *Times* as a sexist institution drove Abe Rosenthal up the wall.

THE WOMEN

"I was the black face in there, but I didn't think of it that way. Not only have I been discriminated against, but all of us women have been discriminated against." Andrea Skinner, a *Times* Sunday magazine news clerk and children's fashion editor, represented women of color at the paper.

She trained at least six men to become her boss. Louise Carini, an accountant, was the most surprising of the plaintiffs. She had been taught to respect God and authority, but her profound sense of right and wrong—and her prayers—strengthened her in the crisis.

Nancy Davis was a telephone advertising solicitor in a department that was virtually all female. When she came to the paper, she had it on a pedestal. She said of her decision to take a public stand that it would be her only chance to participate in history.

THE REUNION

© Photo by Sara Krulwich

Harriet Rabb, the attorney representing the women of *The New York Times*, said of them: "It takes enormous courage to sue a large employer. I really admire the women who do it. In large part, they are not doing it for themselves. They do it for the women who come after them."

It was no accident that the chief named plaintiff in the minorities' suit against the *Times* was also a woman. Benilda Rosario, a black Puerto Rican whose first job at the paper was as a telephone ad taker, told a 1988 reunion about progress and change.

© Photo by Sara Krulwich

When Leslie Bennetts, a gifted, prolific culture news reporter, discovered that her less-experienced fiancé was making $11,000 more a year than she was, she demanded a raise. The *Times* granted a small one but refused to close the gap; the incident led to her resignation.

THE INHERITORS

Carolyn Lee, the *Times*'s first woman assistant managing editor, is uniquely positioned to shape the newspaper's future and is using her power to recruit more women and move them into important jobs. The highest-ranking woman on the paper, she oversees a thousand employees and a hundred-million-dollar budget. She always speaks her mind.

Anna Quindlen, one of only three women ever to be an Op-Ed columnist on the *Times*, makes it clear that had it not been for the women before her who put their careers on the line, she could never have gone as far as she has. Her life has fueled a growing feminism.

THE INHERITORS

Successor to Abe Rosenthal as executive editor, Max Frankel has been quietly putting more women into better jobs, while occasionally inserting his foot into his mouth in public. The unprecedented mutiny at the paper in 1991 over the coverage of the woman who accused William Kennedy Smith of rape showed how dramatically the perceptions about women had changed on the staff—and how much Frankel and some of his top men needed to learn.

The heir apparent: Arthur Ochs Sulzberger Jr., Punch Sulzberger's only son and the *Times*'s deputy publisher, has pushed to close the wide differences between men's and women's salaries and put his managers on notice that they must reject the "comfort factor" of promoting only white men.

it," she said. Curtis told Lesley Oelsner, another reporter in the invited group, that organizing to confront management was the wrong way to proceed.

Those who came into the managing editor's office from the city room on that Friday in May 1972 remember the tableau that greeted them—Rosenthal was already seated at his big conference table, as were Curtis and Huxtable.

Edith Asbury was disgusted. She had tried in vain to persuade Charlotte to sign the letter and had also approached Ada Louise. She had hoped at least that the two most influential women on the *Times* staff would stay neutral. Curtis, in particular, had promoted herself as a liberal and a feminist. Now look at her, aligned with Abe. Oelsner and others were thinking similar thoughts.

Glueck and Block had brought along tape recorders. Rosenthal told the two to turn them off. "His attitude was a wounded 'How could you do this to me?' " Joan Cook remembers. "He said, 'Why didn't you tell me you felt this way? The men come to me and tell me everything.' It was classic Abe—sort of a cross between Caligula and a Jewish mother."

Marylin Bender recalls that the meeting was tense but not acrimonious. "We were there to raise Abe's consciousness, which he didn't want raised," she says. "He did not like surprises. He did not like the idea of our end run around him to the publisher with our letter. He did *not* like not being in command of the situation. I don't remember him chewing the carpet, but he didn't understand what it was all about."

Toward the end, Grace Glueck told Rosenthal: This is not just a newsroom cabal. The dissatisfaction is companywide, and it touches every woman in Newspaper Guild jurisdiction, which means just about all of us. That's why we're sending a letter to the publisher. We don't need your permission to do so.

The meeting with Rosenthal was a standoff. The letter to the publisher and his family was to be delivered at the end of the Memorial Day weekend, only ten days away. By now, fifty-two women had signed it, or almost one out of every ten women working for *The New York Times*. Despite Glueck's comment to Abe, however, it was still a tight little band. The signers were reporters, editors, critics, researchers in New York and Washington, all from the "glamour jobs" in the paper's news and Sunday departments. The secretaries, cashiers, clerks, cleaning women, food handlers, classified-ad takers, accountants had not been included at the start. It began as a revolution of the elite.

Grace Glueck rose early in her tiny East Side apartment on Tuesday, May 30, and hurried down to the *Times*. She went on purpose before office hours, so she would not run into Punch Sulzberger. She took the elevator to the fourteenth floor and left a copy of the letter with a sleepy clerk sitting at the reception desk outside Punch's office. The publisher, to Grace's relief, had not yet arrived. She dispatched a messenger with copies of the letter to each of the Sulzberger family members in New York.

Punch read the letter shortly after settling down at his desk that morning. He was flabbergasted. "Holy crow!" he said to himself. "I thought this was a good place to work!"

Discussions within the family followed. Iphigene, almost eighty, who had fought her own father's opposition to the vote for women before World War I, thought it disgraceful that in the 1970s women were being paid less than men for doing the same work. More was heard from Ruth Sulzberger Holmberg, Punch's sister and the publisher since 1964 of the family-owned Chattanooga *Times*. Ruth believed that she had more experience of the difficulties of a woman trying to get ahead than did her two sisters, Marian and Judy. She had been a cub reporter years earlier, when the *Times* and the newspaper profession in general were virtually all-male; she had been a Red Cross director in combat areas in France following the D-day invasion; in recent years, she had at first been barely tolerated by the conservative Southern business establishment in Chattanooga. In meeting after meeting of the power structure there in southeastern Tennessee, she had been the only woman—as well as the only Democrat and the only Jew. She respected the women who were bringing inequities to the attention of the Times Company. "I don't know of any other way to do it," she told her brother. "I think it had to be confrontational. Suddenly you wake up and you say to yourself—'My God! That's right!' "

Soon after the women's letter had been delivered, Grace Glueck was stopped in a corridor by Sydney Gruson, Punch's best buddy on the paper. "Well, Grace, you finally dropped the other shoe," drawled Gruson, who always tries his best to act as if nothing on earth is important. Grace was momentarily baffled, then remembered the memo about the all-male promotions she had sent to the publisher two and a half years before. "When you sent that note to Punch," Gruson went on, "we were concerned. We were worried because we thought you might be bringing up troops." He sauntered away. You bet we have, thought Grace. In a sense, it was a relief.

The women had finally brought their concerns out into the open. After a month of deliberation—almost nothing happens fast in the upper reaches of the *Times*—the publisher sent an answering memo back to the women signatories, calling a meeting for July 19.

···········

At that very moment, a felicitous conjunction of circumstances was bringing a formidable woman to a high place on the paper—Flora Lewis, Sydney Gruson's former wife. On June 15, 1972, Lewis, recently divorced from Gruson, was put on the payroll and named chief of the *Times*'s Paris bureau. No *Times* woman except Anne O'Hare McCormick a generation earlier had received such a plum assignment. Like Mrs. McCormick, Flora Lewis came late to the paper and had waited long at the door. She was also awesomely intelligent, almost clairvoyant, with a sense of history and a knowledge of the world.

Flora, then fifty years old, had wanted to be on the *Times* since she first saw the newspaper, had been literally close to it since her marriage to Gruson twenty-seven years before. She had followed him as they moved from London to Jerusalem to Prague to Warsaw to Geneva to Bonn to Paris to Mexico; she had borne three children and had worked for the Associated Press, *The Economist,* the *Financial Times, The* (London) *Observer,* the London *Daily Express,* the *Chicago Tribune, Time* magazine, *Newsday, France-Soir* and the Los Angeles Times syndicate, and had done free-lance Sunday pieces for *The New York Times Magazine.* The Grusons had moved seventeen times in twenty years and each time, as was normal for that generation of women, Flora had been forced to seek a new job all over again in a foreign capital. "I've worked for every paper in the world," she used to say ruefully, "except *Ren Min Jih Bao* [the *People's Daily* in Beijing] and *Rude Pravo* [the *Pravda* of Prague]." She often pinch-hit for Sydney, filing stories to the *Times* when he was out of town on assignment. Abe Rosenthal, who had met her years before at the United Nations and thought she was the best damned diplomatic reporter on earth, was scared to death when he was sent to Poland in the late 1950s to succeed Gruson as the *Times* correspondent there. "It wasn't Sydney's act I was afraid to follow; it was Flora's," he once confessed to me.

But Flora would never be hired as long as "Catledge's Rule" prevailed. Turner Catledge had been the top editor all through the 1950s and 1960s. He had retired in 1970. Catledge's Rule was that no *Times* man's wife would ever get on the staff. If a man and a woman married while both were already employees, however—as did Stan Levey and I and many another couple who met at *The New York Times*—there was nothing Catledge could do about it.

Whenever Flora brought up the topic of working at the *Times,* "Turner made his policy plain in a firm and unpleasant way," she recalls. "He told me I had married the wrong man and over his dead body would I be hired. When our marriage broke up, it occurred to the people at the *Times* that perhaps Catledge's Rule no longer applied." Besides, Catledge was no longer there, and Rosenthal was in the saddle, and the women around the office were making a terrific fuss.

Lewis is certain that the surfacing of the Women's Caucus was the final kick in the pants that led to her hiring. "The timing was perfect," she says. "The women had come out in the open, the management was about to meet with them, and now the *Times* could say with great glee, 'Ha, ha—we have a woman bureau chief!' "

Within six months, Rosenthal would send me to Paris as the bureau's second correspondent on the most challenging assignment of my career. I remained for three years, returning to New York toward the end of 1975. I am also persuaded that my Paris assignment was as much the Caucus's doing as Abe Rosenthal's.

⋯⋯⋯⋯

The Women's Caucus prepared itself for the meeting with Punch Sulzberger on July 19. Nothing quite like it had ever occurred at the *Times*. For decades, of course, there had been periodic meetings between the paper's labor relations department and the ten unions in the industry as contracts came up for renewal. The publisher never met directly with the unions, only with his own negotiators. Individuals who were impatient to advance their own careers pleaded their cases in private with their mentors, almost always their superiors within a department. On occasion, small groups had gone to a department head to protest grievances, or a union had argued a grievance case for an individual. This was different.

This time, a group of employees with statistical evidence of discrimination had all put their careers on the line by going over everyone's head straight to the top—to the man whose family had owned *The New York Times* for three generations.

They were going to meet him, and the other men who ran the newspaper, in the sanctum sanctorum, the Board Room on the newspaper's highest floor.

On the eve of the meeting with Punch, Caucus members held an emotional, noisy, crowded gathering in Grace Glueck's apartment on East Sixty-third Street. It was decided that the next morning, they would speak with one voice, the voice of Betsy Wade.

And so it was Betsy who presented the women's case. She was seated to the left of the publisher, who presided at the head of a polished mahogany table so long and broad that it seemed to swallow up all the empty space in a room of majestic proportions.

On one side sat the women. Across from them sat five powerful male executives, among them John Mortimer, the vice president for industrial relations. Mortimer would get to know the Women's Caucus better than any other man there that day, better, in fact, than anyone else in management. It was his forty-ninth birthday. He had been handling labor relations for the *Times* for a decade. Tall and rangy, with a melancholy hound-dog expression until he smiled, he was popular and respected. He believed that getting into combat didn't improve matters "one damn bit." He had seen enough combat to last him a lifetime as an Army sergeant in the South Pacific during World War II. His nonconfrontational manner appealed to Punch, the amiable former Marine.

Like Betsy Wade, Mortimer had grown up in the New York suburb of Bronxville, and like her, he had despised it. It was a white-shoe way of life, he thought, led by people who were born to comfort and who were convinced that the world owed them something. There was a lack of commitment to anything but pleasure. The women he knew in Bronxville had their children and then spent their time playing bridge. John Mortimer sought his childhood pals on the other side of the railroad tracks—they were the sons of the town gravedigger, the town cop, and the salesman in the local haberdashery. And then he went away to boarding school, to Williams College, to the war, and to college again. When Mortimer was graduated, the Taft-Hartley Act had just been passed. "It declared a lot of things to be unfair labor practices, and it was mainly anti-union," he told me. "Liberal people were needed on the management side; somebody who would communicate rather than fight." In 1948 he went to work at the New York *Daily News,* where, he said, "you could have shot a cannonball through the city room without hitting a single woman." When he came to the *Times* in 1962, on the eve of the longest newspaper strike in the city's history, he instantly ran into what he called the "duchy problem"—the warring fiefdoms throughout the newspaper, a bureaucracy of many competing layers. *The New York Times* was a great newspaper with whose philosophy he was comfortable. But it was *complicated,* even Byzantine. It was not easy to change anything.

Mortimer loved the Board Room. There was something about it that reflected the *Times.* It was quietly dignified, not glitzy. There was a sense of history there, with all those photographs of world statesmen around the walls.

When the meeting with the Women's Caucus ended after two hours, Mortimer, who knew more about face-to-face adversarial negotiating than any other person present, felt it had gone very well. "We all agreed in our minds—there weren't any bad guys," he recalled. "Nobody slammed the table, there wasn't any finger-wagging, nobody asked, 'Now what the hell are we going to do about *this*?'"

The only sticky moment had come when Dan Schwarz had insisted that he had promoted lots of women to top jobs, and then the woman across the table had said *she* had been the last woman editor he had hired in the Sunday department, ten years earlier, and Dan got red in the face and kept on arguing. Everybody had laughed, which broke the tension. All had seemed to feel that women and men alike had to reeducate themselves.

But the charges were serious. The women were serious, and

they were well prepared. Mortimer thought, "If we don't solve this problem, we are going to go to a lawsuit. We have got to avert it." He may have been the only person in the room to think that. Both sides, in fact, were congratulating themselves. The road to reason and accommodation seemed clear.

Betsy Wade had appeared unshakable, but she had felt toward the end as if she were going to pieces below the neck. It was a terrific strain doing all the talking. She was clinging to the numbers, the statistics of discrimination the Caucus had laboriously pried from payroll and pension records. "I have the numbers," she told herself, over and over. "I know they are discriminatory. I know it is no accident."

Eileen Shanahan came out of the meeting bubbling with optimism. "They're going to settle this," she thought. "They should have known but they didn't. They took it seriously. They're going to fix it."

As the participants drifted away, there was some joshing among the men. Punch clapped Schwarz on the shoulder and said, smiling, "Dan, Confucius say, 'When they've got you by the balls, don't struggle.' " Schwarz emitted a feeble laugh.

....

The months rolled on. The executives to whom Punch had delegated the job met again and again with negotiators from the Women's Caucus. Fourteen women reporters got "equalization raises," which hardly made a dent in the buildingwide salary gap. A Caucus newsletter was started. Were there patterns of discrimination? "All patterns can be broken," the publisher announced grandly. "That is our wish."

Six months after the meeting in the Board Room, Sulzberger sent a memo throughout the *Times:*

In 1969 I wrote all employees stating our belief in and goals for equal opportunity employment because it was morally, economically and socially right. I wish now to state our equally strong conviction to make sure that women are treated equally well with men at every level of The Times.

We must have equal pay for equal work, full use of the talents and training of women employed at The Times, initiatives in hiring greater proportions of women, especially in positions where women are now excluded, and training opportunities that will allow women to attain jobs of greater responsibility, including the most responsible.

As you know, the intense economic problems of The Times have severely limited hiring and promotional opportunities. This makes it even more important that we consciously act on our goals for women and minorities when these opportunities do occur. I am asking all department heads to share in meeting this responsibility.

And then . . . nothing happened. Department after department was analyzed, but management was coming up with no concrete proposals. "There was a lot of noise at this stage," John Mortimer recalled. "And very little action. I had to make it clear to the decision makers that Punch and I wanted to see results and that they would be evaluated. But when you come down to the old cruncherooni and you tell a manager that you're going to judge him on something like unfairness, when all through his career he's been judged on something else— holding down costs, putting out a first-class product—it's hard to reach him. There was that eternal tendency to push the minority and woman issues way behind them and get tomorrow's paper out. I'd go around every month with a little list and say 'How're you doing?' and they'd say 'Fine, fine, yes, yes, we're going ahead on the women and the minorities.' I couldn't break into the inner depths of these guys. The progress was so glacial we'd all have been ninety-nine years old before we got there."

Mortimer's frustrations were nothing compared with those within the Women's Caucus. The leaders felt they were beating against a velvet curtain. "Plenty of sweet talk to our faces and carrying on just the same behind our backs," said Betsy.

For example, the management promised the Caucus that women who had applied for promotion in the classified-ad department—which was composed almost entirely of women—would be given equal consideration with men. The same week a man was once again, as always, promoted to the supervisor's job over several women with much more seniority. Betsy spilled out her anger and bitterness all the way from New York to Stonington, Connecticut, as she and her husband drove up to their weekend house. It was a pattern throughout the newspaper, it was what the *Times* had done to her own career, she told Jim, promoting men less talented and experienced than she right past her.

She had been with the *Times* sixteen years and had received kudos time after time; only the year before, in 1971, she had been on the elite team that had edited the Pentagon Papers and helped the *Times* win a Pulitzer Prize. What good had it done her? She kept banging her head against a glass ceiling.

By the spring of 1973, the leaders of the caucus knew it was time to get a lawyer. They chose Harriet Schaffer Rabb of the Columbia Law School's Employment Rights Project. She was already building a formidable reputation in the sex-discrimination field as the attorney for the women at *Newsweek,* the *Reader's Digest,* and several prestigious Wall Street law firms.

The Caucus's attitudes about the *Times* bemused her. She described their initial approach as "Please, sir, I have this problem. Can I talk to you about it?"

"They were so womanly, so accommodating," Harriet recalled. "They believed that if you just sat down and talked with management, everything would be okay. You don't do that if you're beyond hope." She perused the Memorial Day letter to Punch and his family, and the minutes of months of meetings. "The Caucus had already so beautifully, strongly presented its position—and it hadn't made any difference at all with the middle-management types who were supposed to carry out the orders from on high," she said. She had come to think that *all* managements, including the *Times*'s, were the same. Their stance was "I certainly am not going to change in any respect because you tell me to."

With the government looking over the *Times*'s shoulder, it might be a different matter.

THE SUIT

When Harriet Rabb decided to take on the *New York Times* Women's Caucus as a client of the Columbia Employment Rights Project in 1973, she was only thirty-one years old, but she was a veteran in equal rights and civil rights law. A small, pretty, delicate-boned woman with a high, thin, almost babyish voice and the palest varnish of a Southern accent, she never, ever, swore in front of a man or an adversary of either sex and looked the essence of a neatly turned-out lady. She was married to Bruce Rabb, a classmate of hers at Columbia University Law School, who had worked in Richard Nixon's White House and came from a wealthy, unshakeably Republican family. Bruce's father, Maxwell Rabb, had been secretary to the Eisenhower Cabinet and would become Ronald Reagan's ambassador to Italy. The FBI considered Maxwell Rabb's daughter-in-law a security risk.

She was born and raised in Houston, in a comfortable Jewish family in a Jewish neighborhood of big old houses and streets with Scottish-sounding names such as Braesheather and MacGregor and Glenhaven. Both her mother and her father were physicians. In their shared offices there was one waiting room for blacks and another for whites—this being segregated Texas in the 1940s and 1950s—but patients of both colors went to the same examining rooms and nobody complained.

Her parents were movers and shakers in every Jewish organization in Houston, including Hadassah, B'nai Brith, and the Zionists of America. Each had been president of their synagogue. Harriet was the sweetheart of a Jewish high school fraternity and desperately wanted to be a cheerleader, but "the idea of having a Jewish cheerleader," she said, "wouldn't have passed the laugh test down there." She briefly dated a Gentile. It ended when she called the boy at home and the father answered. "Harry," he yelled, putting his hand lightly over the phone, "it's that nigger girl calling."

It was always assumed that Harriet would become a professional—if not a doctor, then something else. Looking for colleges where she could escape the role of Southern belle, she and her mother chose Barnard, the alma mater of Iphigene Sulzberger and Betsy Wade; there she majored in government. Harriet married a computer whiz in her senior year and went on to the Columbia Law School. The marriage foundered by the time she got her law degree.

"Not many women from my class at Barnard went into the professions," she said. Twenty years later, in 1983, she went to her class reunion and discovered that of the Barnard '63 women who had wanted to go into law, most had married lawyers—"They married men who did what they later wished to do."

The summer after Harriet's freshman year in law school, a friend at the Law Students Civil Rights Research Council dispatched her to a summer job at Kunstler, Kunstler and Kinoy. "There's some dreadful trouble down in Mississippi," the friend said. The firm represented the family of Michael (Mickey) Schwerner, who had disappeared in Mississippi with two other civil rights workers. They had been shot and killed by the Ku Klux Klan. There followed six years of summer and then full-time work at the law firm, with Arthur Kinoy, as her mentor, "saving the world from reactionaries," as she put it. She represented union members, political outcasts, poor people, Vietnam draft resisters, mothers for peace. She divorced her husband and began going out with Bruce Rabb, who was then occupied with civil rights at the Nixon White House. Harriet's clients included people Nixon was paranoid about: black militants such as Rap Brown, wild man Jerry Rubin, the increasingly far left Students for a Democratic Society, young civil rights firebrands in the Student Non-Violent Coordinating Committee. When the White House banned an SDS demonstration, Harriet would call Bruce, who would get the meeting unbanned. Finally, Kunstler and Kinoy told Harriet that her Republican romance was becoming a serious conflict of interest—either Nixon would fire Bruce or Harriet's clients would no longer trust her. She agreed, quit the law firm, and took a job with Bess Myerson, then New York's commissioner of consumer affairs. She married Rabb and moved to Washington.

"It was then," she said, "that I started paying the price." Bruce was a Republican in a Republican White House. She was a Democrat. No Democratic senator or House member would hire her, because of her husband's position. A public-interest lawyer was willing to take her on—without pay, because her husband had money. Finally, David Bazelon, a Rabb family friend and a distinguished judge on the Court of Appeals for the District of Columbia, offered her a job as a clerk of the court. She had argued some cases before his bench and Bazelon had been impressed. The next day, he summoned her. There were tears in his eyes. "My dear," he said, "I propose you withdraw your application for this job. You have been to some very strange meetings." Her bulging FBI file had been circulated among the judges, and two had violently objected, one saying he would lock the door of his chambers against such a subversive. Bazelon warned Harriet, "They will get you. They will get you and your husband and both of you will be out of work and then what will happen to you?" The FBI had gone to Bruce's file also, and had called the White House and asked his boss, "Do you know what kind of person Rabb is married to?" Bruce kept his White House post, and Bazelon helped Harriet get a job with a young public-interest law firm. But soon the Rabbs moved back to New York, Harriet started work with the Columbia Employment Rights Project, and Bruce was hired by a law firm specializing in corporate securities.

By the time Harriet's path crossed that of the *Times* Women's Caucus, she had been toughened by years of no-holds-barred legal and political roughhousing with Kunstler and Kinoy. She knew that just talking with management would not get the caucus very far. The first thing she wanted to do was to persuade as many women as possible to file discrimination charges against *The New York Times* with the city's Commission on Human Rights and the federal Equal Employment Opportunity Commission. Within six months, eighty-four women who would become active in the Caucus filed individual complaints against the newspaper. They represented almost one-sixth of all the women employed by the *Times;* among them were the fashion editor, the dance critic, the antiques columnist, and a group of secretaries—including the secretaries of the news editor, the editor of the Op-Ed page, Harrison Salisbury, and the managing editor, Abe Rosenthal.

The Women's Caucus was growing fast. Those who had been tepidly interested found themselves becoming militant, even furious, when the statistics the Caucus was uncovering exploded their fantasies and it became clear that they were being discriminated against. Those who would not speak out, however, remained far more numerous. Ursula Mahoney, a picture editor in the Sunday department, recalled with her wry smile, "It took a really hard sell, getting them to put their complaints on the record. A lot of people got timid. All of a sudden, a lot of people were satisfied with their jobs and had wonderful bosses."

But the eighty-four discrimination charges that *were* lodged with the human rights and equal employment opportunity agencies in 1973 forced an affrighted *Times* to move. The management felt it must improve its performance: the public, after all, viewed the newspaper as liberal and humane, and it did not want to be exposed as two-faced.

And so, despite resistance from many editors and supervisors, there was a flurry of hirings, encouraged by Sulzberger and John Mortimer. Most of the women hired were reporters, whose bylines would be visible to the readers. Harriet Rabb found in the *Times*'s own employee records that in 1970 and 1971 combined, only 7 percent, or two out of twenty-nine, of the reporters and editors hired by the paper were women. In 1973, the year following the Caucus's first confrontations with management, 47 percent, or nine out of nineteen, of the reporters and editors hired were women. However, none of the other major grievances, such as salary disparities between the sexes, was being addressed.

By the winter of 1974, Mortimer had forged a new affirmative action plan for the *Times*. The Caucus said the plan looked good on paper but could not be carried out and could not be monitored.

From that time on, the attitudes on both sides began to stiffen. Mortimer hired John Stanton, a labor lawyer whom he called "our tiger." Betsy Wade called him "a ball of pus." Harriet Rabb thought he was either profoundly dumb or a brilliant tactician: "Stanton either did not understand in the early months what the Caucus was protesting about, or he had no personal pride. He feigned ignorance. We would say, 'Don't you see the data?' and finally he'd say, 'Oh, do you think these men have been promoted faster than the women? Is that what you mean?' Is it possible that he didn't get it? A look of candor and wonder would come over his face. Howard Rubin [her associate from the Columbia Employment Rights Project on the *Times* case] and I would look at each other in disbelief."

On April 23, 1974, Betsy Wade went public with the dissatisfaction at her newspaper. It was hardly the statement of a mad radical. She marched up to a microphone at a New York Times stockholders' meeting and had this to say in a firm voice:

My name is Betsy Wade. I am an employee of *The New York Times* as well as a stockholder and I am thus doubly concerned that our board of directors reflect the realities of the 1970s. "Token nominations" to the board have been made. I believe that the time for tokenism is past and that the board must seek out a woman—beyond the members of the Sulzberger family—a woman of standing in the community or in business. Ideally, she should represent the hundreds of women who work for the *Times* and the thousands who own stock in it, as well as the still further hundreds of thousands who read the *Times* and sustain its advertisers. It is a matter of great concern to those of us on the *Times* that we cease presenting to the world the out-of-date image of a board of directors that is effectively all white male with the exception of the women in the controlling family. We need to speak with diverse voices and decide with diverse brains. I look forward in the coming year to the nomination of a woman to the post of director, as I have looked forward, and not in vain, to the promotion of women within the newspaper itself in the last year. Thank you.

To Betsy's surprise, the *Times,* always reluctant to air its own problems, reported her statement the next morning. The two women who had been most prominently promoted during the year past were Charlotte Curtis, the new editor of the Op-Ed page, and Ada Louise Huxtable, who was elevated to the editorial board. The irony that these two had been chosen was not lost on any member of the Women's Caucus.

By the summer of 1974, it was becoming clear that the *Times* was not engaging in any systematic or vigorous effort to give its women equal treatment. Privately, the three Caucus leaders, Betsy Wade, Joan Cook, and Grace Glueck, were already discussing the prospect of a lawsuit.

During the month of August, there was a significant exchange of letters between Betsy Wade, who was in New York City, and Grace Glueck, who was spending the month of August at the MacDowell Colony for writers, composers, and artists in New Hampshire (and organizing croquet games rather than working on a book). Betsy discussed the letters with Joan Cook, who contributed her views.

Wade and Glueck wrote often, discussing possible plaintiffs. Grace is her usual debonair, assertive self: "I'm very concerned about the suit—I mean, getting . . . people together who are willing to stick their necks out. If we can't do it, we'll go down in absolutely ignominious defeat—a great *scandale,* since all of the others who've tried it seem to have won without serious risk of job loss, etc. Can't we convince people of that? . . . I mean, push will probably never come to shove—we stand an excellent chance of settling on the courthouse steps, no?"

A strong feeling of strain, loneliness, and anger permeates Betsy's letters. She reports that she has told Harriet Rabb: "One qualification [for being a plaintiff] is that the suers be prepared to be on the shit list for the rest of their working lives, and she said yes that was so."

Betsy begins one note to Grace, "I think of myself these days as a psychic basket case." She speaks of Abe Rosenthal and Max Frankel, then the Sunday editor, as "vengeful men" who will get even "one way or another." She reports that the chief *Times* lawyer at the stalled negotiations, Jack Stanton, has said, "Why should *we* give *you* numbers to sue us with?"

She signs herself, "Wearily," from her home "here at Wistful Acres."

"Here's how I see it," she writes. "I would certainly sue because nothing can be done to me. Neither, of course, can I personally gain anything because I am well paid and unpromotable [because of her feminist and union activism]. You, Grace, would be willing to sue for pretty much the same reasons. You might get some back pay. Joan would want to sue for the back pay because she is grievously underpaid. Who then? . . . Finding [a group of] good women and true will be tough." She adds that the plaintiffs must be representative of women in many kinds of jobs at the *Times,* not just those in the news department. Glueck and Wade swap lists of possibilities, with candid remarks on each.

"I quite agree with your judgment as to the summer caliber of our soldiers," Grace says. "Believe me, I don't like being on the shit list either, but figure I'm mired in the stuff already because of my desertion of the high-level cultural news post." (Grace had been named assistant metropolitan editor in charge of cultural news in 1972, only weeks after the Women's Caucus met with Punch and his executives in the Board Room. She hated the job and asked to return to art reporting after fifteen months. "Who do I have to fuck to get out of this?" she would inquire of the newsroom at large, laughing airily. Ever well spoken, she corrected herself. "Sorry, *whom* do I have to fuck?" She would have killed anyone who took her question seriously.)

"So," she told Betsy in one letter from MacDowell, stating her readiness to be a plaintiff, "wot I got to lose?"

In September, the Caucus leaders sent all *Times* women a letter that exuded frustration at the lack of progress in the negotiations up to then. It pointed out that, indeed, the lot of women at the *Times* had deteriorated in two and one-half years. It prepared them for the likelihood of a lawsuit. The letter began:

We have been working as a group toward improvement of the condition of women since May, 1972. We have gone through many phases and styles of negotiation, only to end up pretty much where we have been all along: without a real voice in the management of the paper, with salaries below the male average and with consequent poorer pensions, and with little hope of progress toward policy-making jobs and with no women in the higher ranks to whom we could take our case.

In fact, since May, 1972, things have in some ways got worse. The margin between our average salaries and the men's average salaries is getting bigger—right now, the pension figures show a margin of $4,800 a year. . . .

We are an important group because the *Times* is an important publication as well as a big employer. We all honor the *Times* as an outstanding newspaper, and we have all, each in her own way, contributed to the paper's greatness. We think that the *Times* should set an example of fairness as an employer, as it seeks to set an example of fairness in its news columns.

The leaders called for a meeting later that month to decide whether a group of plaintiffs—anywhere from eight to twelve—should sue the *Times* "on behalf of all of us, seeking relief from unequal pay, lack of promotion opportunities and lack of equal treatment in all respects." The Caucus members voted overwhelmingly to take their case to court.

At this time, only six women agreed to be named plaintiffs. Besides the troika of Betsy, Joan, and Grace, there were Louise Carini, an accountant and benefits administration clerk in the *Times*'s accounting office; Andrea Skinner, a news clerk in the Sunday magazine fashion section; and Nancy Davis, a telephone ad taker in the classified advertising department. Eileen Shanahan, the most famous woman in the group and ultimately the most publicly outspoken, would become the seventh plaintiff two years later.

The six brought suit in the United States Southern District Court of New York on November 7, 1974. Betsy chose to use her legal and married name, Boylan, which placed her first alphabetically. Thus the case became *Elizabeth Boylan, et al., Plaintiffs,* v. *The New York Times Company, Defendant.*

....

Of all the plaintiffs, Louise Carini was the most surprising. Everything in her background seemed to militate against her stepping forward to sue her employer. She came from a family that loved God and respected authority; she was a devout Catholic; she was anti-union; all three of her sisters were nuns. In the early years of the Caucus she never went to meetings. She thought reporters on the whole were an eccentric lot, not "normal," like the people who worked on the business side, and she was not comfortable with them. She was frightened of the law, and lawyers, and judges. She was almost fifty-four, the second-oldest of the plaintiffs. Of the six, she had worked the longest at the *Times*—since 1951. On the other hand, Louise had a profound sense of right and wrong. She was a superb accountant and administrator, she had an appealing personality, and she was sick and tired of training one man after another to become her boss. At least six of them had been jumped over Louise's head.

In 1969, Betsy Wade and Joan Cook, who had long been active in the Newspaper Guild, had talked Louise into bringing her complaints to a high official in personnel. Betsy and another union representative had argued Carini's case eloquently in the man's office. Nothing came of it. Louise finally said to herself, "The heck with it—it's not worth the aggravation," but the unfairness rankled, and she was grateful to Betsy and Joan for trying to help her.

Louise was born in the little town of Bettola, Italy, on January 24, 1921, the next to last of the six children of Benvenuto Carini, a miller and farmer, and his wife, Virginia Bongiorno. Her mother "instilled in all of us," Louise said, "a great respect for authority, a respect for God."

When Louise was ten years old, Benvenuto Carini summoned the entire family to New York City. He had preceded them in 1927, when the building boom was attracting thousands of Italian immigrants. Soon after they arrived the Depression's grip tightened, and for many months Benvenuto was out of work. Finally he landed a job with President Roosevelt's Works Progress Administration, picking up litter and stones in the parks. Mrs. Carini cleaned offices at night. They saved for their children; Louise was transferred from the public schools to a Catholic elementary school and then to a Catholic high school run by the Sisters of Charity.

She went to the City College system at night, studying French at first and then taking accounting. She loved mathematics and had always excelled at it. The credits piled up, but she never got her bachelor's degree. She tried to get a job in a certified public accounting firm. "It was almost impossible in the 1940s to get in if you were a woman," she recalled. "They'd never tell you—absolutely never—that it was because you were female." She worked in the claims department of an insurance company and in the billing department of Alcoa Aluminum. In 1945 she moved to the northeast Bronx, to a neighborhood she has lived in ever since.

It is a place of immaculate little two-family wooden houses, tucked close together, with minuscule yards. Nearby are the stone solidity of Our Lady of Solace Church, where Louise has prayed and taken communion for decades, Ruggiero's Funeral Home, which will probably bury her, Scotti's Meat Market, Gambino's fruits and vegetables, and Louis, Salone de Bellezza, which does her hair.

In 1951, when she was thirty years old, Louise Carini came to *The New York Times,* to the general accounting office on the eighth floor, where she remained for the rest of her career. Her starting salary was $54 a week. Despite her innate shyness, she was quick to learn, and her eager, bright-eyed face endeared her to her colleagues. The people she worked for were all men, all much older than she. The *Times* was like a family then, not the corporate behemoth it would become. One of the things Louise was shy about was her speech. She

had never really been at home in English; she felt she mis-
pronounced words and did not use the right words, and so she
took elocution and vocabulary classes at night.

Her fellow workers told her there was a union. Louise was
glad she did not have to join. "I was very bitter about the
unions and what they did to our boys during the war," she
said. "The dockworkers wouldn't load the military supplies on
the ships. My brother Anthony was in the Battle of the Bulge.
My brother Peter was in the Coast Guard. That really upset
me. I never changed my mind. Until, after one of the contracts
was signed—I think after the big strike of the winter of 1962–
63—you either had to join the union or leave. I had twelve
years service by then—so I joined." She and many of the
people in the accounting department had crossed the picket
lines every day during the four-month strike. Those who
stayed out on strike, she said, "didn't seem to hold it against
us."

She did not connect the benefits the Guild had won for all
the workers in its jurisdiction—whether they were dues-paying
members of the union or not—with her own working life. She
had advanced in wages and seniority, she had taken on more
responsibilities, but she was still a clerk, not a supervisor. She
was being held back. She ticked off on her fingers the names
of the men she had taught and trained. By the end of the sixties
she was "fit to be tied," she recalled. "It was getting so bad I
was ready to go to Sulzberger—except he wouldn't know me
from a hole in the wall." That was when the Guild and Betsy
Wade took on her case, in vain.

When Wade asked her to be a named plaintiff in 1974,
Carini prayed for guidance at Our Lady of Solace Church.
And she talked to her brother Peter. Without his encourage-
ment, she said, "I could not have have gone through with it."
Peter, only two years older than she, had been her best friend
since childhood. He was boss of eight hundred electricians in
the city's subway and bus system. He and his wife lived near
Louise. "Every time I got bypassed for something, I'd come

home and rant to Peter," Louise said. "This time Peter said, 'If your manager doesn't think enough of you to appreciate what you're doing, then he's not a good manager and he doesn't respect you. Go for it!' The thought of the lawyers and the judges scared the wits out of me. I had many a sleepless night. It wasn't so much the fear of reprisal—it was my fear of the law. I've seen them on TV programs, cross-examining you cruelly."

Then she met Harriet Rabb, who upset this stereotype with her femininity, her tact, and the feeling she projected that she was there to serve her client. "I came home to Peter, raving about Harriet," Louise said. She joined the suit.

....

Andrea Skinner, a news clerk on the Sunday magazine and the oldest of the plaintiffs, turned fifty-four on November 6, 1974, the day before the suit was filed. She was a black woman, small and gnarled, with a long face and a beautiful, cultured alto voice. She, too, was a symbolic figure, representing the one hundred and thirty women of color who worked at *The New York Times*. She often felt invisible.

When Max Frankel, then Sunday editor and Andy's ultimate boss, learned that she was among the plaintiffs, he sent for Mary Simons, her immediate superior, the editor in charge of the Sunday magazine's food, fashion, and home pages. Max asked Mary to ask Andy, "Have you been discriminated against?" Mary went back to Andy.

"Why didn't he ask me himself if I was discriminated against?" Andy said to Mary. "I can talk. Not only have I been discriminated against, but all of us women have been discriminated against in our job positions and our salaries." Skinner considered herself to be a middle-aged gofer, a flunkey, routing clothes to be photographed from the Seventh Avenue garment manufacturers in and out of the *Times*'s fashion closet. She knew that people thought of her as good old Andy.

Her father had been a lawyer, well known in his profession and in local politics in Minneapolis and Chicago, where Andy spent her girlhood. A black lawyer was quite an extraordinary person in those days. Rufus Augustine Skinner, a handsome and imposing man, born in French Guiana, had gone to McGill University in Montreal and earned his law degree in Minnesota; during Andrea's early years, she remembered, there were only four other black lawyers and one black doctor in the whole of Minneapolis, and one black dentist in St. Paul, the twin city across the Mississippi River. Her mother, born Margaret Rose Fairley in Trinidad, was a seamstress with her own elegant clientele. She was a gifted person who could look at the most complicated dress in a store window and copy it for a customer down to the last buttonhole. She died when Andy was seventeen years old. "I grew up in Chicago in a hard, tough season," Andy said. The Skinners lived in a black neighborhood on the South Side, but the language and behavior they witnessed on the street were not permitted in their genteel Catholic middle-class home. Books, piano lessons, visits to museums, were taken for granted. The older daughter, Rita, was very slow to learn; Andrea Skinner, like Grace Glueck and Joan Cook, was forced to be excessively protective of her sibling, and she was sometimes punished for her sister's misbehavior. Like Glueck and Louise Carini, Skinner had never married.

She spent two years at the University of Minnesota, then transferred to Lincoln University in Jefferson City, Missouri, where she earned a degree in elementary education. After teaching kindergarten in a Cleveland public school, Andrea decided to go east in 1953, to New York City. She took courses in textile design at the Pratt Institute in Brooklyn. In 1954 she went to work for *Mademoiselle* magazine.

At *Mademoiselle* she was a Girl Friday. The only other blacks in the house were the woman who made the morning coffee and the man who cleaned out the office of Betsy Blackwell, the editor. One young twig after another joined *Made-*

moiselle and was promoted into fashion jobs, going out into the clothes market, attending fashion shows. They never let Andy out of the office. When she complained, the answer was always the same: "Think of our Southern advertisers, our Southern stores." One editor said, "Why don't you go to *Ebony* magazine?" Andy replied, "If I'm no good for *Mademoiselle,* why am I good for *Ebony?*" She recalled, "They could never bring themselves to come right out and say it, 'Because you're black.' Never, never."

She had met Patricia Peterson at *Mademoiselle* and had been a baby-sitter for her son. After Pat had established herself as the fashion editor at the *Times,* she asked Andy to come along. Following two years in which she tried Peace Corps training and social work, Andy decided that fashion really was her métier. She arrived at *The New York Times* in 1965. "Let me work with children's fashions," Andy asked Peterson. There were trips to the Caribbean, where Andy's parents had been raised; she scouted the terrain and the talent for magazine photo layouts. There and elsewhere, she chose child models—black, brown, yellow, as well as white—who were a kind of Rainbow Coalition, a dramatic change from the Wonder Bread boys and girls who had formerly filled the children's fashion pages. Peterson, and then Simons, backed her up. She spent many days out "in the market" at Seventh Avenue wholesale design houses. Finally, under Simons, Andy received one merit raise.

She well remembered the meeting in the Board Room in July 1972. "That group of men, all sitting there, very rigid and stern, at that long, long table," she said. "The men were on that side. We were on this side. They were saying in their minds, 'What do you want? Why are you here, lady?' "

She hesitated very little when Joan Cook asked her to join the suit. "I wanted to be part of it," she said. "I had been a news clerk forever. I was the black face in there, but I didn't think of it that way. I thought of it from a woman's point of view. It was scary, but I figured I really had nothing to lose. They couldn't have fired us. So I went out on a limb."

••••••••••

Nancy Audrain Davis in 1974 was twenty-nine years old, the youngest by far of the plaintiffs. She was a big, friendly, enthusiastic person, just an inch under six feet tall, who thrashed into a room like a handsome hunting dog, all paws and wagging tail. She was a telephone advertising solicitor, in a department that was one of the most blatantly female ghettos at *The New York Times*—a department in which it seemed impossible for any woman to get ahead. Nancy had come to the *Times* only two and one-half years before, in March 1972, and had already made a name for herself as a pushy, uppity young woman. She had applied nine times for jobs that would advance her, and nine times she had been turned down. Like every other plaintiff, she had initially been thrilled to get a job on *The New York Times*. Unlike all the others, she did not stay there long.

Nancy Audrain, the youngest of three children and the only daughter, came of pioneer midwestern stock on both sides of her family. The family icon was "Aunt Becky" Heald, a woman who had been scalped by marauding Indians and wore a bonnet for the rest of her life. Nancy grew up in Alliance, Ohio, about an hour's drive from Cleveland, in a comfortable house set in a big lawn brightened with daffodils, daisies, and lilacs. She joined the Boosters Club in high school and was the valedictorian of her class. The Audrain parents and their two sons were conservative Republicans. They all doted upon Nancy. They were her "shield," she thought, sure to stand with her whatever she did.

Nancy went to Ohio Wesleyan University and then on to the American Academy of Dramatic Arts in New York City. But acting was not for her, and she drifted from one temporary job to another. When she came to *The New York Times*, she considered it her "first real job." By then, she had been married for two years to Joseph Charles Davis, a jazz musician whom she had met one summer during her college years, while she was waiting tables at a resort in Lake Placid, New York.

As for the *Times*, "I had it on a pedestal," she said. "I thought that the *Times* was a daily wonder. I had enormous respect for the product. I expected the *Times* to be an equal opportunity employer, a leader for the rest of the newspaper business and for the country. I was astonished that the *Times* reacted like a corporation being sued. They closed ranks and tried to win, rather than trying to do the right thing, or opening their eyes."

Nancy saw female talent all around her in the big, open room on the sixth floor, where women with headsets solicited classified ads over the phone. She found her colleagues intelligent, capable, energetic. She also saw inequality. There were very few men, and almost invariably they were promoted to outside sales positions within six months to a year of their hiring. The women *never* got into outside sales. That was where the spice and variety were—and the big money, both in salary and in commissions. She began testing the system right away—as soon as she heard of an outside job opening, she applied for it. She felt that many of the women stagnating within the classified department, particularly the older, more experienced ones, were discouraged. "Some of them were so discouraged they stopped trying," she said. "There was no lack of qualified women—women far superior to me."

From the time Nancy Davis joined her name to *Boylan* v. *The New York Times*, she felt the tension. "I felt observed constantly," she said—by whom, she was not sure. Her conservative family was baffled. "What is it, Nan?" her worried mother asked. "Do you really have to do this?" Nancy Davis thought she did. Her husband's roving, bohemian, nocturnal life, her brush with the stage, and now her rebellion against the most respected newspaper in America were a far cry from the Boosters Club in Alliance, Ohio. "I entered into the suit because it was so obviously right," Nancy said. "I didn't think I was particularly gutsy. It was the one time in my life—the only time there will ever be—for me to participate in history."

Harriet Rabb disagreed with Nancy's statement that it was not gutsy of her to become a plaintiff. "It takes enormous courage to sue a large employer," Harriet said. "It is a long, slow, painful, difficult, and ego-destroying process. I really admire the women who do it. In large part, they are not doing it for themselves. They do it for the women who come after them."

Nancy Davis's name remained on the list of plaintiffs, but she left the *Times* for another job two years later. She was not at the newspaper for the final, most rending stages of *Boylan* v. *The New York Times*.

CHAPTER 10

THE SINGLE
WORST MOMENT

Clifton Daniel, a man so poised and worldly that he gave a deeper dimension to the word "suave," was clearly embarrassed. It was at the end of a November day in 1975, and Daniel, the chief of the *Times*'s Washington bureau for almost three years, had just called Eileen Shanahan into his office. "I don't know how to tell you, except to tell you," he said to Shanahan. "The executive editor [Abe Rosenthal] has asked me to inform you that after the standard raises the Newspaper Guild has negotiated for all employees, you will be making a salary of $33,583." Here Daniel veered into the third person, changing his inflection and putting quotes around the next phrase: *"and that's enough for her."* He was obviously quoting Rosenthal's refusal to give Eileen a merit raise.

"Clifton was so uncomfortable I almost felt bad for him,"

Eileen recalled. From that day on, it was war between Rosenthal and Shanahan. And on that day she decided she would not stay much longer at the newspaper she loved and to which she had added much luster over a period of thirteen years.

The trouble in the Washington bureau had begun earlier in November, when the Guild shop steward tacked up a roughly accurate list of thirty-two reporters' salaries on the bulletin board. No names were given, but each reporter could spot his or her own wage. Some bureau members felt they were not being paid what they were worth in relation to others. All six women reporters were incensed: very quickly, they figured out that every one of them was in the bottom half of the salary listing. The single black woman, Nancy Hicks, ranked last. Eileen was the highest-paid woman but was still halfway down the scale.

As she looked at the list, she did not—for once—instantly blow her top. She thought it over. Then she wrote a letter to Clifton Daniel. She told him that she wanted to send an identical letter to Abe Rosenthal. Daniel pleaded with her not to send it. She went ahead. The meeting with Daniel in which he told her of Rosenthal's scornful response came toward the end of that month.

Eileen's letter to Abe had begun: "I cannot remain silent in the face of my discovery that my pay is below the mid-point for Bureau members." She pointed out the numerous "herograms" and letters of praise she had received from bosses at every level, not only for work on the national economic policy beat, but for her willingness and ability to jump in wherever needed, as in the New York City bankruptcy crisis of the mid-1970s.

"I had always assumed that I was the victim of a degree of salary discrimination, probably based on the unjust rationale that I didn't need the money because I have a husband with a good job. (The rationale is unjust because it is never applied to men with working wives or those whose wives have independent means.) But in my darkest hour, I never imagined that my pay would place me in the lower half of the Bureau's reporters. . . .

"I really can't believe that my salary position represents anyone's considered judgment concerning my worth to the paper. If it does, I will have to look elsewhere for a job.

"If it doesn't, I hope that I will have prompt and adequate evidence of that fact in my paycheck."

She suggested that a $40-a-week merit raise above the $33,583 she would receive because of the Guild contract settlement would be "fair." Rosenthal never replied directly, sending his "that's enough" message through Clifton Daniel. Once one of Shanahan's fans, Abe had turned his back on Eileen forever.

···········

Meantime, the pretrial discovery process ground inexorably on in New York, turning up one horror after another. Prodded by Harriet Rabb, Judge Henry Werker of the federal Southern District Court in New York, who had jurisdiction over the case, had ordered the *Times* to produce payrolls for its entire work force for ten years, the personnel record of each employee, and the private memos and letters of ten *Times* managers in the business and news departments, including those of Abe Rosenthal.

Abe was outraged that his memos would be read by the opposition's lawyers. He called the discovery process and the lawsuit "a kind of social blackmail." Compounding Rosenthal's and the *Times*'s problems was *another* suit brought in 1974. In this case, the newspaper's minority employees were charging racial discrimination. "My God!" said Punch Sulzberger, "they're chewing on us at both ends!" The chief named plaintiff was a young black Puerto Rican woman, Benilda Rosario, a classified-ad taker with guts and imagination. Blacks, Hispanics, gays, and women were all feeling angry and misused at the *Times*. A widespread perception of Abe Rosenthal on the news floor was that he was a homophobe, an antifeminist, and uncomfortable with blacks, to say the least. This produced a typical city room witticism: "*The New York Times* is an equal-opportunity oppressor."

And the salary gap between men and women at the newspaper kept widening.

Even though the threat of suit was forcing the *Times* to hire more women, they were being brought in at lower wages all over the building. By 1977, economic statisticians hired by Rabb who analyzed the payrolls discovered that men at the *Times* were paid on the average $98.67 a week more than women, or $5,160 a year. For that amount in 1977, a parent could pay a child's tuition plus books and pocket money for one entire year at any first-class private college, including Harvard, Wellesley, or Dartmouth.

One of Rabb's statistical experts, Dr. Orley Ashenfelter of Princeton University, noted that $1,425 of the difference could be attributed to education and years of experience. That left a $3,725 gap that could not be explained away. The purchasing power of the dollar then was about double that of today.

The Caucus lawyers and statisticians found that Grace Glueck, the only woman to serve as an assistant metropolitan editor before the suit was brought in 1974, had earned $2,435 less than the man who immediately preceded her, $7,126 less than the man who succeeded her, and $6,675 to $12,511 less than the men who were also assistant metropolitan editors during Glueck's tenure.

Marylin Bender had become editor of the Sunday business and financial section in 1976 at a salary of $36,000. Her immediate predecessor, Richard Mooney, had earned $50,988. Like five male assistant metropolitan editors, Mooney had been given a dollop of *Times* stock and was on the "publisher's payroll," which conferred bonuses and significantly better pension and health benefits on those employees whom Punch Sulzberger deemed up-and-coming. Bender was not on it.

Flora Lewis, the Paris bureau chief, was one of only three women who were. There were ninety-two men on the publisher's payroll.

Rabb's experts also learned from the *Times* payrolls that Shanahan was twelfth in seniority in the Washington bureau of thirty-two reporters, but down in nineteenth place on the salary scale and earning almost $3,000 a year less than the average salary of male reporters in the Washington bureau. She was making $12,334 less annually than R. W. (Johnny) Apple, Jr., and $11,426 less than Charles Mohr, the two highest-paid correspondents. Both were marvelous newspapermen. Both had come to the *Times* after Eileen.

The numbers were bad enough. The private memos that surfaced during the discovery process revealed example after example of personal bias and condescension. The files of Dan Schwarz, the Sunday editor, produced this lulu, a response to Heather Bradley in the London bureau, who had recommended a young woman for a job: "We'll take your word on Pamela Kent, of course. What does she look like? Twiggy [an extremely skinny English model]? Lynn Redgrave [plump]? Perhaps you ought to send over her vital statistics, or picture in a bikini?" Somehow, Schwarz never seemed to strike the right note in twitting women.

Robert MacDougall, in reviewing the work of employees in the circulation and promotion departments, wrote of one woman: "Very pleasant. Good at shorthand and typing. Her chief ambition is probably to get married. Has a good figure and is not restrained about dressing it to advantage."

Ed Pelz, the personnel director, had this to say in a progress review of a woman mail clerk: "Smart. Has a lot of common sense. . . . Has the interest of The New York Times at heart—more so than anybody else. Loses very little time—comes to work when she's sick. . . . Saves a lot of money for The New York Times by her thorough knowledge of mail rates. . . . Weak Points: May lack education, and may overdress. . . ." To which Ben Amato, head of the outgoing mail department, added, "Promotability: Yes. She would be good as a female supervisor. I would make her my first assistant if she were a man."

Pelz was somebody whom Clara Rotter never forgot. Clara began at the *Times* in 1946 as a roving stenographer for all kinds of exacting people, including one of the most imperious of all, Cyrus Sulzberger. Sulzberger, chief of foreign correspondents and a first cousin of Punch's, sent her flowers in gratitude for her never-say-die efficiency. She later became legendary in the New York theater world in the job where she spent decades—as the *Times* drama department secretary who did not know the meaning of the words "impossible" and "no." Playwrights and press agents quailed when Clara called. They knew they could not put off her relentless requests for information and services. But early in her career, when she was working for Pelz in personnel, he came to her desk to tell her, "Miss Rotter, you know, there are not many jobs that you could occupy, because you are a very good worker, but your looks are not great." Clara was devastated but did not show it. Then she thought, "Well, I'm no glamour girl, but that was a terribly indelicate, tactless thing to say." She did not forgive Pelz. Soon afterward, the drama critic Brooks Atkinson, the platonic love of Clara's life, brought her into his department in the job she seemed born to do.

Memories such as Clara Rotter's, poignant and diminishing of women, were passed from one employee to another. There were also the overheard conversations between men at *The New York Times*. The following remarks between two editors in the Sunday book review became a Caucus favorite:

First editor: "Did you see —— when Abe passed her that cake at lunch? You could almost see her nipples pucker."

Second editor: "Yeah. These broads' nipples always pucker for power."

Other editors, in the feminist and litigious climate of the 1970s, began to look around furtively before making what one male feminist at the paper called their tits-and-ass cracks.

Meantime, the lawyers for the *Times* were as busy as Rabb and her colleagues, combing the paper's personnel dossiers for damning evidence—of anything from alcoholism to incompetence—to use against the women who were suing the paper. They were also seeking to have the suit dismissed altogether. They described the plaintiffs' charges as "frivolous." "This is a case," they argued, "where . . . highly paid women, who have been well treated by The Times, now assert for some reason undeterminable from their papers herein that they have suffered discrimination because of their sex. But their claims . . . are totally devoid of substance and rationality."

"It's as if they believe that once a woman makes more than $17,000 a year, she loses her constitutional rights," Harriet Rabb retorted.

For one moment, even Judge Henry Werker seemed to be leaning to that point of view. When it was revealed at a hearing that Betsy Wade made $36,473 a year and was the highest-paid copy editor on the newsroom floor, the judge was said to have suggested to Rabb and her associate, Howard Rubin, that they find themselves a more suitable "victim" as their chief named plaintiff. Wade, who was charging that the *Times* had promoted eleven men over her during a period of eight years, could hardly contain her anger. "I make the amount of money I make," she said, "because I am one of the best editors the *Times* has, and because, after all, if I couldn't have the [promotion], they thought that maybe if they gave me the money I would shut up."

Eileen Shanahan became the seventh and final named plaintiff of the suit shortly before she resigned from the *Times* to take an important government job in January 1977. Harriet Rabb had warned her that being a plaintiff would be painful. She added that if Eileen said yes, "It will strengthen the suit for everyone." Shanahan responded that she was eager to join. In addition, she did not want to remain in a workplace where she was becoming increasingly embittered.

During her years in the Washington bureau, she had

worked harmoniously as the second in rank on the economic beat with Edwin Dale, whose mental fireworks dazzled even a group of singularly bright people. When Dale was offered an assignment in London in the fall of 1976 but for private reasons turned it down and left the paper, it was assumed by Eileen and many of her colleagues that she would be elevated to chief economic correspondent. Among other things, she had annually assigned, edited, and helped write the *Times* coverage of the federal budget. Nonetheless, the job went to Clyde Farnsworth, who was brought back from Paris. Eileen had been regularly looking for a post elsewhere, and this was the last straw. The very week that Shanahan learned she would not get Dale's job, in November 1976, she received an offer from an old friend, Joseph Califano.

Califano, the secretary-designate of Health, Education, and Welfare in President-elect Jimmy Carter's Cabinet, asked her to become his press officer, with a rank of assistant secretary. Her friends urged her to accept. Given Rosenthal's hostility, and his absolute power, her career at the *Times* could never go any farther. Eileen joined Califano's staff on the day Carter was inaugurated—January 20, 1977—but, like Nancy Davis, she continued as a plaintiff, although no longer a *Times* employee. And, more and more, she spoke out in interviews and at feminist forums against the sexism she had perceived at her former newspaper. It drove Rosenthal up the wall.

The discovery process that allowed Harriet Rabb, her colleagues, and the statisticians to go through the *Times*'s payroll figures, employee files, and private memos moved the lawsuit to its next important stage. On April 11, 1977, Judge Werker—after studying Rabb's massive documentation, which showed the probability of systematic discrimination at the *Times*—approved her petition to declare *Boylan* v. *The New York Times* a class-action suit.

That meant that the seven plaintiffs were not just a tiny group of disgruntled individuals but were representative of all the women under Newspaper Guild jurisdiction, as well as management secretaries: about 550 women, in sum—virtually all the women then working for the paper. Betsy put the notice of Werker's certification up on the bulletin board in the *Times* city room. "We won!" was her jubilant if premature postscript. Instead, the atmosphere grew ever tenser.

Marylin Bender, the Sunday business editor, remembers a luncheon she went to that year at which Punch Sulzberger was host. It was in the publisher's private dining room on the eleventh floor, where Punch regularly invited important guests. Bowls of the unsalted pecans Sulzberger favored sat on the table. The *Times*'s maître d'hôtel, André, oozing lugubrious formality, dispensed the iced tea sweetened with orange juice, another Sulzberger standard. Among the *Times* executives present were Sydney Gruson, Abe Rosenthal, and Charlotte Curtis, as well as Guy Garrett, a black director of labor relations. The guests were former United States Representative Martha Griffiths, a ten-term congresswoman and a legend in Michigan politics, and Eleanor Smeal, the newly elected president of the National Organization for Women, or NOW. According to Bender's notes, the talk turned to the Equal Rights Amendment. Sulzberger smiled uncertainly at his guests and said, "Well, I have three sisters—I'm outnumbered, I guess." Then he turned to Garrett. "Guy," he said, "what law are those women suing us under?"

"Title Seven of the Civil Rights Act," Garrett replied.

Punch looked puzzled. He said, "Why can't a private company have men around if it wants to?"

Bender asked him: "Do you really consider this to be a private company?"

Sure, Punch said, it's publicly traded, but it's privately owned. Bender knew full well that the Sulzberger family had a controlling interest in the shares. She replied that anyone doing business with the government was subject to federal antidiscrimination laws. Punch responded with a laugh: "Yeah, we deliver twenty-five papers to West Point and the CIA and the Pentagon." (His remark was wholly facetious—

federal offices from the White House on down subscribe daily to *The New York Times.*)

"He began talking about the cultural conditioning of women," Bender recalled, "and said it was unfortunate, but society expected women to be married and stay home. Griffiths and Smeal were agape."

The embarrassing luncheon creaked to an end. The visitors were scandalized. In the hallway, Charlotte Curtis pulled Marylin aside. She was at the point of tears. She felt betrayed. The Caucus saw Curtis as a hypocritical adversary, but she had a different view of herself. For years she had thought she was boring from within, influencing the publisher about the cause of women in the working world. She was an intimate of Punch and his wife's. She had fought for her protégées on the family/style page, she had assigned and prominently displayed stories about women's politics. She considered herself a feminist, while caring passionately about the paper. Her rationale for not joining or supporting the Women's Caucus had always been that she wanted to remain neutral. Charlotte now told Marylin that she questioned the strength of Punch's commitment to "do the right thing" by his women employees. Still, she made no move to support the women's suit.

The gap between the *Times*'s public stance on discrimination and what it was doing in secret—fighting the women's suit tooth and nail—was becoming surreal. "Don't think of this company as the liberal *New York Times,* think of it as the Georgia Power Company," Harriet Rabb kept saying. "They don't treat their women any differently."

For example, the New York Times Company told its stockholders in a report summarizing the proceedings at the 1977 Annual Shareholders' Meeting: "The Company is not only in compliance with equal employment opportunity laws but in many areas is far ahead of legal requirements. At the present time, 20 percent of women employees are in management positions; 8 percent of management positions are filled by blacks or other minorities."

Marylin Bender read that and gasped. "My God!" she said to herself. "Where in *hell* did they get those numbers?" In the newsroom the reality was different. If one counted the hundreds of heads on the third floor, "there was only me—little, underpaid me—in a supervisory job," she said with a cutting laugh.

The *Times* published a high-minded, much-quoted editorial at the end of 1977 about "reverse discrimination," headlined "THE COMPLAINTS OF WHITE MEN," that also contrasted with the reality inside the paper. It began well enough:

As the lists of our company officers [the masthead above the editorials] testify each day on this page, we are an institution run mostly by white men. As in most other institutions, women and non-whites came later than white men into the hierarchies from which our managers have been chosen.

Then the tone turned self-congratulatory:

Recognizing the inadequacy of the result, and faced with social and legal pressures that we ourselves helped to generate, we have undertaken corrective measures, affirmative action, to expand opportunity in our company, in our profession, and in our country. Sex and race are factors in our appraisal of qualified applicants.

Clearly, that effort is far from complete. Its success will show up only in future generations.

The *Times* editorial opposed the views of those who said the civil rights laws had led to discrimination against white males:

The law cannot suddenly decide to be neutral when for so long it favored white men. . . . To the complaint of white men that [affirmative action] complicates their lives as a group, there is only one honest reply: Sure it does. But if they are being deprived to some extent, it is only . . . that they are losing opportunity which they would not have had without past discrimination.

James Goodale, the urbane head of the *Times*'s legal department, was quoted as saying that the newspaper was "at the top of the list" in progressive hiring practices, and that the suit was attacking the *Times*'s "institutional credibility." He was asked by a reporter from *Ms.* magazine: Then why do so many intelligent women employees at the *Times* believe they are being discriminated against? "You'll have to ask them," Goodale smoothly replied.

He kept repeating in interviews that the *Times* would never settle with the women; that its management was determined to go to trial. He told reporters, "*The New York Times* has taken, throughout its history, the position that this country [*sic*] should not engage in discrimination of any kind. We have been the leader of opinion on this question. We are fighting this case because to settle would be to compromise the integrity of *The New York Times* by implying that our editorials over the years have been hypocritical."

Throughout the winter of 1977–78, the case was moving into a final stage with the interviewing of potential witnesses and the taking of depositions, a form of pretrial interrogation and sworn testimony.

Harriet Rabb took depositions from eighteen *Times* executives while management's lawyers were deposing the plaintiffs and witnesses for the women's case. An image kept recurring in Rabb's mind. "I saw two huge ships," she said. "They were steaming straight toward each other at about a half a mile an hour. They saw each other, but they were not altering direction. They were on a collision course."

The taking of the depositions was unnerving for the plaintiffs—for none more so than for Eileen Shanahan, even though she was no longer at the paper. "She had made Abe angry," Harriet Rabb said. "She continued to speak in public against the lot of women at the *Times*. Abe was put out with Betsy Wade. He thought Joan Cook was misguided. But I'm telling you, he and the lawyers reserved a special place in hell for Eileen."

The deposition the *Times* lawyers took of Shanahan, with Rabb in attendance, lasted all of one day. Harriet described the session as "brutal." The two went to a restaurant at dusk to calm down. "Eileen's a brassy dame, but she let me see how painful and lacerating and bruising the encounter was," Rabb recalled.

On the other hand, Jane Brody, who was due to be called as a witness on behalf of the Women's Caucus, rather enjoyed the day her deposition was taken. She described the young *Times* lawyer who took it as being open-mouthed and "aghast" at her testimony.

Jane, who had earned a degree in biochemistry from Cornell University and a master's in science writing from the University of Wisconsin, had written the popular "Personal Health" column since 1976, as well as books on healthful living and eating. A tiny woman with flashing dark eyes, a Brooklyn accent, and volcanic energy, she projects authority in person and on the page. A year or so after beginning her column, which took off almost from day one, she discovered with the aid of a male colleague that she was making one hundred dollars a week less than the lowest-paid man in the science department.

"I was furious! I was insulted!" she said. "And especially since I was the breadwinner of my family. My husband is a lyricist. He had a regular job when I married him but his company left New York in 1971. He decided to stay home and take care of our twin boys, who had just turned two. I became the primary wage-earner. There were men in the science department who were not married, or married with no children, or in two-career marriages, and they were all earning more than I was. The whole issue of salary was compounded by the attitude of my male superior, Hank Lieberman, who believed women's place was in the home and did not hesitate to say so. I literally got pats on the fanny while my colleagues got raises."

She also told about her fight against male squeamishness at

The New York Times. The copy desks' prudishness and itch to bowdlerize had been the curse of reporters for many years. She was the first person to get "sexual intercourse" on page one of the *Times,* the first to get "ejaculation" into the paper at all, and it was the 1970s before she was able to do that. When she wrote a story on a technique of using the rhythm method that involved taking samples of cervical mucus, the news editor decided that the term "cervical mucus" was far too nasty for the delicate sensibilities of *Times* readers and cut it from the article without informing Brody. With this excision, he also cut the sense from the piece.

With a single exception, Rabb's interviews with the powerful men on the other side were civil. Seymour Topping, the managing editor, was immensely cordial. A former foreign editor, Top had admired Betsy Wade and her work for years, considering her a "great newspaperwoman." He often told other editors and reporters, "If she weren't a woman, she'd be in the bullpen," the critically important desk that is the nerve center of the news on the *Times*'s third floor. Privately, he thought the suit had blighted her career and turned her bitter.

Rabb described the manner of Max Frankel, then head of the editorial page, as "crushingly polite." "He had decided," she remembered, "what should be the appropriate demeanor. He had thought it all through. It was controlled behavior—a very mannered performance."

Arthur Gelb really surprised Harriet. He was merely the deputy managing editor, but Rabb knew from her clients that it was he who actually ran the news side of the paper with his best friend, Abe Rosenthal. It was always "Abe 'n' Artie" this and "Abe 'n' Artie" that at *The New York Times,* the two pals forever twinned, Mutt and Jeff, little Abe and skyscraper Artie, flapping shortsightedly around the city room, looking for somebody to buttonhole to carry out one of Artie's one thousand daily ideas. Reporters called the pair the sentimental gangsters because of the way they rewarded their friends and punished their enemies. Artie was and is somewhat reminis-

cent of Lyndon Johnson, constantly pressing the flesh, seeming even taller than he is, a nonstop talker. In Gelb, Rabb was
expecting Rasputin, or at the very least Machiavelli. "And in
walks this cocker spaniel," Harriet said, "with long ears and
over-large feet that kind of stepped on things." She was flabbergasted. "He wanted it to be fun and friendly. He wanted
admiration," she said. It was Artie to the life.

Like Gelb, Punch Sulzberger struck the Caucus's counsel as
affable and forthcoming. "I think he wanted to make a nice
impression," Rabb said. "He wanted me to see that he was a
decent fellow." Sulzberger, as usual, was vague about details.
She asked him, "Who in your opinion are the first-rate women
reporters?" Punch came right back with "Flora Lewis and
Nan Robertson." Rabb waited for more names. Punch
thought and thought. And finally, Harriet asked, "What
about Judy Klemesrud?"—a reporter whose lively, imaginative stories had been showing up for years all over the paper.
"Judy Klemesrud?" Punch repeated, slowly. "Who's Judy
Klemesrud?" When Harriet told that story at a packed Caucus
meeting soon afterward, every one of us in that room let out
a gasp of disbelief.

But nothing had prepared Harriet Rabb for Abe Rosenthal,
not even all the tales she had been told of his ego and his
wrath. She had been brought up in a household where voices
were never raised. Only one other deposition in all her career
remains as vivid in her memory. She took it when she was very
young, of an older lawyer who was angry and supercilious and
objected to every one of her questions. Finally he said,
"Maybe we should adjourn this deposition until you learn
how to practice law." She was shattered.

It was an older and much tougher Harriet who faced Rosenthal in 1978. She had been awestruck by the man's letters and
memos, the words and thoughts that pierced to the heart of
the matter as if shot from a gun. "I felt like I was getting some
kind of fabulous training in journalism," she said. He was a
tremendous writer, even in his private communications, one

who could pack more into six sentences than others could say in twelve, who wasted not a single phrase, who could paint a landscape in a paragraph. What Rabb had discovered, as she perused file cabinets full of Abe's papers during the legal discovery process, was what other reporters and editors and the readers of *The New York Times* had long known about Rosenthal—that once, particularly when he was covering the United Nations in its yeasty early days, or serving as a foreign correspondent, he had been a breathtakingly good reporter.

From the moment he entered the room at Cahill, Gordon & Reindel, the *Times*'s law firm in the Wall Street district, Rabb could see that Rosenthal thought the whole business was a goddamned affront.

They faced each other over a table for three days. They were three of the longest days in Harriet Rabb's life. By the time the interview was over, the deposition ran to 571 pages and weighed six pounds. No other testimony from a potential witness on either side came anywhere near it for length. Nobody else among the executives of the *Times* was so important to the case, so famous, quick-witted, gifted, controversial, and feared. He ran the editorial side of the *Times,* all of it. He delegated nothing. Even his publisher, way up on the fourteenth floor, knew that. Abe decided what stories went into the paper and where. He hired, promoted, switched people around, sent them into limbo. Abe's shit list, as it was commonly known, grew bigger every year, and sometimes people could not figure out why they were on it, or, just as often, why Abe had decided to take them off it. Gradually Rosenthal had become more and more isolated as he rose to the top. By 1978, only a tiny circle of yes-men was left around him, cronies who cocooned the executive editor from reality.

And there, just across the table, was this little Southern lady who had rifled through his personal papers, prodding, insisting on answers. "By the time he came into that room he was already strung tight," Rabb remembered. "He did not want to be called to account—by y'all in the Women's Caucus, by the

court process, by the lawyers, by me." Rosenthal yelled at
Rabb, waggled his finger at her, jumped up from his chair as
if to storm out, and, according to Rabb, frequently demanded
of Floyd Abrams, the famed First Amendment lawyer who
would argue the *Times*'s case in court: "Do I have to answer
this?" "You have to," Abrams replied.

At one point, Harriet asked Abe to compare the work of a
woman reporter with that of a man reporter in business news:

Rosenthal—"I think this is idiotic, frankly."

Rabb—"I'm sorry you think it's idiotic."

Rosenthal—"I think it is."

Rabb—"It is at the heart of this lawsuit."

At times, she said, "He was beside himself. He . . . was
. . . just . . . crazed." It was intimidating, but she was determined to be professional, to do her business and get out of
there. She would ask Rosenthal quietly, "Do you need fifteen
minutes to collect yourself?" or "You appear to have lost
control. Would you like to step outside for a moment?"

Abe occasionally exhibited affection and respect for some of
his women employees, most notably for Flora Lewis, his Paris
bureau chief. He had recently considered naming her to head
the Washington bureau, if she would take it. She was the only
woman in his employ that he would so honor. (As Flora
remembers it, Rosenthal offered her the bureau in case his first
choice, Hedrick Smith, turned it down. "It was as though he
had said, 'If my fiancée jilts me at the altar,' will you stand
in?' " Flora said. "No man would ever have offered another
man a job in that way." After a long pause she said yes,
convinced that Smith would take the post. He did.) Abe told
Rabb that there was no male Flora Lewis. Why is it so hard
to find one? Harriet asked. Because, Abe answered, she is a
brilliant and almost unique correspondent. Harriet held up a
memo from Rosenthal to the publisher. "This memo suggests
that Flora Lewis proved her worth and that she deserved a
raise," she said. "I want to know why you decided to raise her

only $2,560 if, as the memo suggested, you hired her at $3,000 to $4,000 less than you might have."

Rosenthal wandered around some kind of answer, to the effect that he had also given some men jobs at lower salaries than they were worth.

At times he "slashed and burned," in Harriet's words, describing some women's work as puerile, simplistic, poor, uninspiring, merely competent. He singled out one female reporter, "with psychic problems," who had once refused an assignment to cover the president of the United States. Another could not be trusted to cover women's politics because she was an "advocate."

The other *Times* executives whose testimony Harriet had taken thus far had retreated into the same polite evasiveness that the management had exhibited throughout its negotiations with the Women's Caucus. Not Abe Rosenthal. His temper rose toward apoplexy when he spoke of Betsy Wade and Eileen Shanahan. Reading what he said about them, I found it difficult to believe that these were the same women I had known and with whom I had worked all those years.

Of Wade he said: "I recall people saying that she had a foul temper; that she shouted at people; that she used obscenities and was very difficult to get along with; cried rather too much." He could have been describing himself, including the tears. He denigrated dignified, thoughtful, totally professional Betsy—who was described in the *Times* house organ as "one of the best damned editors who ever held down a place on a *Times* copydesk," an editor who could do "a man's job with a woman's delicacy," and "one of the glories of the newsroom"—as lacking the imagination and news judgment needed for her promotion to a more central job.

Eileen was similarly trashed. Rosenthal, whose rages laid the newsroom waste, described Eileen as irascible and short-tempered. There was no question that Shanahan frequently flew off the handle, shrieked at people, and called them names.

I had witnessed such scenes myself and invariably told her to pipe down. Against this could be weighed the woman's joy and pride in her work, her integrity, her almost limitless generosity of spirit. She was a wonderful friend, an exciting journalist. Abe conceded that her writing was lucid, intelligent and grammatical, but said this explicator of complex topics was not "broad-gauged" enough to be the chief economic correspondent in Washington. He accused her of bias and distortion in economics, of frequently showing "derision or contempt" for some people or subjects and unwarranted admiration for others. He felt "absolutely" that it was better for the paper that Eileen had gone. He had told the publisher as much when Punch worried about the rising numbers of gifted people resigning from the *Times*. Once, it had been the newspaper nobody left.

While the depositions were being taken, Harriet Rabb was telling their substance to us at meetings of the Women's Caucus in the winter and early spring of 1978. The thought that Abe was prepared to say all this and more from the witness stand about two women of character and talent I had long admired, who represented the very best on a great newspaper, filled me with sadness. I was sad for them, for me, for the man Abe Rosenthal had become.

Abe and my husband, Stanley Levey, had both started as young reporters on the *Times* in 1944. They were buddies from the very first. Soon their professional paths diverged, but they never lost touch. Stan began to cover the labor movement; Abe went to the United Nations bureau and then abroad to India, Poland, and Japan. His was the kind of copy that leaped out at you from the page, simply bursting with color and emotion. You walked with him wherever he went. I saw other reporters who were going abroad studying his bulging clippings folders in despair, knowing they could never bring Calcutta or Lodz or Osaka alive the way Abe did. I read him too, and was awed. I did not meet him until 1963, when I discovered what a marvelous friend he could be. Stan had just quit the *Times* after nineteen years to go with CBS News in Washington. Abe was about to come back to New York as the new metropolitan editor, and the city room was crackling with excitement. One day shortly before our departure for Washington, a long letter came from Abe in Tokyo. It was overflowing with love and a sense of loss. He had looked forward to having us both as reporters in his city room. He felt as if a big chunk of capital had been suddenly withdrawn from his bank account. "I don't know Nan yet," he said, "but I can read." It was gracious and touching and beautifully written. Stan saved it for years.

We began to see Abe in New York and Washington. I had rarely witnessed this kind of friendship between two heterosexual men, one in which they openly expressed their closeness and trust.

In June 1970, while Stan and I were vacationing in Istanbul, my husband suffered a crippling heart attack. We spent three months in a Turkish hospital, five thousand miles from home. I lived in his room, sleeping on a cot at the foot of his bed. I learned enough Turkish to get by. It was impossible to reach friends and family in the United States through Istanbul's antiquated phone system. And so I sent important messages via telex to Abe Rosenthal, who instantly routed them on to Stan's son Bob, a reporter at *The Washington Post*. Abe moved heaven and earth to try to reach us by phone. Even the spectacularly resourceful operators at the *Times* could not do it. He had to fall back on telexes. I could almost feel his frustration and dread and affection throbbing over the wires. At last, Stan and I were airlifted by a military hospital plane to Germany. He suffered a setback there and was rushed to an Air Force hospital in Wiesbaden. I was able to call Abe. I told him that half of Stan's heart was gone, that he would never work again. I could hear Abe weeping. Within minutes he sent a telex. I taped it to the foot of Stan's bed. Ghost though he had become, it still made him smile with his old radiance. The cable said, "ANN [Abe's wife] AND I SEND LOVE EVERY HOUR ON

THE HOUR AND ALL THE MOMENTS IN BETWEEN." I cannot think of this without tears.

Stan died in Washington during open-heart surgery six months later. He was fifty-six.

During the dark years that followed, Abe was a staunch and sensitive friend. He sent me to Paris to join Flora Lewis. He encouraged us and expressed enormous pride in our work. He welcomed me with open arms when I returned, crestfallen, after several years in Paris to seek treatment for alcoholism and severe depression. In 1977, following eighteen months of sobriety, my grief and anger over Stan's terrible end had pushed to the surface, no longer smothered by drinking. I broke down completely. Instead of swallowing some alcohol or committing suicide, I took myself to the Payne-Whitney psychiatric clinic. Abe was one of the few friends who visited me there. He comforted me and assuaged my shame. A part of me will be grateful always.

We remained friends, but ideologically, we were miles apart. I was a feminist. I was a union maid. I was appalled by his increasingly tyrannical behavior. It was hurting people I loved and respected.

And as the women's suit rolled inexorably toward trial, I became hopping mad. One day in the summer of 1978, I told my friend Nora Sayre, "I'd like to sock Abe Rosenthal in the jaw."

Even Charlotte Curtis, disillusioned with Punch Sulzberger and the attitude of his executives, broke her public silence about the women's suit. "The women's charges against the paper are generally true," said the highest-ranking woman on it to Judith Coburn of *New Times* magazine. "There have been changes since the suit was filed [more women hired and promoted], but whether parity has been reached is another question. I eagerly await the trial to find out."

Ms. magazine said the approaching trial—in the context of sex-discrimination lawsuits and official complaints filed with the Equal Employment Opportunity Commission by the women of *Newsweek, Time, The Washington Post, Newsday, Reader's Digest,* the Associated Press, and NBC, to cite the most prominent cases in the press and broadcasting—"already promises to be the Title VII World Series."

John Leonard, one of only two male editors at *The New York Times* to give a deposition in favor of the women's suit (the other was John Van Doorn, who had been his deputy in the book review), had a darker outlook. If the trial came to pass, he said, it would be "nothing less than the single worst moment in the history of this newspaper."

Reputations, he was convinced, would be ruined on both sides. Beyond the protagonists, the paper many Americans admired above all others would be besmirched. John well remembered the trouble he had had when, as head of the book review back in the early seventies, he tried to hire a woman editor. One of the most creative thinkers and writers ever to work for the paper, he was deeply sympathetic to the women's movement. He was aghast when he came to the review to find that out of a dozen editors on his staff, only one was a woman—whom the others essentially ignored. He began interviewing prospects for two vacancies on the review, among them the novelist Toni Morrison.

When Daniel Schwarz, the Sunday editor, heard that Leonard was interviewing only women, he was not pleased. "He called me in," Leonard recalled, "and he said, and I quote him, 'You don't want to hire a woman. They can't take criticism and they cry a lot.' " Leonard retorted: "Dan, you've just gone through three heart attacks, one suicide, and two or three alcoholics who are killing themselves, and they have all been men on your staff." The charge was true. Schwarz muttered that the Sunday department was still in a hiring freeze.

···········

Katharine Darrow, one of the *Times* lawyers who was intimately involved with *Boylan* v. *The New York Times,* remembers the summer and early fall of 1978, preparing for the trial, as one of the worst periods of her life. "It was like going through hell," she said.

At first, her attitude about the women's lawsuit had been purely legalistic. In the early seventies, when the women brought their grievances as a group to Sulzberger, she was very young, very much a new lawyer. "The only question in my mind was: Can I defend the case if I believe the company has violated the law?" she said. "I felt there was a difference between violating the law and discrimination against women. I thought at the beginning that *The New York Times* had the better of the case."

But gradually, Kathy Darrow changed her mind.

"The more I was involved, the more I learned about the history, the more I knew about all sorts of discrimination occurring at the *Times*," she recalled. "My sympathy for the women as a class grew. I discovered there had been years and years of discrimination at the *Times*, always more than at other newspapers. There had been some amelioration on the news side. On the business side, the conscious, systematic discrimination was undeniable. Management wouldn't promote women, didn't want women around."

She felt no discrimination against herself. She was proud to work for the *Times*, and for James Goodale, who had hired her. "Jimmy trained me, he gave me opportunities, he taught me how to be a lawyer," she said years later, now elevated to a vice president's job at the paper. "I owe everything to him."

Katharine Prager Darrow was no stranger to discrimination. Her parents had fled Nazi Germany to Chicago, where she was born. In her teens she had become involved with Quaker groups in Philadelphia who were working to help the poor. At the University of Chicago she joined a law student civil rights research group and worked off-campus with black civil rights leaders. In 1965, the year Martin Luther King marched on Chicago, her firm defended many of the demonstrators. She was disillusioned by the complexity, the difficulty, of race relations. Her first marriage was collapsing. She moved to New York, worked briefly for the Legal Aid Society, and then entered the Columbia Law School to complete her studies. She helped found the *Columbia Civil Rights Review.* She was determined to do some public service legal work eventually. In the meantime, she decided, she would find out what corporate law was all about, "fully expecting," she said, "that corporate law was not what I was going to do."

So she went out to interview for a summer job in 1968 at "what seemed to be every law firm in New York City." She had ranked fifteenth in a law class of 150 at Chicago, about 10 percent of whom were women. Early on she had qualified for the *Law Review.* Nobody wanted her in New York. One interviewer, noting her civil rights record and her transfer from Chicago to Columbia, accused her of instability. Another offered her a job but retracted the offer after the interviewer found that his firm had already hired a woman for the summer. "I was in despair," she said. "The process was agonizing." Then Goodale and *The New York Times* took her in and changed the direction of her life.

Kathy Darrow came to the *Times* as a summer intern with a year still to go as a student at the Columbia Law School. "It was terrifically exciting," she remembered. "I was just a kid. A whole world opened up to me. I wasn't a New Yorker, so at first I didn't have a strong feeling about the *Times.*" By the end of that summer, however, after hobnobbing with management charmers such as Sydney Gruson and Michael Ryan, meeting the people behind the bylines in the newsroom, and becoming saturated with the history of the place, she was a *Times* groupie. "It was the most wonderful and important event of my life, other than having my children," she said.

Goodale put her on the permanent staff shortly after her graduation from law school. In the spring of 1971, she left *The New York Times* for London with her second husband. Goodale kept in touch by telephone. When the Women's Caucus surfaced, his calls increased; he pleaded with Darrow to rejoin the staff. She returned in the fall of 1973. The *Times* needed a woman lawyer on its team.

In 1976, at the age of thirty-three, Kathy Darrow was named assistant general counsel. She was two years younger than the chief opposition lawyer, Harriet Rabb. Harriet felt Kathy was the only lawyer on the other side who grasped every nuance of the women's case.

By August 1978, a vision of horror was rising before the eyes of all. "If the case comes to trial," Kathy thought, "it will be like the worst divorce that ever happened." Floyd Abrams, who would present the *Times*'s defense, was briefing the management, preparing for a six-week trial. The court date for *Boylan* v. *The New York Times* was set for early September.

"We knew that people were going to get up on that stand and say terrible things about each other in public," Darrow said. "Not until the very end were our guys really focusing on what would happen *after* the trial, after all these hideous stories were out in the open. Even taking the depositions, people cried, people were devastated, and there was nobody there but the lawyers to hear them."

"It will be more awful than a divorce," Kathy thought, "because the worst part of it is, these people who get divorced will then have to live with each other afterward. How are they going to work together? How are they going to look at each other? How will they get a newspaper out?"

And then, on August 10, 1978, a citywide strike and lockout hit all three New York general daily newspapers, including the *Times*. It would last for eighty-eight days and become the second-longest newspaper blackout in the city's history. Thus in darkness and public silence the women's suit against *The New York Times* entered its final stages. There would be no major newspaper open in New York to report the developments and their resolution.

Crossing the strikers' picket lines every morning into the nearly empty *Times* building were the members of management, including Kathy Darrow, Jim Goodale, Punch Sulzberger, and John Mortimer, the man in charge of labor relations.

Since 1972, Mortimer had spent more time negotiating with members of the Women's Caucus than had any other *Times* executive. He recalled in an interview that he felt particular respect for Betsy Wade and Joan Cook. Grace Glueck he did not know as well, but he found her authoritative and well-spoken. "Fantastic Grace," he called her. He saw the emotion in Betsy, the romantic idealism, the all-consuming commitment to the Cause. "Both she and Joan were serious and dedicated," he said. "They weren't about to settle for any baloney. They were strong, passionate advocates, but they weren't obnoxious about it. Joan was a little more tough-minded than Betsy, quicker to get down to cases. Betsy was always looking at the far horizons. I think they were soul mates in many ways."

But beginning with the 1978 newspaper strike, Mortimer was diverted altogether from the women's case. "I was completely engulfed in strike negotiations," he recalled. "I did nothing else. It was frantic." The lawyers were running things now.

With the discovery process and the deposition-taking behind them, the attorneys on both sides were meeting regularly all through August in the stage of litigation immediately before trial—preparing what is called a pretrial order. The objective of it is to focus the issues of the case, to have a clear sense of the points of agreement and disagreement, and to determine the bottom lines. "It's putting on your war paint and trying to settle the case all at once," Rabb explained. "It's like renovating your apartment and trying to sell it at the same time. It's crazy." By this time the atmosphere was poisonous.

Day after day the attorneys argued across tables, uptown at Rabb's offices, downtown at Cahill, Gordon. "If they were going to say something rotten about one of our women, we'd say something rotten about their men," Harriet Rabb recalled.

"We knew vile things, and they knew vile things. We'd wave papers with damning facts at each other. We had a vast pile of shared, accumulated knowledge—it would wreck not just individuals, men and women alike, but the *Times*. The stuff that bothered me the most was not just the private peccadillos or troubles, like who was a drunk or kept three women and a dog on the side for his pleasure. It was 'She's not good at her job,' or 'This guy is a perfect case of upward failure.' To strike at somebody's conception of his or her standards of professionalism is devastating. The thought of having it dragged to the light scared the socks off me. The lawyers on the other side would ask, 'Are you really prepared to do this?' Or we'd say, 'Is this what you are prepared to do to win?' We never answered each other."

Privately, Rabb was just as convinced as Darrow and Abrams and, ultimately, Jack Stanton that if it came to a trial, nobody would win. Jim Goodale held out for an airing in open court until almost the last moment. A dozen years later, he still remembered the day when he finally gave in, with "both Kathy Darrow and Jack screaming and yelling, saying it would be very painful for everybody involved." Their arguments about the expected damage to the paper and to individuals finally outweighed Goodale's determination to go to trial. He believes to this day that the *Times* was "fair to all its employees, including women."

By early September of 1978, Punch Sulzberger certainly wanted to settle, and he gave his approval eagerly. He would *not* get up on the stand and say these god-awful things about his employees. The trial date was postponed until later in the month, to give the lawyers time to haggle over terms.

Harriet Rabb, who said that the *Times* had been determined not to give the women "even a *peppercorn* in back pay," described what happened next: "A lawyer for the *Times* [probably Stanton, the paper's general attorney] called me and said that he had been authorized by his clients for the first time since the litigation started to *really* talk settlement. I asked if he was prepared to talk money. He was. The *Times* called it annuities because they didn't want to call it back pay." She added sarcastically, "If you call it a big yellow bus, it's a big yellow bus even if it looks a whole lot like a wristwatch."

The two sides met late one night soon thereafter in the Employment Rights Project's office at the Columbia Law School. There were four attorneys representing the *Times,* as well as Harriet and two of her colleagues. The *Times* lawyers requested two conditions: that as part of the settlement the lawsuit charging discrimination be withdrawn; and that there be no continuing court enforcement of the settlement terms.

Harriet said: "Why should we ever do that? Persuade me why we should do that. We filed suit in 1974; the women have been struggling and arguing with you since 1972. Why in the *world* should we withdraw this lawsuit?" To the second point, about court monitoring of the terms, she answered: "After all, you'll make reports to us about whether you're meeting the goals, and what will we do with the reports if you're not meeting the goals and the court isn't looking over your shoulder? Eat them?"

And then, said Rabb, "the *Times*'s general attorney looked me square in the eye and said, 'Harriet, you'll just have to trust us.'" "That is out of the question," Harriet replied icily.

It was an infuriatingly patronizing remark, but perhaps not quite so bad as one a *Reader's Digest* lawyer had made to her, Harriet thought. In 1977, when Rabb, representing the *Digest*'s women, suggested that the magazine's negotiators put a crucial point in writing, the *Digest* attorney intoned, "Sixty million Americans trust us. So can you." The *Digest,* like virtually every other publication and network sued for sex discrimination in that decade, settled with its women before going to trial.

One day toward the end of September, Harriet summoned the plaintiffs to her office. By then, the major terms that became the settlement were on the table: they included hiring and promotion goals and a $350,000 monetary package. "This is the best offer we are going to get from the *Times*," she told them. "I think we should settle." In addition, she said, Judge Werker was a conservative, and the tide in the courts was turning against cases like theirs—the burden of proof was being put more and more upon individual plaintiffs. Furthermore, the depositions of the *Times* management were hurtful to the reputations of some women at the *Times*.

Joan and Grace Glueck were reluctant. Can't we hold out a little longer? they asked. The back pay they're giving us is really very little. Can't we get something better? No, said Harriet. Grace found Rabb's presentation "intimidating." At last, she and Joan reluctantly voted for settlement. In Washington, Eileen Shanahan, the only plaintiff who could not attend the meeting in person, also voted for a settlement she found unsatisfactory.

There remained some specifics to be ironed out. In case negotiations broke down again, as was possible, the judge set yet another trial date, Friday, October 6, 1978, at 10:00 A.M. Still, it looked more and more as if the settlement terms would be announced on that day.

On the evening of Thursday, October 5, Eileen Shanahan flew up to New York from Washington to write a press release for the Women's Caucus. She met Betsy and Joan in Harriet's offices. "The mood was very like closing the college paper at 2:00 A.M. We told bum jokes and laughed a lot. My terrible doubts about the settlement were lost in the fun. I wanted to tell the world in that press release that even a great institution like *The New York Times* can discriminate against women. I wanted to say, 'Have no doubt that a lesser institution can do this too.'"

The next morning, the adversaries from the *Times* converged on the federal courthouse, a stone skyscraper sitting incongruously on a columned stone temple near New York's City Hall. There had been a settlement. A magistrate of the court would announce the terms, and the two sides would then comment upon it in separate news conferences within the courthouse.

The citywide newspaper blackout was almost two months old. A sprinkling of reporters and photographers from strike-born alternative newspapers, some magazine writers and out-of-town newspaper correspondents, and several television crews waited for them on the courthouse steps. Broadcasters thrust microphones under the chins of the women plaintiffs and the *Times*'s lawyers. Pictures were taken, sound bites recorded.

In one of the hearing rooms, U.S. Magistrate Sol Schreiber read off the fourteen pages of the final settlement terms to a standing-room audience.

Monetarily, the *Times* got off lightly.

The newspaper would pay a not-so-grand total of $350,000 to settle the lawsuit. The 550 women represented in the class action would be given $233,500 of this in back pay, which the *Times* still insisted on calling annuities, but which could be cashed at once. The most senior employees, those with twenty years' service or more, would be given the most money— $1,000 each—and the others would be paid on a sliding scale downwards. The sum of $15,000 would be divided among the named plaintiffs and other women who had testified in depositions. The sum of $1,500 would be used to defray the costs of the *Times* Women's Caucus in enforcing the court decree, which meant the women would be monitoring the *Times*'s compliance with the decree, including its reports to the court. The *Times* would pay $100,000 of the total of $350,000 to cover the plaintiffs' lawyers' fees and expenses. The fees were to be used by the Columbia Law School clinical programs to fund the training of law students, including those in the Employment Rights Project. Harriet Rabb and Howard Rubin got no money from the settlement.

In settling, the *Times* also agreed to a new affirmative action plan, promising to place significant numbers of women at every level in every news and business department. The plan would continue in effect under the court decree for four years, until the end of 1982. The management was directed to give the women's lawyers yearly reports of its progress. Magistrate Schreiber, about to retire from the bench, would serve without fee during that time as the court's monitor. The magistrate ended his reading of the terms by saying, "I think it would be a mistake if one reached a conclusion that there was a victory."

Both sides contradicted Schreiber the moment he left the scene. The plaintiffs and Rabb took up their posts in a narrow corridor nearby, handing out their press release and giving interviews.

Harriet Rabb called the new affirmative action plan unprecedented. "The unprecedented aspect of the affirmative action plan is the *Times*'s commitment to place women in one out of every eight of the top corporate positions during the four-year life of the settlement," she told the press. "I know that there has never been an affirmative action plan in the media, and I believe there has never been one in any other industry, which set goals for filling the top corporate offices."

The positions included those of publisher, president, and all the vice presidents. In the news and editorial departments, the goal was one woman for every four men in the top positions of executive editor, managing editor, the editors of the foreign, national, and metropolitan desks, the financial editor, the sports editor, the Washington bureau chief, and the editors of *The New York Times Magazine, The New York Times Book Review,* and "every major section of the newspaper." (Immediately after the settlement, the *Times* named LeAnne Schreiber as the sports editor.) The *Times* also promised women one out of four top jobs in the business departments, such as managers in the retail, classified, and national advertising departments—all of this by 1982.

Howard Rubin of the Columbia Employment Rights Project, who worked with Rabb from the beginning, had this comment: "I hope this settlement will lay to rest forever the ignorant, bigoted notion, asserted by one of *The New York Times*'s experts, that women, particularly those with families, are not really interested in attaining responsible, demanding jobs and are, therefore, less valuable employees."

As for the money, Harriet had this to say: "The fact is, the *Times* will pay, and the amount it will pay per plaintiff is comparable to or better than what has been achieved in other sex-discrimination cases in the media. The cash amounts in the *Reader's Digest* and NBC settlements were widely publicized, but the numbers of women involved in those cases were five to ten times larger than the number of women covered in the settlement at the *Times*."

This was so. A total of 5,635 women in the class-action lawsuit at the *Digest* got a whopping $1,375,000 in the settlement Rabb negotiated. However, divided among them, the money averaged out to $244 each. At NBC, 2,700 women got $540,000 in back pay, or an average of $200 apiece. In addition, NBC set aside $860,000 for a women's job-training program. The back pay the *Times* gave its women employees averaged $454.54 per person.

Still, the mathematics were disheartening. Marjorie Hunter of the Washington bureau, already smarting from the conviction that she was underpaid and underappreciated, exploded later to Eileen Shanahan: "Five hundred dollars! [She was in the fifteen-to-twenty-year category of seniority.] What the hell is that? What did we go through this for—for nothing?"

From the hour the settlement terms were announced, the *Times* management team maintained the pose they had assumed long before—that nothing whatever had been wrong. As soon as Magistrate Schreiber had departed the hearing room at the federal courthouse on October 6, James Goodale, by then an executive vice president of the Times Company, gave a press conference inside the room. Goodale and the *Times* could have been gracious on that day. They were not gracious. The whole tone of Goodale's statement on behalf of the newspaper was bellicose and mean-spirited, yielding not one single point.

Goodale began by saying: "We regard today's announcement as total vindication of The New York Times and as full refutation of the charges against us."

He went on: "Unlike most settlements of other women's class actions, this agreement does not require any new or retroactive salary increases, any unscheduled promotions, any major changes in the Company's ongoing affirmative action program, or any pledge to revoke discriminatory employment practices. No such actions were required at The Times because affirmative action and equal opportunity have been and are inflexible Times policy. The termination of this lawsuit is in distinct contrast to the multimillion-dollar agreements made by other companies in similar suits."

The *Times*'s lawyers also made sure that the following language was embedded high up in the final decree of settlement:

"The Times does not admit any discriminatory employment practices, past or present. . . . no findings of any kind have been issued by the Court. There has been no determination that The Times has violated any law, regulation, rule or order of the United States or any agency of the United States government with respect to discrimination in employment."

At the same time, the paper agreed to the new affirmative action plan and promised to carry it out. That day, I thought, the *Times*'s public utterances had boiled down to this: "We didn't do it, and we won't ever do it anymore."

While Goodale was still reading his statement, and after the plaintiffs and Rabb had given their own press conference in a courthouse corridor, Shanahan walked into the *Times*'s news conference. Goodale's statement made her boil over.

When he had finished, Eileen walked up to him. "He gave me a big hello," she recalled. "I had thought he was a good guy, a great libel lawyer, a First Amendment believer. He pushed us to the Supreme Court on our right to publish the Pentagon Papers in 1971. And here he was, with this lying statement. I didn't know whether to give him what-for about the lies right out there in public or to turn on my heel after a frosty response. I chose the frosty response." (Shanahan celebrated when Goodale left the *Times;* he quit in 1979 when a rival was made president of the company and Goodale felt there was nowhere left to go on the paper. He became a partner in Debevoise & Plimpton, a blue-chip New York law firm.)

⸺⸺⸺

During the four years that the court decree was in effect and the settlement was being monitored, the *Times*'s public stance and its private performance continued to be at odds.

In the paper's printed report of its 1978–79 annual meeting, the management, ever in a state of total denial and self-congratulation, told its stockholders: "A class action suit brought by a group of women employees of The Times was successfully terminated in 1978 with an agreement that called for no significant changes in the Company's continuing affirmative action program or employment practices. We were gratified by the magistrate's description of The Times's affirmative action program as one of the strongest in the country. We have endeavored to be leaders in this vital area, and we pledge to so continue."

Punch Sulzberger was quoted as saying, "We have made an enormous amount of progress not only with women but with all minorities."

By the early eighties, however, Emily Weiner, then head of the Women's Caucus, was calling the *Times*'s compliance with the court decree "woefully inadequate" in categories "dealing with influence and power." Finally, Margaret Hayden, Rabb's successor as the Caucus's attorney, wrote an irate letter to Magistrate Schreiber, complaining that the *Times* treated the goals listed in the decree as "meaningless hypothetical figures having no practical application."

Boylan v. *The New York Times* was the last Title VII discrimination case that Harriet Rabb ever took. She was drained. She would do no litigation at all for another three years.

Not one of the plaintiffs regretted becoming a plaintiff, even though not one thought it had helped her in her own career. But all thought the effort was for others, those who would come after.

About two years after the settlement, I experienced a moment when I wondered whether it had all been worthwhile. I was lunching in the *Times* cafeteria with a young woman reporter from the business and financial section. She had come to the paper the year the women's suit was settled. "There is no sex discrimination at the *Times,*" she declared to me in 1980. "I got here on my own merits and I'm going to get ahead on my own merits." She had no notion of what the women who came before her had done that made it possible for her to get a job in a section of the newspaper that had been virtually closed to women of my generation. Eileen Shanahan, of course, was a notable exception—and she *was* an exception.

I said to myself, "Is it for this that we laid our careers on the line? Is it for this that we struggled for six long years? This kid doesn't even remember there was a lawsuit."

I did not realize how much the Women's Caucus had accomplished until 1988. Ten years to the month after the suit was settled, several generations of *Times* women gathered together to tot up the pluses and the minuses and tell their stories in a union hall just down the street from the building where it all began.

Only then did I see that although a few women had had to pay dearly for their leading roles in the Caucus, many more had benefited greatly from the suit against the paper. I saw, too, that what we were celebrating at that reunion was nothing less than the single most important collective event in the history of women at *The New York Times.*

CHAPTER 11

THE UNION HALL

The intersection of Forty-third Street and Eighth Avenue in the Times Square neighborhood is one of the sleaziest crossroads in America, a living nightmare inhabited by teen whores, pimps, drag queens, drunks, addicts, homeless women in the final stages of decay, and violent men bent on sack and pillage at the very least. Live peepshows and filthy moving pictures alternate with crumbling tenements, and every vice in the world is up for hire. Tunnel vision alone can get the passerby through it unscathed. There are only two decent places in view. On Forty-third, half a block to the east, looms the *New York Times* building, crowned by its chateau-like tower. Just yards to the west of Eighth Avenue is the Martin Luther King Labor Center, known to all simply as 1199. The building that houses Dr. King's favorite union, Local 1199 of the Drug, Hospital, and Health Care Employees, is nondescript except for the brilliant mosaic-tile strip that stretches across its entire front. The style is pure Socialist Realism, the work of a WPA artist of the 1930s, Anton Refregier, in bold primary colors that practically bounce into the street. The mosaic depicts white-uniformed nurses and orderlies bending over a patient on a gurney, a laboratory worker pouring liquid into a retort, earnest children perusing books and examining a globe of the world, happy picnickers, singers, a guitar player, and two huge hands, one black, one tan, holding a message from Frederick Douglass: "If there is no struggle there can be no progress."

On Tuesday evening, October 18, 1988, the pitch and decibel levels were many notches above normal in the ground-floor art gallery of 1199, as about a hundred and fifty women packed into the room, occupying every chair and standing shoulder to shoulder along the walls. There were screams of recognition, hugs, and laughter. Betsy Wade and Joan Cook stood grinning at a table near the door, hawking ten-dollar white-on-black T-shirts that said "Free *The New York Times.*"

Ten years to the month had gone by since the *Times* and the Women's Caucus had settled a sex-discrimination lawsuit against the paper on the very day it was due to go to trial. Now, several generations of *Times* women were gathering to remember that unique communal effort—and to count up the gains and the losses of a decade.

Six of the seven named plaintiffs, who had sued on behalf of all the women at the *Times,* were there. The missing plaintiff was Louise Carini, the deeply religious accountant who had prayed for courage as the legal process dragged on through the 1970s. Louise, who had retired in 1986 after thirty-five years with the paper, was vacationing in New Orleans. Eileen Shanahan had come up from Washington, as she had so many years before for the first meeting of the Women's Caucus with the management in the dauntingly august Board Room of *The*

New York Times. After leaving the *Times* in 1977 and her stint as press spokesman for the Health, Education, and Welfare Department in President Jimmy Carter's administration, she had gone on to *The Washington Star* and then to the Pittsburgh *Post-Gazette* as an assistant managing editor. She had returned to Washington to become the founding editor of *Governing,* a handsome monthly magazine covering state and local governments, published by *Congressional Quarterly.*

Betsy Wade Boylan, the chief named plaintiff in *Boylan* v. *The New York Times,* was writing a weekly column called "The Practical Traveler" for the Sunday *Times* travel section; she had been moved to that quiet backwater after an extraordinarily distinguished but ultimately aborted upward trajectory in the news editors' ranks. Few doubted that her vigorous leadership in the lawsuit had derailed her career. Joan Cook was grinding out small stories and unimportant obituaries on day rewrite, the Bermuda Triangle of city room assignments. Grace Glueck was holding steady as an art news reporter on the culture staff. Nancy Davis had left her dead-end *Times* job as a telephone classified-advertising soliciter in 1976, after only four years on the paper, and was advertising director of *Music & Sound Retailer* magazine. Andrea Skinner was still in a news clerk's job in the Sunday magazine's fashion department, with the title of children's fashion editor and periodic bylined stories and picture spreads on children's styles. Harriet Rabb, the lawyer who had fought the women's case from beginning to end, in 1988 the assistant dean of the Columbia University Law School, was also in the room at 1199 that October night.

The three principal bêtes noires of the Women's Caucus were gone. Charlotte Curtis had died of cancer at the age of fifty-eight in 1987. Her final years at *The New York Times* were described by some of those who knew her well as sad and isolated. In 1974 she had been elevated to the post of editor of the Op-Ed page, but the higher she went in rank, the less clout she seemed to wield. More than one member of the editorial board thought she was over her head as Op-Ed's editor, dealing with topics and people far weightier than she was used to covering. By the time she got her own weekly column at her request and went back to writing, the Curtis zing and bite had vanished and the column was buried in obscure nooks of the newspaper. When Anna Quindlen was appointed deputy metropolitan editor in 1983, the first woman ever to get that job, Charlotte told her: "You will only ever have as much power as they wish you to have. Don't fool yourself as to what this promotion means. Do the best you can do for yourself and other women, and don't blame yourself if that turns out not to be enough." Anna called the advice a mitzvah—a gift—but she did not seem to hear the melancholy overtones.

Ada Louise Huxtable, by contrast, went triumphantly into the sunset with a MacArthur Foundation "genius award" in 1981. She left the paper to enjoy a tax-free quarter of a million dollars spread over the next five years; she wrote and consulted and served on prestigious boards and architecture juries. In 1990, aged sixty-nine, she was elected to the fifty-member American Academy of Arts and Letters, one of the most important honors in the arts.

Abe Rosenthal stepped down as executive editor at the age of sixty-four in 1986. He began to write a column on the Op-Ed page called "On My Mind," which was instantly dubbed "Out of My Mind" by his still-smarting former news staff.

At the Caucus's tenth-anniversary reunion in 1988 there were women who had never met the lawsuit's plaintiffs. They knew why they were there, however, and because of whom. The plaintiffs' stalled careers at the *Times* were in distinct contrast to those of the women who came after them. The nineteen speakers of the evening included the national editor of *The New York Times,* the Sunday business editor, the picture editor, a member of the editorial board, a columnist and former deputy metropolitan editor, the reporter covering the

Supreme Court of the United States, and several managers from the business side of the newspaper.

Half of the speakers had been hired after the Women's Caucus filed suit against the *Times* in 1974, jolting the management into taking more women on its staff, and most had joined the paper in or after the year the suit was settled. The "Class of '78" members present at the tenth anniversary included the Caucus's young president, Emily Weiner, thin, dark, and intense, the first woman hired in the map department; Carolyn Lee, sprung from generations of Tennessee farmers, the first woman picture editor of the raucously male photo department; Karen Arenson, the Sunday business editor, who followed Soma Golden and Marylin Bender in that job; and Leslie Bennetts, a talented and prolific cultural news reporter who had left the paper midway through 1988 to write for *Vanity Fair* magazine. Anna Quindlen, a superb writer, had been hired in 1977 at the age of twenty-four as a city room reporter. By then, the suit seemed certain to be heading for a trial that would ruin the newspaper's public image as a benign and liberal institution, as well as tarnish the reputations of some women working there.

Quindlen—who had risen quickly, becoming "About New York" columnist and then deputy Metropolitan Editor—made it clear from the beginning of her remarks that had it not been for Betsy Wade and Grace Glueck and Eileen Shanahan and Joan Cook, she could never have gone as far as she did. She talked about how lonely it was in a man's world there in the upper ranks of the *Times,* with only Carolyn Lee for female company beside her at the page one meetings every afternoon. (Soma Golden, the national editor since 1987, often absented herself and sent her male deputy.)

"[Carolyn and I] habitually sat together, on one side of the desk; so habitually that sometimes copy people would come in and drop [Carolyn's] pictures in front of me because, as you know, we all look alike!" said Anna with a grin. "And Seymour Topping [then managing editor] leaned across and said to us, in a very friendly fashion, 'Ladies, the two of you don't always have to sit together.' And Carolyn said, 'Why not? You guys always do' [*laughter*]." Anna went on, "In the perpetual game of 'whose is bigger' I always lost [*more laughter*] until the ninth month, when I was able to say, 'Mine is alive!' (That night in 1988, Anna was eight months pregnant with her third child.)

Anna told the audience that the dearth of women in the *Times*'s highest posts made it obligatory for her, as a woman in power, to practice "reverse discrimination" if necessary to encourage women's careers. One of her finds was Isabel Wilkerson, a black reporter who became the *Times*'s Chicago bureau chief. Another was Maureen Dowd, whose résumé and clippings had languished in a huge pile of applications until Quindlen plucked them out and told her peers, "This woman writes better than anybody on the paper!" and Dowd was hired. She proved Anna right, going on to become the *Times*'s first female chief correspondent at the White House. In speaking of her second imperative, Quindlen paraphrased the great maxim that those who cannot remember the past are condemned to repeat it.

"I do not want to repeat what Betsy went through, or what Joan went through or what Grace went through, for anything," she said. "The fact is that in some ways . . . we are different and in some ways, which we all know and understand, we are better. We ought to use those ways in which we are better to help make that newsroom a better place. There are plenty of the boys there to do the things that boys do, but in those rare cases when there are women in positions of power, they have a moral obligation to not only help other women, but to foster some of the special qualities which make us do an exemplary job as executives. . . . Tonight, I just want to say thank you. I want to say thank you not to Abe Rosenthal, not to Max Frankel, but to a small, devoted cadre of women—and I'm not sure I would have had the guts to be one of them—who made it possible for me to have eleven very good years at *The New York Times.*"

The story that Leslie Bennetts told her audience that night about her decade on the *Times* began badly and ended worse, with years of achievement in between. She had been a star of the first magnitude on the *Philadelphia Bulletin* when Abe Rosenthal hired her in 1978 at the age of twenty-eight. Leslie began her remarks by describing an encounter with Seymour Hersh, one of the world's greatest investigative reporters. He had won the Pulitzer Prize before he joined the *Times* by exposing the 1968 massacre by American soldiers of unarmed old men, women, and children in the South Vietnamese village of My Lai. Rosenthal introduced the two in his office the day that Leslie was hired. A fortnight later, on one of her first days on the job, she and Hersh found themselves in the same elevator. Leslie said hello. He gave her a curt nod. They rode up in total silence. She was shy and admiring in the presence of this peerless investigator and couldn't think of anything to say. The elevator doors opened; Hersh started to leave.

"And then," Leslie recounted, "he turned to me and said in the angriest tone of voice, 'You know perfectly well you never would have been hired if it hadn't been for the women's suit, don't you!' And then he got out of the elevator and the elevator doors closed behind him." She was stunned by his vehemence, particularly since Hersh had never seen any of her work and was in no position to judge it.

That was Sy Hersh. I must be fair to him: I sat near him for months in the Washington bureau while he threatened and cozened and cajoled his sources over the phone, and I am here to say that Hersh was impartial in his treatment of the sexes— he was frequently and brutally rude to both. I well remember what he said to me when it was announced that I was being sent to the Paris bureau early in 1973 to join Flora Lewis as her number two. I was ecstatic, and so were all my women friends. I did not know Flora, but as Rosenthal would say, I could read. Sy rushed to my desk that day and said loudly and without preliminaries: "Flora's a bitch and she'll cut you off at the knees!" I was staggered and hurt, and then I gave him the tongue-lashing he so well deserved.

Leslie Bennetts is a total professional. On the *Times* she was fast, productive, a tough reporter and elegant writer who had an impact on the style page, the national staff, and finally as a reporter in cultural news. She told the women at the tenth-anniversary celebration: "Over the years it did seem to me that discrimination, in its many forms at the *Times,* became a lot less overt. Certainly a lot of men became a lot more used to working with women on a daily basis."

In the spring of 1987, something happened that embittered Leslie permanently. She was then a general assignment reporter in culture news, with a focus on theater; she was living with Jeremy Gerard, a former drama critic on *Newsday* who had come to the *Times* as the drama reporter. "We were talking about marriage," she told her audience in the union hall, "and not surprisingly, the subject of salaries came up. At the time, I had been . . . a daily newspaper reporter for fifteen years. He had been a daily newspaper reporter for five years. I had been at the *Times* for almost ten years; he had been at the *Times* for less than one year. Imagine my surprise when I learned that . . . he was earning $11,000 more a year for doing the same job that I was."

Leslie hit the ceiling. She began a series of frustrating conversations with the culture editor, William Honan. Finally, after six months, Honan called her in to announce, "as if he were bestowing the queen's diamonds on me," that she was receiving a merit raise—her first—of $3,500 a year. Bennetts responded: "This is great, except by my calculations this still leaves me $7,500 behind [Jeremy], and . . . since I've been here for ten years, if I'm $11,000 behind the guys, that's $110,000 that you owe me." According to Leslie, Honan "then made it very clear that he was grievously disappointed in me for not getting down on my hands and knees and being properly grateful."

She went to several senior editors and was told that was all they could do for her in one calendar year. Notes Leslie took at the time showed that Warren Hoge, then the assistant managing editor for news personnel, told her, "Even if discrimination exists, there exists no mechanism to remedy it."

In 1988, Bennetts took up the cudgels again. "It's a new calendar year. I think you should give me a new raise," she told her editors. She asked again why she should be paid less than her male counterparts, particularly those not as experienced as she. This went on for six more months. She called the new round of talks "unpleasant." They led nowhere. And then Tina Brown, editor of *Vanity Fair* magazine, came along to offer Leslie "a great deal more money and a great deal more freedom" to write major articles on a variety of subjects. Leslie's last day at *The New York Times* was Friday, July 29, 1988, the day she and Jeremy Gerard were married.

If Leslie's tale was a dark one, Roberta Weinberger bore bright tidings to the anniversary celebration from the business side of the *Times*. Roberta, a manager in the advertising department, was a veteran of the paper and of the Women's Caucus. She had come to the *Times* at the age of thirty-four in 1968 as a classified-ad taker in the big room on the sixth floor then called the "Gestapo kindergarten." The women who labored there, plugged into telephone headsets the live-long day, had to raise their hands for permission before going to the bathroom. They could not bring food to their desks. If they had names that were considered "too ethnic"—like Weinberger, for instance—they were given names with a WASP flavor, the theory being that advertisers didn't want to give their money to Jews, or the Irish, or Italians. For years, Roberta Weinberger was Roberta Jeffries. All that had changed in twenty years.

Roberta told the reunion audience that the progress achieved on the business side showed in the numbers and placement of women: In 1968, of 67 managers in advertising, 2 were women, or about 3 percent. In 1988, of 103 managers,

37 were women, or 36 percent. In 1968, women formed 2 percent of the outside sales staff, with its superior salaries, perks, and commissions; in 1988, women filled 50 percent of the 150 outside sales jobs. "Those numbers," Roberta said, "show just how far we have come and what our efforts have been." The *Times,* she said, at least on the advertising side, had not only carried out the letter of the law but had enthusiastically embraced its spirit.

Sharon Yakata, a tiny, effervescent young woman, one of the new generation of leaders in the Caucus, had a similar story to tell about the circulation department. Sharon, who was hired in 1976 and went to circulation three years later, was the circulation sales development manager in 1988. She described the circulation department as it was when she joined it: "a very blue-collar, male-dominated area . . . there was one woman who was a manager. One sole woman, and I was hoping she'd be here tonight. She had been a manager in that department for twenty years, alone, and nine years later, today, there are now fifteen women who are managers in the circulation department. One of the five directors is a woman, and women represent about 25 percent of all the managers in that area. Now these, I think, are tremendous changes over a relatively short period." They had occurred everywhere on the business side, she said, with more and more women visible at all levels.

"You might ask," said Sharon, "if the progress has been so terrific, what do we need a women's group for?"

She answered her own question. Women need networks as much as men do; they need a support group such as the Women's Caucus to define and push for their goals: promotions, equal salaries, child care, flextime, elderly parent care. Just as important, she said, was her view of a women's group "as a teaching arm of the company, an army of employees to retrain colleagues and managers with more traditional, archaic attitudes about the role of women in the company. I know that sounds a little preachy, but I just really do feel that so many of the prejudices that exist are rather subtle. It's hard to get around those things, and I think it requires all of us, in gentle ways, to retrain our bosses and colleagues to think differently about women."

Sharon said she really believed that *The New York Times* was a different company from what it had been fourteen years before, when the Women's Caucus filed its suit. Male managers were more comfortable and secure working with women, "unintimidated by their presence in the workplace and in positions of power." She concluded, "I think we can thank the women who were courageous enough to file the suit in the first place."

The tenth-anniversary reunion lasted three hours, with speaker after speaker bouncing up to the podium to tell her tale. There were horror stories and there were stories of triumph. The empathy of the audience mounted to such a peak that when E. R. Shipp got up to say she was reminded of the fervid testifying at a Baptist revival meeting, the applause almost drowned her out. Shipp had been hired in 1980, the year the *Times* settled with the minorities that were also suing the newspaper. She was moved to confess that she had felt less discriminated against as a woman at the *Times* than as part of a black minority keenly aware of the "limitations that are still set for blacks and other racial minorities" there. She mourned the lack of contact between blacks and whites, and added: "I think we should pool our resources."

"A lot of the things I'm hearing [tonight] are new," she said, "which is also saying . . . that we haven't done a good enough job of communicating the history to those who have come after the lawsuits."

It was Grace Glueck who had led off the evening by speaking about the origins and early years of the Women's Caucus—aiming her comments particularly at the younger women, such as E.R., who had only a shadowy notion of what had happened in the 1970s.

Only two other plaintiffs spoke: Nancy Davis, who described the "classic female ghetto" of classified advertising as she knew it in the early 1970s, and Eileen Shanahan, who joyously urged those present to "sue the bastards again!," which provoked laughter and clapping.

When she came up from Washington, Eileen said, she knew she was going to see old friends and find out how they were doing, and meet some younger women she knew by their bylines alone. What she did not expect was that she would be thrilled. "I am thrilled to hear women stand up here and say, 'I'm good, I'm the best. I was the best-qualified person for that job and I still am and I'm not grateful that they gave me the job; I deserved it!' I have to tell you that that is the most tremendous difference."

Shanahan commented that the women of our generation were flattered when men said to us, "You think like a man." Eileen said it took Gladys Spellman, a Maryland county commissioner who was later elected to Congress, to show her the error of her ways. Eileen heard Spellman recount that, at one of her speaking engagements, a man on the platform said, "Gladys, you think like a man." Spellman replied for all to hear: "I know, I'm not myself today; I'll be better tomorrow." Shanahan's retelling of the story brought down the house.

Geneva Overholser—who had come to the *Times* editorial board from the *Des Moines Register* in Iowa and then returned after two and a half years as the *Register*'s editor—had this to say: "For people like me, who were practicing journalism in the hinterlands back in the days of this suit, names like Betsy Wade and Eileen Shanahan were heroes' names. And not only did this suit make people know that great institutions like the *Times* can discriminate, but [it showed] that people with gumption could do something about it."

Another speaker that night was Carolyn Lee, the picture editor. Within a little more than a year she would be named the first woman assistant managing editor in the history of *The New York Times*. She would also be uniquely positioned to shape the future of women—and of minorities—at the newspaper, for as of January 1, 1990, Carolyn would be in charge of personnel for the entire editorial staff, one thousand strong, with a budget of $100 million and the power to hire from outside or promote or transfer within.

That October night at 1199, Carolyn spoke the longest of anyone. She was then forty-three years old, and she had already turned in superior performances on the national desk, on the central news desk, called the bullpen, and in the photo department, where she not only changed the Joe Six-Pack image of the place by bringing more women photographers and editors into it, but became a hero to the men and women of her staff because she fought for them always.

Lee dwelt at length on her experiences of discrimination in the newspaper business *before* she got to the *Times,* as if to remind her listeners that women everywhere had to struggle to get ahead. She introduced herself in her soft Southern voice as "another of those who, without incurring any risk at all, benefited from the courage and character of those women who filed suit against *The New York Times.*" She had come to the paper the year the suit was settled.

Like many of the women she spoke to, Carolyn had run into discrimination on her first job, at the Houston *Post.* In her initial eighteen months there, she had handled every job from copy editor to assistant news editor, laying out the format of the inside of the paper and being responsible for the production of those pages. She discovered shortly after she had recruited a man fresh out of the University of Missouri journalism school that he was making twenty dollars a week more than she was.

She complained to her bosses. She had been working very hard at a variety of demanding tasks. The answer she got was "Money is not a measure of what we think of your work." Carolyn was greeted by a wave of understanding laughter.

The assistant managing editor told her that he suspected she had become unhappy in her job. Tell me about it, he said. Tell me what's wrong. She spent about forty-five minutes complying with his request: This person's in the wrong job. We could do this. We're not realizing our potential for this other thing. She concluded, "There's so much we could do—I want to do great things for this newspaper."

The assistant managing editor of the Houston *Post* weighed her suggestions in silence. Then he said, "You know, Carolyn, you ought to have an affair."

Soon thereafter she went to the *Courier-Journal* in Louisville, Kentucky. She ultimately became the news editor. The man who had been passed over for the job Carolyn got, and who made her life "miserable" during the entire time she was there, she said, made between twenty dollars and forty dollars a week more than Carolyn did during her seven years on that newspaper.

When she decided to leave for the *Times,* after the *Times* had wooed her for two years, the *Courier-Journal*'s assistant managing editor remarked: "Well, Carolyn, I don't know why you're doing this. You know the only reason they want to hire you is because you're a woman."

"Well, I don't care," she replied. "I can do the job. It doesn't matter why they're hiring me. They'll find out they've hired someone who can do the job."

"I'd *like* to say," Carolyn told the women at the tenth-anniversary reunion, "that that remark about 'they're only hiring you because you're a woman' was the last time I had to think about equal or unequal opportunities for women. Certainly it was not."

For a long time, she said, she had put away those thoughts in a mental closet. Suddenly, when she was asked to speak, some memories surfaced and she became angry all over again. She remembered the male editor with credentials identical to hers who was hired at a substantially bigger salary than she was making after two years on the *Times.* She remembered the raises she had asked for that had been denied. She remembered the colleagues who told her, when she was promoted to the central news desk, that the only reason she had been promoted was that Barbara Crossette had just vacated the post, having been sent abroad, and that it was the "women's slot" in the bullpen—"a slot they fondly called 'the cow pen,'" Carolyn recalled. "I thought I was the person best qualified for that job, and I still think so."

Shortly before the Caucus's tenth-anniversary celebration was announced, Carolyn was asked, "Do you mind if we put your name on the program of speakers?" The approach was so timid, she said, that it was a measure of how far women had *not* come at *The New York Times*. "Support groups are wonderful," she said. "We all need a sympathetic ear, we all need a matching anecdote from time to time, just so we know we aren't alone in fighting this battle." She urged the members in her audience to apply for job openings: "You might not get the job this time, but you're somebody who'll be thought of the next time a job opening comes around. Unless we make these efforts for one another and for our- selves, the fact is . . . that white men will go on choosing white men to run the newspaper. They're very comfortable with white men. Or sometimes worse, they will say to them- selves self-consciously, 'We have to have a woman'—or a black or whatever—and they will as likely as not choose the wrong person because they've not gotten to know that many women, that many blacks. . . . unfortunately, when one woman fails, all women are set back. When a white man fails, it's just an aberration."

At times, Carolyn said, she got to feeling very low. She did not want to become like those women whom all of us had encountered, women at the end of their careers, who were very bitter and could "only talk about how they were held back because they were women. I don't doubt that they were held back, or that I was held back at times and might be yet again because I'm a woman," Carolyn said. What she hoped for, she said, was that at the end of *her* career, she would be able to count the gains that she had made, not just for herself but, much more important, for other women.

That was the lesson the Women's Caucus had taught Carolyn Lee.

CHAPTER 12

PROMISES

In December 1990, Arthur Ochs Sulzberger Jr. sat in his Art Deco office on the eleventh floor of the *Times.* It was twelve years after the sex-discrimination suit against his family's newspaper had been settled. He began a conversation by saying he had never known firsthand what it had been like for women in the past at the *Times.* He wanted to talk about what he hoped it would be like for them in the future. He would soon have the power to shape that future. He is Punch Sulzberger's namesake, his only son, and the next publisher of *The New York Times.*

At the time, he was thirty-nine years old but appeared much younger. He has the family's appealing good looks in abundance, with wide-set eyes circled by fashionable oversized glasses, delicate bones, and a head covered in thick, dark curls.

He is immaculately turned out; clothes sit well on his slender frame. Unlike his father, he is tough and sharp and has no time for fools and shows it. He is bright, witty, very fast at the verbal footwork, sometimes indiscreet, a leg-puller and a wise-cracker, and, according to almost everybody who has dealt closely with him, committed to the cause of women and minorities at the paper his family has owned since 1896.

The staff often refers to him as young Arthur. Just as often, because he is the sprout of Punch, the employees call him Pinch behind his back. Unlike Punch, who was thrown into the deep end of the pool in 1963 when he was abruptly made publisher after years of wandering about with few responsibilities, young Arthur was long and carefully groomed for the job. In effect, he asked for it when he was still a boy.

He is the son of Barbara Grant, Punch's first wife; they were divorced in 1956 after a troubled marriage that lasted eight years. Punch remarried soon thereafter, and so did Barbara, and both had children with their second spouses. Barbara had custody of Arthur and his sister Karen. Sometime in the mid-sixties, between his thirteenth and fourteenth birthdays, he went to his mother and told her lovingly but firmly, "Mom, I have to live with Dad; I want to get to know my dad." She assented. It was a decision that fixed his professional future forever. After graduation from Tufts University in Medford, Massachusetts, where he was an indifferent student and took a degree in political science, he became a reporter on the Raleigh *Times* in North Carolina. "You don't learn journalism at the [New York] *Times* if your name is Sulzberger," he said.

During one of his visits to Topeka, Kansas, where his mother had moved with her third husband, Barbara introduced him to the girl who lived across the street, Gail Gregg. They were married in 1975 in the backyard of her parents' house. Gail, a graduate of Kansas State University, had been on the journalism track all through high school and college. While Arthur was on the Raleigh *Times,* Gail earned a master's degree in journalism at the University of North Carolina, reported for the Associated Press, and ran a weekly newspaper. When the two went to London, Arthur worked for the A.P. and Gail for its competition, United Press International. In 1978, Arthur finally joined the reporting staff of the *New York Times* bureau in Washington. The other bureau members, to their surprise, liked and respected the boss's son. Gail continued to work for U.P.I., then went to *Congressional Quarterly*. In 1981, the pair moved to New York, where Arthur was a *Times* reporter and assistant city editor. In 1982, he left the newsroom—reluctantly at first—to work on the business side as an advertising salesman, followed by a stint in production and corporate planning and a three-month cram course at the Harvard Business School.

In April 1988, Punch put his son on the masthead as deputy publisher. Gail—after years as a free-lance writer and a term as a prestigious Bagehot Fellow in economic reporting at Columbia University—switched careers completely. In the early eighties she began to study art and went on to become a professional painter. There are two children, Arthur Gregg, born in 1980, and Ann Alden, born in 1982. The parents refused to name their son Arthur Ochs Sulzberger III: that seemed a little too dynastic, and besides, young Arthur hated the "Junior" after his own name. Nobody ever called him Junior.

Gail considers herself a feminist, "in theory if not invariably in practice." Her husband considers himself a feminist as well. He is an ardent fan of the writer Marilyn French and keeps in his desk a typed page of excerpts from her book *Beyond Power*. One of his favorite quotes deals with how men often engage not in a dialogue with women but rather in "a monologue with an echo."

About a year after Punch made young Arthur his deputy, the son began to gather groups of middle and senior management people together to hear what was called The Speech. Some in his audiences were upset by what they heard.

There was one statistic he gave them that he believed would have more impact on the future of *The New York Times* than any other: The U.S. Census had projected that by the end of the nineties, 80 percent of all new American employees would be women, minorities, or first-generation immigrants. That did not give the male, white *New York Times* much time to get its house in order. He said the company was not adequately prepared to deal with the changes that were certain to come.

He told his managers that the *Times* had to treat its own people as well as it tried to treat its public—to be fair, honest, open, and responsive. Too often, young Arthur said, the newspaper forced its employees to choose between their home life and their work life, rather than creating a balance between the two. The fundamental questions of parental leave, child care, and flexible scheduling, affecting mainly women, had to be addressed.

He said that the *Times*'s commitment to integrating women and minorities into the highest levels of management went to the very heart of what the newspaper stood for. He warned that managers would be judged more and more on the effectiveness with which they hired and encouraged a diverse work force. Finally, young Arthur put his listeners on notice that all of them, like himself, must reject what he called the "comfort factor" of promoting only white men, and must commit themselves to risk.

That is what he promised. It is one measure of the man who will run *The New York Times* in the years to come.

During my interview with him in 1990, young Arthur was eager to show how women's salaries were catching up with men's. He flipped through sheets of statistics, pointing out that new employees on every level—those hired within the last five years—were benefiting most.

In 1987 the average salary of men in the news division hired within the previous five years was $13,000 higher than the average salary of women hired during the same period; in 1990 there was no gap between the average starting salary of men and that of women in the division. In 1987 men in the business division with six to ten years of experience earned, on average, $25,000 more than women with the same experience. In 1990 the gap between the average starting salaries of men and women had narrowed to $7,000, and, young Arthur said, progress in this direction would continue until there was parity. It was the long-term women workers, those with twenty-one or more years of experience on the *Times,* who would never make as much as the men with equal seniority. One reason was that until very recently, women simply had not been given the chance to rise into the better-paid ranks of middle management, let alone the higher levels.

It gets Anna Quindlen's goat. On New Year's Day, 1990, at the age of thirty-seven, she became only the third woman to have a regular column on the Op-Ed page of the *Times.* But, she said, "every time guys like Max Frankel [the executive editor, who succeeded Abe Rosenthal in 1986] talk about the status of women, they should repeat four words: 'Look at the masthead. Look at the masthead.' "

The masthead, at the top of the editorial page, tells people where the real power lies within *The New York Times.* On the highest line is the name of the publisher, and just below is that of his son, and then there is a space, followed by sixteen names. By early 1991, only two women were listed there.

From the business side of the paper, there was Elise Ross, the senior vice president for systems, who runs the giant computers that run the newspaper. She is the only woman among the six vice presidents, who report directly to Lance Primis, the newspaper's president. (Primis has enlightened ideas about women and has done much to help them; he did not, however, hire Elise, a technical whizbang who came to the *Times* long before Primis became president in 1988.)

From the news side of the *Times,* there was Carolyn Lee, who began her job as the assistant managing editor for administration in 1990, on the same day that Anna Quindlen first appeared on the Op-Ed page. The two women are close. It is

Carolyn—one of five assistant managing editors who report directly to Frankel, and the highest-ranking woman in the history of the news staff—who has the power to hire and encourage women and minorities in the ranks of reporters, photographers, and editors. She is using that power. She also possesses a rare gift: she speaks up, she speaks her mind, but with such grace and good humor that almost nobody takes offense.

The important women managers in the news division but *not* on the masthead in the winter of 1991 were the editor of the national desk, Soma Golden; the editor of the Sunday book review, Rebecca Sinkler; and the editor of the Sunday arts and leisure section, Constance Rosenblum. Nancy Newhouse was the Sunday travel editor, Angela Dodson the editor of the style department (traditionally a woman's post). Laurie Mifflin, a former deputy sports editor, was the education editor. Women were deputy editors on the Sunday magazine and in the business, science, photo, and graphic art departments. Four of the fifteen members of the editorial board early in 1991 were women: Diane Camper, who is black; Mary Cantwell; Joyce Purnick, formerly an excellent City Hall reporter, who is Frankel's second wife; and Dorothy Samuels.

The *Times* was certainly doing better by its women in 1990. The women knew that it was not yet nearly good enough.

Nancy Newhouse, who came to the paper in 1977 as editor of the new home section and became editor of the style department and then of the Sunday travel section in 1989, suggested laughingly, when I told her that I was writing a book about the women of the *Times,* that it be titled *The Kingdom of the Powerless*—a play on *The Kingdom and the Power* by Gay Talese, published in 1969. Gay's subtitle was *The Story of the Men Who Influence the Institution That Influences the World.* That was fitting, since Talese virtually ignored the women employees of the newspaper—with the notable exception of Charlotte Curtis, then in her heyday; and of Patricia Riffe, Clifton Daniel's secretary, whose beauty he chose to comment upon, as well as "that nice hip motion she has when she walks."

Newhouse is just one of an outspoken group of women managers hired in the late seventies or eighties who acknowledge that they were beneficiaries of the women's lawsuit but believe that many male executives remain unliberated. This group broke through the "glass ceiling" only to find what one called the "interruption factor."

One day Nancy Newhouse was talking to David Jones, for fifteen years the national news editor and the first of his rank to hire significant numbers of women to edit copy on his desk. During their conversation, the interruption factor took hold of Dave. Nancy stopped him in his tracks. "You're not hearing what I'm saying," she told Jones. "You're reacting before I finish my thought."

"That conversation with Nancy set me thinking," Dave recalled. "I said to some of the other editors, 'You know, I think she's right. I wonder how much we do that?'

" 'Absolutely not!' cried one editor. 'I don't believe it!' said another."

A woman editor said managerial meetings on the news floor at the *Times* had given her anxiety attacks and sent her into therapy because "we are drowned out, not listened to, we are dismissed, passed over. It makes me crazy. The men running the *Times* now truly do not believe themselves capable of sexist feelings. They have serious wives. They help with the dishes. But they are still looking for, and are only comfortable with, people in their own image—in other words, other white men. They have a joking camaraderie together that walls us out." She sounded like young Arthur Sulzberger, only madder.

Another woman editor added, "We all face a more subtle form of discrimination in meetings here. It's hard to make yourself heard in a roomful of men. They use sports metaphors, team language. We say things differently; our voices are higher pitched, and for some reason, men think we can't be serious. It's like women in broadcasting—it took a long time before their voices were deemed 'important' enough to deliver significant stories on the air." That very day, she attended a meeting in which she offered an intriguing story idea about changes in child care centers in New York. Her idea fell into a little pool of silence. Then the assistant managing editor running the meeting said repressively, "Let's get back to Iraq."

Carolyn Lee warned Frankel that the shutting-out of women in high-level planning meetings was so bad that at least a couple of them were keeping track of how many times they had been interrupted. She gave specific examples; Max reacted with incredulity and then promised to do better in the future.

Carolyn has voiced her opinions under even the most daunting circumstances. Shortly after she became the first woman assistant managing editor, young Arthur Sulzberger invited about one hundred and fifty of the paper's executives to a retreat-cum-brainstorming session about the future of the *Times* at a country resort. Frankel, whose style with women is ponderously gallant, told the assemblage that he was pleased to welcome Carolyn Lee as the latest "adornment" to the paper's masthead. "Thank you," Carolyn said, "but I have not worked so hard all these years to be called an *adornment.*" A woman editor who was there said, "The men gasped, they were scandalized; the women were silently cheering." Max apologized on the spot.

The incident brought to mind something that had happened to me shortly after I won a Pulitzer Prize in 1983 for my story about an attack of toxic shock syndrome that nearly took my life. Clifton Daniel, by then retired, came by my desk. We embraced. He held me at arm's length and he said with a smile: "What's a little bitty thing like you doing winning the Pulitzer Prize?" I let him have it. Clifton was a friend, but after the ordeal I had gone through I found his remark thoughtless and patronizing. I deserved the prize, and I knew it and I said it.

When I told this story soon thereafter to a group of newspaper editors and reporters in New Jersey, a murmur of understanding came from every woman in the room. The men there looked utterly puzzled. "Aw, Daniel was just being affectionate," one said to me. "Why don't you relax?"

Nancy Newhouse discovered that even when they died, women were being ignored by the newspaper. One day she was browsing through the obituary pages and noticed that among seventeen obituary articles, not one was of a woman. "I could not believe it," she said. "I mean—women are not dying? Their lives are not worthy of notice? I was livid and I was determined to bring it up in the next news meeting. I knew I'd get dumped on." And she was. Editors laughed. Frankel made a caustic remark. Allan Siegal, an assistant managing editor, snickered and said, "You mean you want *more* women to die?" Finally Phil Boffey, then the science editor, came to Nancy's rescue. "It's true," he said, "that women in their seventies and eighties might not have had careers, but we should look into this." Nancy said that Siegal—who studies the paper as closely as if searching for devils on the head of a pin—"obviously was making mental notes, and from then on, there has been a woman on the obit page every single day."

Few male editors at the *Times* have seen more clearly than Dave Jones what it is that women can add to a newspaper. He brought so many women onto his national desk that he was known as "the Phil Spitalny of *The New York Times*." (Spitalny's "All-Girl" orchestra was a hit on radio in the thirties and forties.) Dave, now an assistant managing editor, is hardly the warm, fuzzy type—he has the deadpan manner of a Mississippi riverboat gambler. He said he was flattered that people thought he had helped women along, "but the fact is that the women did it themselves, on their own merit and ability." They have added real diversity and sensitivity to the daily report, he said, as well as material of interest to the large number of women readers. Whereas some men on the national staff tended to pass over or downplay such subjects as birth control or toxic shock, the women would say, "Wait a minute—this is a hell of a story."

Dave learned early how hard was the road for professional women. "Maybe it was my wife's experience decades ago," he said. "I think it changed my thinking decisively." Jones and his wife, Mary Lee, were both editors of the student newspaper at Penn State University in the early 1950s. After graduation and their marriage, Mary Lee Jones became a reporter at the Dayton *Journal Herald* while Dave served his stint in the Air Force at a nearby base. "She was making sixty dollars a week, and they would not give her a five-dollar raise," he said. "When I got out of the Air Force, I applied for a job at the same newspaper. I said I wanted a salary of one hundred dollars a week; they practically went white and then they offered me one hundred dollars a week and I said, 'Stuff it.' I was so angry at the way my wife had been treated, I've never forgotten it."

Jones remembered what Eileen Shanahan had told him about her first job interview back in 1962 with Clifton Daniel. Daniel asked Eileen what her ultimate ambition was, and although she had some thoughts about becoming an editor one day, she babbled eagerly, "Oh, all I ever want is to be a reporter on the best newspaper in the world."

"That's good," Eileen quoted Daniel as saying, "because I can assure you, no woman will ever be an editor at *The New York Times.*"

By early 1991 in the newsroom, however, about a third of the copy editors were women. Twenty-seven percent of the photographers and photo editors were women; 30 percent of the employees in graphic arts and on the desk that lays out the paper were women. Twenty-three percent of the reporters, correspondents, and critics were women—only 10 percent higher than in 1972, when the women of the *Times* began organizing. In 1990, the new hires of nonminority women reporters amounted to only 18 percent of the total.

While the paper's record shows improvement in important areas, it is nothing to crow about—considering that women compose half the population and that there are no longer any significant cultural or educational differences between white men and women in the United States. By 1990, however, the *Times* was hiring almost as many minority women reporters as minority men reporters.

The two persons presiding most closely over these changes on the news side have been Carolyn Lee and Max Frankel, her immediate boss. "Max may put his foot in his mouth about women and blacks, but look at his performance," Carolyn said. "Three-quarters of the women in management jobs on the news side have been put there by Max."

Frankel put his foot in his mouth twice in public in 1990. The first time he offended women. The second time he managed to offend both women *and* blacks. While trying to refute a charge that his paper had fewer stories by and about women on the front page than other major papers do, he told Eleanor Randolph of *The Washington Post,* "If you are covering local teas, you've got more women [on the front page] than *The Wall Street Journal.*" The next day, dozens of women employees and a few males came to work sporting tea bags on their lapels; buttons showing a teapot crossed by a diagonal red line were worn soon thereafter by both women and men on the staff. New York's *Village Voice* commented: "Frankel's 19th-century relegation of women to wifely Darjeeling-and-scone duties would be objectionable from any editor, but when it comes from the head cheese of the paper that sets the world's news agenda, it's not just offensive, but dangerously stupid."

About fifty women of the *Times* met to protest, their biggest get-together since the 1988 Caucus reunion. This time the meeting was held right on the premises. What came out of it was a letter to Max, in which they asked, "Did you mean what you said? If not, what did you mean? . . . . It was painful to be contacted by colleagues across the country who suggested our executive editor did not value our contributions. And there is additional concern that this incident could impede efforts to recruit and promote women at The New York Times."

Max apologized handsomely, if somewhat obscurely. "I assure you that my sin was chronological, not ideological," he wrote back. "If I were 20 years younger, I surely would have found a better example" of an important women's activity than giving tea parties.

Six months later, he did it again. At a symposium on women and the media at Columbia University's Graduate School of Journalism, he said it was easier for him to fire women than blacks because there were now more women in the newsroom. "We've reached a critical mass with women," he explained. "I know that when a woman screws up, it is not a political act for me to go fire them. I cannot say that with some of our blacks. They're still precious, they're still hothouse in management, and if they are less than good, I would probably stay my hand at removing them too quickly."

He later told black journalists that even though he had tripped over his own "fat lips," the Times had no double standard. Rebecca Sinkler, the Sunday book review editor, commented: "I think we're lucky to have Max Frankel because he's so completely politically incorrect—the man's well intentioned but antediluvian. He's not hypocritical enough to mind his mouth—he shows us what really is on men's minds. I thank him for that, for being unguarded, for getting it all out there, because anything hidden under a mask of hypocrisy is harder to fight."

"He does what Ed Koch [the former mayor of New York] does," another influential woman said. "He gives voice to certain bigoted truths."

Still later, Frankel explained to me what he meant by his "critical mass" statement:

"What I meant was that I as manager of this wonderful organization can afford to have a woman fail without having a political crisis on my hands. I do aim for fifty-fifty [men and women on the staff]. Fortunately, enough women have already succeeded in high places here so that we can also have them fail. What I was doing was revealing my own state of mind—really. When Branch Rickey recruited Jackie Robinson, he had to say, 'Boy, this guy had better be great.' He had to be better than anybody else. My mother used to say to me, 'Max, you're a Jew—you've got to be better than anybody else.' Now major black ballplayers are routinely scolded, traded, kicked out, and nobody calls it racism."

But the fuss kicked up over Frankel's "tea party" and "critical mass" comments was as nothing compared with the outrage that erupted against him among the employees of *The New York Times* in April 1991. The anger focused on the paper's profile of the woman who had accused William Kennedy Smith, Senator Edward Kennedy's nephew, of rape at the Kennedy estate in Palm Beach. Printing the story, with its unsavory "she asked for it" tone as well as the alleged victim's name, was Max Frankel's decision. It was the worst decision of his career. It brought shame to the newspaper and those in charge and scorching criticism from readers and periodicals across the country. It pitted the staff against Frankel and his top editors in a confrontation that involved three hundred members of the newspaper, almost half of them male. The meeting in the ninth-floor WQXR auditorium—the only room in the *Times* building big enough to contain such a crowd—revealed as no other single event in memory how dramatically most staffers' perceptions of women had changed. It also revealed how Max Frankel's perceptions, and those of most of the men closest to him, had *not* changed.

The profile of Smith's accuser ran in the *Times* on Wednesday, April 17, on an inside page. An unidentified friend from high school mentioned that the woman had "a little wild streak," and there were details about her bar-hopping, her child born out of wedlock, her poor grades in school, her many speeding tickets; it was reported that her mother, once

a secretary and a welder's wife, had moved up the social and
financial ladder with her daughter after having an affair with
a multimillionaire, who eventually married her. One *Times*
reporter echoed the almost universal reaction by saying:
"They made [Smith's accuser] look like a slut."

The morning the profile appeared, the *Times* building exploded. Becky Sinkler, the Sunday book review editor, was so
incensed that she charged downstairs from her eighth-floor
office and burst into Frankel's conference room, where a meeting was going on. John Lee, an assistant managing editor,
looked up smiling and said, "Don't you think we had a terrific
story this morning?" Becky snapped: "It's a disgrace! That's
why I'm here." She said the faces of the men around the table
"simply froze." Joe Lelyveld, the cool, disengaged managing
editor, blurted out, "What do you *mean*?" Sinkler told them
the story was an outrageous smear—sexist, class-ridden, a
nasty piece of work riddled with negative quotes from anonymous sources, a violation of the paper's high journalistic standards. Frankel, overhearing the raised voices through an open
door next to his office, rushed in to say to Sinkler in a voice
thick with anger: "I woke up this morning so proud of that
story. We had more reporting, more facts in that story than
any other paper in the country."

By the next morning, it was obvious to Max and his associ-
ates that something was terribly wrong. Reporters and *Times*
fans from all over the nation were calling, wondering what on
earth had happened to the Good Gray Lady.

Young Arthur Sulzberger was privately appalled by the
profile. The uproar and the bitter debate, inside and outside
the *Times,* was also reaching a baffled Punch Sulzberger in
London.

That Thursday morning, April 18, Allan Siegal, an assistant
managing editor, who had watched the television news programs and knew that "an enormous flap" was brewing over
the *Times*'s performance, said to Frankel: "You know, we
ought to call the staff together and give them an opportunity

to talk to us rather than talk around us." He was concerned
that their anger had no place to go, and that it would leak, as
always in the past, to eager ears at *New York* magazine or *The
Village Voice* or *Spy*. The WQXR auditorium was reserved for
early Friday afternoon.

Frankel, Siegal (the spokesman to the outside world for the
Times's news side), and Soma Golden, the national editor
whose desk had processed the Palm Beach profile, faced the
staff from the platform. People poured in by the hundreds,
filling the seats and packing the side aisles and the back. Fifty
members of the Washington bureau listened to the proceedings as they were piped down to the capital on a speaker-
phone. "They've got blood in their eyes," Al Siegal said in an
undertone to Max. He could "feel the anger radiating up off
the auditorium like the heat radiating off a summer highway."

What really radiates off the tape-recording of the next
ninety minutes is not so much anger as anguish and deep
sadness, expressed by both women and men speakers from the
floor, about how the *Times* had tarnished the very journalistic
standards that they and the paper's readers had long admired.
There are none of the "boos and hisses" *Time* magazine later
reported; nobody shouts or interrupts, the reporters and editors ask tough questions without losing their dignity, but their
distress is palpable. What also comes strongly off the tape is
Max Frankel's total avoidance of responsibility, and his pre-
occupation with the newspaper's image rather than his own
values. Soma Golden comes off no better. "It was not a damning portrait of somebody asking for it," she says. "It was a
portrait, period. . . . Everybody's outraged. I don't understand
that. . . . I can't account for every weird mind that reads *The
New York Times*." At this point a moan of revulsion rises from
the audience. Only Siegal, one of the most scrupulous word-
by-word readers of the paper, takes any blame. He confesses
that he read the profile "much too hastily," agrees with the
objections to the anonymous "wild streak" quotation, and
speaks of how the uproar has sensitized him to the emotions

the delicate subject arouses. Asked why there was not a profile of William Kennedy Smith, the alleged rapist, Soma replies, "We're working on it." (A sympathetic story ran May 12, almost a month later, the day after Smith was indicted.)

Anna Quindlen, like many, felt betrayed by her own newspaper. In the column she wrote for Sunday, April 21, she compared the *Times*'s discretion about the name of the victim in the 1988 Central Park jogger case with the paper's current conduct in the Palm Beach affair. In the final paragraphs, her disgust sizzled off the page:

In the face of what we did in the Central Park case, the obvious conclusion was that women who graduate from Wellesley, have prestigious jobs [the victim was an investment banker], and are raped by a gang of black teen-agers will be treated fairly by the press. And women who have "below-average" high school grades, are well known at bars and dance clubs, and say that they have been raped by an acquaintance from an influential family after a night of drinking will not.

If we had any doubt about whether there is still a stigma attached to rape, it is gone for good. Any woman reading the Times profile now knows that to accuse a well-connected man of rape will invite a thorough reading not only of her own past but of her mother's, and that she had better be ready to see not only her name but her drinking habits in print. . . .

The day after the column appeared, young Arthur Sulzberger hugged and kissed his friend Anna in the middle of the newsroom, telling her, "It was brave of you to write that column." Thirteen of the highest-ranking women editors gathered soon thereafter in a supportive, females-only meeting in Frankel's conference room. A crestfallen Soma Golden was there, and was comforted. The women pushed Max to run an Editor's Note of apology. It ran Friday, April 26, along with a full and fair—and unprecedented—article summarizing the negative repercussions of the episode inside and outside the paper. Frankel was quoted as saying, "This is a crisis because many people feel The Times betrayed its standards."

The Editor's Note said in part: "The article drew no conclusions about the truth of [the accuser's] complaint to the police. But many readers inferred that its very publication, including her name and detailed biographical material about her and her family, suggested that The Times was challenging her account.

"No such challenge was intended, and The Times regrets that some parts of the article reinforced such inferences."

Anna Quindlen told a friend: "First they blamed the victim. And then they blamed the reader."

I asked Al Siegal what lessons he had learned from all this. "I never thought that rape was something people took lightly," he replied, "but the power of the subject to provoke volcanic rage is a revelation to me, and the pain and the grief that women commonly experience about it is staggering. I knew how to handle sensitive material about Jews and Arabs, but not about this. Now I will be hypersensitive and cautious. I've heard a lot of screaming from the depths of people's souls, and I'll remember. That awareness alone could serve me as an editor."

There were other lessons. First, from beginning to end, it was the women of the *Times* who pushed and prodded and called the paper and its most powerful editors to account and insisted upon action. They received their staunchest support from younger male staff members. Second, the WQXR meeting would never have been called under Abe Rosenthal—who believed at the end that *he* was *The New York Times*—nor under any of his predecessors. (If the article had been run during Abe's regime, however, he almost certainly would have taken entire responsibility for it, because that was his nature and because he thought he and the *Times* were one and indivisible.)

Perhaps Max Frankel was born too soon to comprehend the women of this generation, or those of his own generation, like myself, who were irrevocably changed by the modern women's movement. He has always given the impression of being a weighty thinker, but I sometimes wonder—as do many of those who work for him—if Max will ever understand us in his gut.

....

No *Times* woman writer since Charlotte Curtis and Ada Louise Huxtable has been as admired or had as much public visibility as Anna Quindlen. Unlike Charlotte and Ada Louise—and many men—the older Anna gets, the more of a feminist she becomes. Gloria Steinem remarked on the phenomenon that women may be the one group that grows more radical with age. When we are still in school, she explained in *Outrageous Acts and Everyday Rebellions,* we have not yet experienced "the life events that are most radicalizing for women: entering the paid-labor force and discovering how women are treated there; marrying and finding out that it is not yet an equal partnership; having children and discovering who is responsible for them and who is not; and aging, still a greater penalty for women than for men."

Anna Quindlen's emerging voice on the Op-Ed page is unmistakably the voice of a woman. In both her womanly and family-oriented point of view and in the way she sees the world through the eyes of ordinary Americans, she differs from the *Times*'s Big Picture male pundits and from her two illustrious women predecessors on the page. The voices and the subjects of Anne O'Hare McCormick and Flora Lewis were, on the whole, without gender.

Anna is half-Italian, half-Irish, born July 8, 1952, in a Philadelphia suburb to Prudence Pantano and Robert Vincent Quindlen. She was the eldest of five children. Her family was very middle-class, very Roman Catholic. She was hooked early on journalism, becoming editor of the student newspaper at a high-class convent academy in West Virginia and then in a public high school in New Jersey.

"In journalism, you could do all the things good girls were not supposed to do," Anna said with relish. "You were obligated to ask rude questions. They made you go to strangers' homes; they made you ask how much money people earned. I mean—*Jesus*—it was like a dream come true."

She entered Barnard College in New York. One day in 1971, her father gathered his children together around the kitchen table and told them that Prudence had cancer. "She isn't going to get better," he said. Anna, a sophomore, withdrew from college for a year to manage everything at home. The cancer spread. "Father made Mother promise to hang on until Christmas," Anna said. "At Christmastime, he said, 'How about Easter? Easter comes early this year.' And she said, 'The hell with Easter.' " As she remembered, Anna's eyes filled with tears. Prudence Pantano Quindlen died on January 18, 1972. Her oldest daughter was nineteen.

She went back to Barnard in the fall of 1972. "I had made a giant leap into maturity," she said. "I felt that about 90 percent of what was going on around me was incredibly trivial. I was determined to milk every single experience of my life. Forever after, people would say, 'Slow down! How come you're in such a hurry?' I didn't believe life lasted long enough for me to slow down."

Right after graduation in 1974, Quindlen joined the *New York Post*. "It was a real down-at-the-heels, seat-of-the-pants newspaper," Anna said fondly. "It was great. People said, 'Ah well, we got it wrong today. We'll get it right tomorrow.' Even the typewriters were funky. It was a good place to grow up in. Nobody held your mistakes against you, the way they do here."

Abe Rosenthal hired Anna in 1977. She was a success from her first bylined feature story, a fresh piece about Valentine's Day. She became the first woman and one of the best writers ever to do the "About New York" column, whose high standards had been set by Mike Berger. Later, readers followed just as eagerly the story of her life and family in the "Life in the 30's" column, which Anna originated. *New York* magazine, which named her as one of the "Treasures of New York" in 1990, called the column as gripping as a densely plotted novel: "Would criminal lawyer Jerry Krovatin [Anna's husband] always be the love of Quindlen's life, the Rhett to her Scarlett? Would her two sons, Christopher and Quindlen, have difficulty adjusting to Maria, their new baby sister? And who would describe . . . the terror of confronting a hairy, Godzilla-like monster under the bed?"

Her column on the Op-Ed page is a forum, *New York* magazine said, for Quindlen to deal with the "real monsters under the bed"—to attack the Catholic Church, of which she and her husband are members, for its campaign against abortion or its treatment of homosexuals, or to describe the problems of crack babies or mothers who leave their children in car trunks while they work second jobs. Without question, one of the hardest columns she ever had to write was the one that censured her own beloved newspaper for its coverage of the alleged rape victim in Palm Beach.

Only four months earlier, on Thanksgiving Day, 1990, Anna had dedicated a birthday column to her daughter, Maria, who had just turned two. Anna called it "The Glass Half Empty." It was one of the angriest and most deeply felt essays she ever did for the *Times.* Behind that sparkling face, that unshakable optimism, were years of pent-up rage.

Anna said that in the previous twenty years, she had gradually learned to live in the world as it was: "The fact that women were now making 67 cents for every dollar a man makes—well, it was better than 1970, wasn't it, when we were making only 59 cents?"

Now, she wrote,

when I look at my sons, it is within reason to imagine all the world's doors open to them. Little by little some will close, as their individual capabilities and limitations emerge. But no one is likely to look at them and mutter: "I'm not sure a man is right for a job at this level. Doesn't he have a lot of family responsibilities?"

Every time a woman looks at her daughter and thinks "She can be anything" she knows in her heart, from experience, that it's a lie. Looking at this little girl, I see it all, the old familiar ways of a world that still loves Barbie. Girls aren't good at math, dear. He needs the money more than you, sweetheart; he's got a family to support. Honey—this diaper's dirty. . . .

My daughter is ready to leap into the world, as though life were chicken soup and she a delighted noodle. The work of Prof. Carol Gilligan of Harvard suggests that some time after the age of 11 this will change, that this lively little girl will pull back, shrink, that her constant refrain will become "I don't know." Professor Gilligan says the culture sends a message: "Keep quiet and notice the absence of women and say nothing.". . .

Maybe someday, years from now, my daughter will come home and say, "Mother, at college my professor acted as if my studies were an amusing hobby and at work the man who runs my department puts his hand on my leg and to compete with the man who's in the running for my promotion who makes more than I do I can't take time to have a relationship but he has a wife and two children and I'm smarter and it doesn't make any difference and some guy tried to jump me after our date last night." And what am I supposed to say to her?

I know?

You'll get used to it?

No. Today is her second birthday and she has made me see fresh this two-tiered world, a world that despite all our nonsense about post-feminism, continues to offer less respect and less opportunity for women than it does for men. . . .

The reader mail was mixed. Some applauded Anna. One said she should be passing on to her daughter not anger, but rather a sense of empowerment. Another said, Don't be ridiculous! Women are favored in our society. "A shrink wrote, 'This is an inappropriate emotion to feel on your daughter's birthday,' " Anna said with a grimace. It may be some consolation to her that no previous staff columnist *ever* got a feminist blast like that on the Op-Ed page of *The New York Times.*

Anna brought up the subject of the women's lawsuit with me in a 1990 interview, reiterating that it had paved the way for everything she had achieved at the *Times.* Of Abe Rosenthal, she said: "Abe likes family relationships—the father-daughter-mother-sister stuff. And all of a sudden his five sisters rose up and kicked him in the tush. The message of the class-action suit was: You must deal with me on my *own* terms—professional, legal, rational, matter-of-fact. If he were writing a column about the women's suit, I wonder what he would say now?"

Both Quindlen and Rosenthal work in the serene think tanks of the tenth floor, where the eggheads dwell. Abe is no longer the paper's radioactive core, dangerous and leaking unbelievable energy. In his cozy office late in 1990, he seemed the most mellow of men after four years of writing his Op-Ed-page column. He sank down in his upholstered leather chair. He thought back on what the city room had looked like when he first came there from Tokyo as its lord and master in 1963.

"It looked like a monastery," he said. "It was not an accident. I grew up around women, my mother, my five sisters. I am not comfortable in a locker room. When I came home from Tokyo in 1963, there was no systematic advancement of women anywhere. There was no affirmative action plan. There were certain places you wouldn't send women reporters, certain assignments you wouldn't give them. They were paid less; they were patted on the head." Abe reminded me that he had hired Flora Lewis, made her a bureau chief, and sent both Flora and me to Paris. "That's when the big arguments came around here," he recalled, "when I appointed not just one but *two* women to Paris. A lot of the men could not stomach the idea. They predicted a catfight."

Abe would not go as far as Punch Sulzberger did in saying, from hindsight, that if the women's suit had not happened, the *Times* never would have gotten off the dime. "The suit was very important, and much flowed from it, but it was not the totality of my life, it was not the total Rosenthal," he said. "I had a lot of things to do in the 1970s—like saving the whole goddamned fucking newspaper!" (The *Times* was then in deep financial trouble.)

Abe said that the taking of the depositions for the trial had bothered him deeply. He remembered Harriet Rabb, the Women's Caucus lawyer, and those three days of questioning. "I thought: You're suing *me*? Me, Abe Rosenthal, who likes women? I'd never been cross-examined before. They were constantly trying to get me to denigrate reporters for *The New York Times,* to say 'This man got a raise, this woman didn't get a raise.' Come to think of it, when you take men or women, it works out about fifty-fifty—half of the members of both sexes are incompetent. I felt the lawyers were pushing me. I saw blood being spilled on the courtroom floor, having to get up and say these things in public. I was indignant."

Suddenly, his mood lightened. He grew sentimental. He spoke of the day in the mid-1980s when he had finally ordered the *Times* copy desk to use "Ms." as an honorific for women, long after other major newspapers had done so. He recalled the outpouring of praise and affection from women throughout the country, the flowers that Gloria Steinem had sent him. "I did not know, until I lifted that ban on 'Ms.,' how overly long I had resisted it," he said. "I forbade its use because I didn't want the *Times* to be used politically. The women on the staff, the women everywhere, were so happy, I was stunned. I should have done it earlier."

He leaned forward. "You know, the women's liberation movement really had a profound effect on this whole country," he said. "I think you should call it a men's liberation movement because it liberated *men,* because it opened our eyes and our ears and our hearts. It liberated us from our own stereotypes. I think that the women's movement made men better." That was Abe Rosenthal, on a day late in 1990.

············

Sometime that fall, young Arthur Sulzberger was enthusiastically discussing the future of *The New York Times* in his eleventh-floor office with Penny Abernathy, who manages a $100 million budget for the paper's news staff of one thousand people worldwide.

During the conversation, young Arthur said to Penny: "I want to leave my son a different newspaper from the one I'm inheriting."

Penny was thrilled. She went down to the third floor, where she and Carolyn Lee, her boss, occupy the northwest corner of the newsroom. She told Carolyn what Arthur had said. Carolyn smiled, very sweetly.

And then she said: "Did you mention to young Arthur that he also has a daughter?"

Acknowledgments

All the living employees and former employees of *The New York Times* whom I have quoted by name in this book deserve my heartfelt thanks for their unstinting cooperation. So do members of the Sulzberger family. There were many others whom I interviewed but whose stories did not fit into my narrative, or who—extremely rarely—asked that their names not be used in a few direct quotations. They have my thanks also.

I am grateful to still others behind the scenes who gave generously of their time and expertise, such as Mary Marshall Clark and Susan Dryfoos of the New York Times Oral History Project; John Rothman, the New York Times Company archivist; Linda Amster, Judith Greenfeld, and John Motyka of the *Times* reference library; Louise Francke and Michael Sklaroff of *Times Talk;* and Robert Fowlow and Robert Medina of the *Times* morgue. I would like to single out for special thanks all seven plaintiffs of *Boylan* v. *The New York Times:* they were endlessly patient and forthcoming, as was their chief attorney, Harriet Rabb, professor of law and director of clinical education at the Columbia University Law School in New York City.

Journalists outside the *Times* who were particularly helpful were

Bonnie Angelo of *Time* magazine; Frances Lewine, an Associated
Press veteran now with Cable News Network; Tom Morgan; and
Isabelle Shelton, formerly of the Washington *Evening Star*.

My thanks go also to Donna Allen, of the Women's Institute for
Freedom of the Press in Washington, D.C.; Sister Mary McCaffrey,
archivist of the College of St. Mary's of the Springs in Columbus,
Ohio; Patricia King, director, and Eva Moseley, curator of manu-
scripts, of the Schlesinger Library on the History of Women in
America at Radcliffe College, Cambridge, Massachusetts; Barbara
Vandegrift of the Cora Rigby Archive of the National Press Club in
Washington, D.C.; and Ronald J. Grele, director of Columbia Uni-
versity's Oral History Project.

This book would never have come together without the sensitive
guidance of my editor, Robert Loomis of Random House. I owe
thanks as well to the gifted Jennifer Ash of Random House for her
editing suggestions; and always, gratitude for the support and inspiration of my literary agent, Lucy Kroll, and for the able assistance
of Barbara Hogenson.

Bibliography

My shelves contain dozens of books on the newspaper world, but those I found particularly helpful in my research—the volumes that taught me the history and informed and enriched my own memories—were the following:

ADLER, RUTH. *A Day in the Life of The New York Times.* Philadelphia and New York: J. B. Lippincott Company, 1971.

———. *The Working Press: Special to The New York Times.* New York: G. P. Putnam's Sons, 1966.

BAKER, RUSSELL. *The Good Times.* New York: William Morrow and Company, 1989.

BELFORD, BARBARA. *Brilliant Bylines: A Biographical Anthology of Notable Newspaperwomen in America.* New York: Columbia University Press, 1986.

BERGER, MEYER. *The Story of The New York Times: 1851–1951.* New York: Simon and Schuster, 1951.

BREASTED, MARY. *I Shouldn't Be Telling You This: A Novel.* New York: Harper & Row, 1983.

CATLEDGE, TURNER. *My Life and The Times.* New York, Evanston and London: Harper & Row, 1971.

COSE, ELLIS. *The Press: Inside America's Most Powerful Newspaper Empires—From the Newsrooms to the Boardrooms.* New York: William Morrow and Company, 1989.

CROUSE, TIMOTHY. *The Boys on the Bus: Riding with the Campaign Press Corps.* New York: Random House, 1972.

DANIEL, CLIFTON. *Lords, Ladies and Gentlemen: A Memoir.* New York: Arbor House, 1984.

DRYFOOS, SUSAN W. *Iphigene: My Life and the New York Times.* New York: Dodd, Mead & Co., 1981; New York: Times Books, 1987.

EDWARDS, JULIA. *Women of the World: The Great Foreign Correspondents.* Boston: Houghton Mifflin Company, 1988; New York: Ballantine Books, 1989.

FURMAN, BESS. *Washington By-Line: The Personal History of a Newspaperwoman.* New York: Alfred A. Knopf, 1949.

GOULDEN, JOSEPH C. *Fit to Print: A. M. Rosenthal and His Times.* Secaucus, N.J.: Lyle Stuart Inc., 1988.

HALBERSTAM, DAVID. *The Powers That Be.* New York: Alfred A. Knopf, Inc., 1979.

KLUGER, RICHARD. *The Paper: The Life and Death of the New York Herald Tribune.* New York: Alfred A. Knopf, Inc., 1986.

MCCORMICK, ANNE O'HARE. *Vatican Journal: 1921–1954.* Compiled and edited by Marion Turner Sheehan. New York: Farrar, Straus and Cudahy, 1957.

———. *The World at Home: Selections from the Writings of Anne O'Hare McCormick.* Edited by Marion Turner Sheehan. New York: Alfred A. Knopf, 1956.

MILLS, KAY. *A Place in the News: From the Women's Pages to the Front Page.* New York: Dodd, Mead & Company, 1988.

ROSS, ISHBEL. *Ladies of the Press: The Story of Women in Journalism by an Insider.* New York and London: Harper & Brothers, 1936.

SALISBURY, HARRISON E. *Without Fear or Favor: An Uncompromising Look at The New York Times.* New York: Times Books, 1980.

SULZBERGER, CYRUS L. *A Long Row of Candles.* New York: Macmillan Company, 1969.

TALESE, GAY. *The Kingdom and the Power: The Story of the Men Who Influence the Institution That Influences the World.* Cleveland: New American Library/World Publishing, 1969.

Index

NAN ROBERTSON's *New York Times* article on her near-fatal attack of toxic shock syndrome saved countless lives, elicited two thousand letters from *Times* readers, and won her the Pulitzer Prize.

Born in Chicago, she was graduated with honors from Northwestern University's Medill School of Journalism in 1948. Before coming to the *Times*, she was a correspondent in Paris, Berlin, Frankfurt, and London for several American newspapers, including the New York *Herald Tribune* European Edition, now the *International Herald Tribune*.

On *The New York Times*, she reported for the women's page and the city desk in New York, was a correspondent in the Washington and Paris bureaus, and covered the performing arts in New York.

In addition to the Pulitzer, Ms. Robertson has three times won the Newswomen's Club of New York's Front Page Award and the New York Newspaper Guild's Page One Award. She has been a fellow at the MacDowell Colony and at Duke University and has been a Woodrow Wilson National Visiting Fellow every year since 1983. In 1991 she won Northwestern University's Alumnae Award.

Her book *Getting Better: Inside Alcoholics Anonymous*, the first major book ever written on A.A., was a popular and critical success. She lives in Washington, D.C.